D1130973

CATCHING CAPITAL

CATCHING CAPITAL

The Ethics of Tax Competition

Peter Dietsch

OXFORD
UNIVERSITY PRESS

OXFORD
UNIVERSITY PRESS

Oxford University Press is a department of the University of Oxford.
It furthers the University's objective of excellence in research, scholarship,
and education by publishing worldwide. Oxford is a registered trade mark
of Oxford University Press in the UK and in certain other countries

Published in the United States of America by
Oxford University Press
198 Madison Avenue, New York, NY 10016,
United States of America

© Oxford University Press 2015

Cataloging-in-Publication Data is on file at the Library of Congress.

978-0-19-025151-2

1 3 5 7 9 8 6 4 2

Printed in the United States of America on acid-free paper

For my parents

CONTENTS

* These sections are largely based on Peter Dietsch & Thomas Rixen, 'Tax Competition and Global Background Justice', *Journal of Political Philosophy* 22, no. 2 (2014): 150–77. I thank my co-author Thomas Rixen for his permission to use this material here.

ACKNOWLEDGMENTS

A book is the reflection of how the author views the conceptual landscape, at least at the time of publication. Yet, this view has not been arrived at in isolation. It builds on the insights of others, on countless discussions with colleagues and on comments one receives in the process of writing. Authors might deserve credit for putting it all together, but the ideas that emerge are very much the product of research as a social endeavour.

While I am happy to take full responsibility for the arguments defended in this book, I would like to thank those who have helped me develop them. First on this list is Thomas Rixen, with whom I have co-authored several papers on international tax governance, including one that feeds into parts of the first two chapters of this book. Having discovered a model of collaboration as productive and pleasant, one hardly wants to work alone anymore. I have also benefited enormously from written comments from and/or discussions with Allison Christians, François Claveau, Miriam Ronzoni, and Christian Schemmel.

The Montreal political philosophy community around the Centre de recherche en éthique (CRÉ, formerly CRÉUM) and the Groupe de recherche interdisciplinaire en philosophie politique (GRIPP) have provided me with an exceptionally stimulating work environment. Here, special thanks go to Allison Christians, Pablo Gilabert, Will Roberts, Robert Sparling, and Daniel Weinstock, who participated in a workshop on the manuscript in 2013, and to Charles Blattberg, who provided detailed comments on the introduction.

During my sabbatical in 2011–12, I had the privilege to spend a year in the research unit on global governance at the Social Science Research Center Berlin (WZB). Thank you to Michael Zürn, who directs the unit, as well as to Thomas Rixen for inviting me and to the Alexander von Humboldt Foundation for financing my stay. A lot of the work towards the book happened at the WZB, helped along with feedback from, in addition to those already mentioned, Martin Binder, Pieter de Wilde, Matthias Ecker-Ehrhardt, Benjamin Faude, Tim Gemkow, Anja Görnitz, Monika Heupel, Gisela Hirschmann, Michal Parizek, Autumn Lockwood Payton, Christian Rauh, Matthew Stephen, Xaver Keller, Lora Viola, and Frank Wendler.

Without listing the numerous conferences and workshops where parts of this book have been presented, and with apologies to those who should be on this list but are not, I would like to say thank you for their comments to Arash Abizadeh, Jason Alexander, Alex Anderson, Reuven Avi-Yonah, Martin Blanchard, Richard Bradley, Geoff Brennan, Gillian Brock, Kim Brooks, Neil Brooks, Barbara Buckinx, Paula Casal, Rui Castro, Ryoa Chung, Rutger Claassen, Simon Cotton, Geert Demuijnck, Laurent de Briey, Jurgen de Wispelaere, Marc-Antoine Dilhac, David Duff, Avigail Eisenberg, Colin Farrelly, Thomas Ferretti, Marc

Fleurbaey, Rainer Forst, Alexandre Gajevic Sayegh, Philipp Genschel, Stefan Gosepath, Axel Gosseries, Joe Heath, Iwao Hirose, Waheed Hussain, Christian Jobin, Xavier Landes, Jacob Levy, Dominique Leydet, Christian List, Catherine Lu, Colin Macleod, François Maniquet, Dominic Martin, Frédéric Mérand, Michaela Mihai, Elizabeth Milton, Christian Nadeau, Pierre-Yves Néron, Wayne Norman, Ludmila Oliveira, Ronen Palan, Julian Reiss, Tom Sorell, Christine Straehle, Christine Tappolet, Laura Valentini, Laurens van Apeldoorn, Gijs van Donselaar, Philippe van Parijs, Jean-Pierre Vidal, Alex Voorhoeve, Nicholas Vrousalis, Michael Webb, and David Wiens.

I have learnt a lot from John Christensen, Markus Meinzer, and Richard Murphy at the Tax Justice Network, and I admire their work. Thank you to François Claveau, Xaver Keller, François Letourneux, and Georg Simmerl for invaluable research assistance. The detailed comments of two anonymous referees have helped me to substantially improve the book from the manuscript initially submitted. While this is my first book and I thus lack comparison, I can hardly imagine a more efficient and helpful editor than Peter Ohlin at OUP.

Parts of the book have been previously published in article form. 'Tax Competition and Global Background Justice,' by Peter Dietsch and Thomas Rixen, (*Journal of Political Philosophy* 22, no. 2 [2014]: 150–77) feeds into parts of chapters 1 and 2. My article, 'Rethinking Sovereignty in International Fiscal Policy,' (*Review of International Studies* 37 [2011]: 2107–20) is in part reproduced in chapter 4. I thank my co-author, as well as the respective publishers, for the permission to use this material here.

The research for this book has been financially supported through grants from the Alexander von Humboldt Foundation, the German Academic Exchange Service (DAAD), the Fonds de

Recherche du Québec—Société et Culture (FRQSC), the Social Sciences and Humanities Research Council of Canada (SSHRC), and the Direction des Relations Internationales at the Université de Montréal.

Last but not least, I would like to thank my family, Cynthia Milton and our daughters Lena and Nora, who give meaning to this project and to everything else.

Introduction

Once there was a bird that could live either on land or under the water. He lived in the air with the other birds until the king of the birds came demanding his taxes. Immediately the bird flew to the sea and said to the fish, 'You know me. I'm always with you. That idle king of the birds has been asking me for taxes.' The fish welcomed him and he stayed with them, 'comforted and consoled,' until the king of the fish came around asking for taxes. Whereupon the bird shot out of the water, flew back to the birds, and told them the same story. So he continued without ever paying any taxes.

—Leo Africanus, *The Cosmography and Geography of Africa*

The story of the amphibian bird is the story of capital owners today.[1] While not all of them exploit to the full the possibilities of reducing their tax burden, these possibilities do exist. Capital is mobile globally, whereas politics has remained largely local. If 'globalization' tends to be a vague and slippery term, one of its very tangible and precise aspects is the continuing trend towards capital mobility. By contrast, the *governance* of the increasingly global economy still by and large lies in the hands of nation-states. And fiscal policy is no exception. On

---

1. Leo Africanus, *The Cosmography and Geography of Africa*, cited by Natalie Zemon Davis, *Trickster Travels: A Sixteenth-century Muslim Between Worlds* (New York: Hill and Wang, 2006), 110. Leo Africanus's real name was al-Hasan al-Wazzan.

the contrary, given its importance to the functioning of governments, the latter are jealously guarding their control over tax matters.

One significant by-product of this mismatch between the economy and its political regulation is that those subject to the latter can play off different regulatory regimes against one another. In the fiscal context as one particularly important realm of regulatory competition, both individuals and corporations can often pick and choose, though not always legally, between different tax regimes.[2] They have an incentive to shift their capital to jurisdictions where they will receive favourable tax treatment.

This situation creates an incentive for states to make their fiscal policy as attractive as possible so as to attract capital from abroad. They do so not only by lowering tax rates but also by adjusting other aspects of regulation, such as disclosure requirements, bank secrecy, or the regulation of financial institutions more generally. The resulting *tax competition* is defined as interactive tax setting by independent governments in a noncooperative, strategic way. Taking the fiscal policies of other states as parameters, they design tax policy to attract a mobile tax base from abroad up to the point where this requires too high a sacrifice in terms of tax revenue losses at home. Tax competition illustrates the first sense in which this book is about 'catching capital.' Some states design their fiscal policy in order to attract, or to 'catch,' capital from abroad. In fact, tax competition has become one of the principal policy variables employed by governments to shore up the 'competitiveness' of their economy[3]— to attract capital and the jobs, as well as the economic growth this capital brings in its wake. Even those who do not themselves initiate aggressive fiscal policies find themselves forced to react by participating in this tax competition in order to prevent substantial capital outflows.

2. See Ronen Palan, 'Tax Havens and the Commercialization of State Sovereignty', *International Organization* 56, no. 1 (2002): 151–76.
3. See Lyne Latulippe, 'Tax Competition: An Internalized Policy Goal', in *Global Tax Governance - What is Wrong With It and How to Fix It*, ed. Peter Dietsch and Thomas Rixen (Colchester: ECPR Press, forthcoming).

Note that tax competition happens at all levels of governance, from municipalities to provinces to states. However, this book focuses exclusively on tax competition between states. Models of tax competition predict, and empirical evidence confirms, that small states in particular stand to gain from tax competition because, for them, the benefits from inflowing capital tend to outweigh the costs in terms of forgone tax revenue.[4]

We can distinguish three principal kinds of tax competition, which will be analysed in more detail in chapter 1. First, states compete for *portfolio capital*. Individuals shift some of their wealth in the form of cash deposits, equity, and security holdings offshore—which in fact means nothing other than 'abroad' in the financial world—in order to avoid paying capital gains tax. Given that individuals are taxed on the basis of residence, this is in fact illegal and constitutes tax evasion. Tax evasion hides behind the veil of secrecy provided by, for instance, banking regulations in tax havens such as Switzerland. Recent estimates put the share of European wealth that is held offshore at 10 percent, which equals about US$3.7 trillion.[5] This percentage is thought to be considerably higher for Latin American countries (50%) and in the Middle East (70%).[6] A study by the Tax Justice Network (TJN) estimates the worldwide wealth hidden in tax havens at $21–31 trillion.[7]

---

4. See Sam Bucovetsky, 'Asymmetric Tax Competition', *Journal of Urban Economics* 30, no. 2 (1991): 167–81.

5. See Boston Consulting Group, *Tapping Human Assets to Sustain Growth*, Global Wealth Report (Boston: Boston Consulting Group, 2007), 14, cited by Vanessa Houlder, 'Bound by the Call of Duty', *Financial Times*, 27 June 2012.

6. Tax Justice Network, *Tax Us if You Can. The True Story of a Global Failure* (London: Tax Justice Network, 2005), 4, accessed 9 December 2011, <http://www.taxjustice.net/cms/upload/pdf/tuiyc_-_eng_-_web_file.pdf>.

7. See James S. Henry, 'The Price of Offshore Revisited: New Estimates for "Missing" Global Private Wealth, Income, Inequality, and Lost Taxes' (report for Tax Justice Network, 2012), accessed 10 June 2013, <http://www.taxjustice.net/cms/upload/pdf/Price_of_Offshore_Revisited_120722.pdf>.

Second, states compete for the *paper profits* of multinational enterprises (MNEs). Using a whole menu of sophisticated techniques that will be described in somewhat more detail later, MNEs shift their profits from states with high tax rates on corporate profits to those with low ones. While there are restrictions on the way these transactions are done, they are not in principle illegal. For example, using a number of tax arrangements involving subsidiaries in Ireland, the Netherlands, and Bermuda, Google Inc. managed to cut its overseas tax rate to 2.4 percent in 2009. By comparison, the U.S. corporate income tax rate is 35 percent and the high-tax countries outside the United States in which Google mostly operates equally have rates of well over 20 percent.[8] Another tax-avoidance tool that has gained in popularity recently, but has been around at least since the 1980s, is the corporate inversion. A company in a high-tax jurisdiction relocates its headquarters to a low-tax jurisdiction while going about its business largely as before. Since regulators have tightened the screws on this kind of transaction over the years, today it is mostly done through the acquisition of a foreign company. For instance, in 2012, the Eaton Corporation, a power management company originally from Cleveland, acquired Cooper Industries, based in Ireland, for $13 billion, and reincorporated there, expecting 'to save $160 million a year [in taxes] as a result of the move.'[9] The fact that even lesser known and relatively small corporations can save amounts in the hundreds of millions of dollars is an indication of the significance of the problem. The above examples are by no means exceptional

8. I borrow these figures from Jesse Drucker's article, 'Google 2.4% Rate Shows How $60 Billion Lost to Tax Loopholes', accessed 17 July 2012, <http://www.bloomberg.com/news/2010-10-21/google-2-4-rate-shows-how-60-billion-u-s-revenue-lost-to-tax-loopholes.html>.
9. David Gelles, 'New Corporate Tax Shelter: A Merger Abroad', *New York Times*, 8 October 2013.

cases. MNEs have become experts in tax arbitrage, and when regulators move to close one loophole—as the Obama administration is attempting to do with corporate inversions—two new ones will be found to replace it. A recent joint report by Citizens for Tax Justice and the Institute on Taxation and Economic Policy shows that out of 288 Fortune 500 companies that were profitable in every single year between 2008 and 2012, 111 of them (39%) paid zero taxes or less—that is, they received a refund—in at least one of the five years.[10] For MNEs, not paying taxes has become part of what it means to stay competitive.

Third, states compete for *foreign direct investment* (FDI). In contrast to the first two, this type of tax competition actually involves the relocation of real economic activity. The classic example in this category is Ireland. For years, its low tax rate on foreign corporate profits attracted up to 25 percent of FDI by U.S. corporations in Europe.[11] In some cases, what is presented as FDI turns out to be tax fraud in disguise. Using a practice called 'round-tripping,' wealthy individuals will first move their funds offshore to evade paying taxes, and then re-invest them at home declared as FDI, which in some cases gives them further tax advantages. This phenomenon explains why Cyprus was the largest foreign investor in Russia by a huge margin,[12] and why most FDI in India comes from Mauritius.[13]

10. Robert S. McIntyre et al., 'The Sorry State of Corporate Taxes: What Fortune 500 Firms Pay (or Don't Pay) in the USA and What They Pay Abroad—2008 to 2012' (report by Citizens for Tax Justice and the Institute on Taxation and Public Policy, Washington, D.C., 2014), accessed 21 March 2014, <www.ctj.org/corporatetaxdodgers/sorrystateofcorptaxes.pdf>.
11. See *The Economist*, 'A Survey of Ireland', 16 October 2004.
12. *Financial Times*, 'Russian Money Streams Through Cyprus', 6 February 2013.
13. Ronen Palan et al., *Tax Havens: How Globalization Really Works* (Ithaca, NY: Cornell University Press, 2010), 56.

Against this background, I can now pose the two central questions of this book: Is there anything wrong with the phenomenon of tax competition from an ethical viewpoint? If so, what should we do about it?

This brings us to the second sense in which this book is about 'catching capital.' Under a system where states compete to attract capital—the first sense of catching capital—a lot of capital in fact slips through the fiscal net. Tax competition and the loopholes it promotes mean that a lot of states are no longer able to effectively tax capital at the rate their citizens see fit. While they are formally sovereign over their tax matters, they de facto lose control over aspects of their fiscal policy. This, as we shall see, is one of the principal normative challenges that tax competition presents us with. From the perspective of these individual states, but also from a systemic perspective, the question is how to make sure that those who have a right to tax capital are able to do so. Put differently, from a collective viewpoint, how do we have to design the international tax regime in order to make sure that it can effectively 'catch capital'?

In his important new book, Thomas Piketty has recently argued that the drastic increase in wealth inequalities in Western countries, notably in the United States, calls for higher taxes not just on the return from capital but also on the underlying wealth itself.[14] Tax competition is relevant to his argument in two ways. First, given the enormous private wealth that is hidden in tax havens, and given that Piketty bases his estimates of wealth inequalities by and large on tax data, he is in fact likely still to underestimate actual wealth inequalities.[15] Second, tax competition is one of the

14. Thomas Piketty, *Capital in the Twenty-First Century* (Cambridge, MA: Belknap Press, 2014).

15. Piketty himself makes this point. See Piketty, *Capital in the Twenty-First Century*, 467.

principal obstacles that stand in the way of the increased taxation of capital that Piketty recommends. Any serious effort to 'catch capital' in the fiscal net presupposes an effective way of tackling the problem of tax competition.

In sum, there are two meanings to the term 'catching capital.' *Empirically*, the fact is that within tax competition, states vie to catch capital. While some succeed individually, they fail collectively because the loopholes that tax competition encourages often allow capital to slip through the net. *Normatively*, I will argue that the global community should collectively structure *international* fiscal policy such that a more effective way to catch capital through taxation becomes possible.

Pursuing this latter objective raises a number of issues. If some coordination in tax policy is required to respond to tax competition, what will be the implications for states' fiscal sovereignty? Can one regulate tax competition without calling for an outright harmonization of tax rates? If so, how should we strike a balance between the fiscal autonomy of one particular state and the externalities this autonomy creates for other states? And supposing that reforming the system through multilateral regulation of tax competition is not politically feasible, are there compensatory duties that the winners of tax competition owe the losers? Last but not least, could it be that regulating tax competition will be economically inefficient?

1. THE POLITICAL PHILOSOPHY OF INTERNATIONAL TAXATION

In a nutshell, this book presents a normative assessment of the phenomenon of tax competition. In itself, this is a novel contribution to the literature. While different disciplines touch upon aspects of this project, they all remain incomplete in one way or another.

In political philosophy, the discussion of tax issues is only just beginning to move onto the intellectual agenda.[16] Two prominent examples are Liam Murphy and Thomas Nagel's *The Myth of Ownership* and Martin O'Neill and Shepley Orr's edited volume, *Political Philosophy and Taxation*.[17] Explicit references to the phenomenon of tax competition are few and far between among political philosophers.[18]

In economics or, more precisely, in public economics as the subdiscipline that deals with fiscal issues, the dominant criterion for assessing the practice of tax competition is efficiency. While there is no consensus on whether tax competition is efficient or not, almost all economic models propose to evaluate tax competition exclusively in terms of this one dimension.[19] One significant exception is Hans-Werner Sinn's *selection principle*. While he participates in the debate about the efficiency of tax competition, he

---

16. For a useful overview, see Daniel Halliday, 'Justice and Taxation', *Philosophical Compass* 8, no. 12 (2013): 1111–22.

17. Liam Murphy and Thomas Nagel, *The Myth of Ownership: Taxes and Justice* (Oxford: Oxford University Press, 2002); Martin O'Neill and Shepley Orr, eds., *Political Philosophy and Taxation* (Oxford: Oxford University Press, forthcoming).

18. Notable exceptions are Gillian Brock, 'Taxation and Global Justice: Closing the Gap between Theory and Practice', *Journal of Social Philosophy* 39, no. 2 (2008): 161–84; Alexander Cappelen, 'The Moral Rationale for International Fiscal Law', *Ethics & International Affairs* 15, no. 1 (2001): 97–110; and Miriam Ronzoni, 'The Global Order: A Case of Background Injustice? A Practice-Dependent Account', *Philosophy & Public Affairs* 37, no. 3 (2009): 229–56. Brock discusses challenges of international taxation similar to the ones at the heart of this book, yet her account of potential solutions differs in that she focuses on various kinds of global taxation rather than principles to make national taxation more effective. Cappelen analyses the current distribution of international rights to tax through the lens of theories of distributive justice. Ronzoni, whose work I shall discuss in more detail later, identifies tax competition as an instance of background injustice.

19. For a useful survey on the economic literature on tax competition, see Philipp Genschel and Peter Schwarz, 'Tax Competition: A Literature Review', *Socio-Economic Review* 9, no. 2 (2011): 339–70.

emphasizes that efficiency alone is too narrow a criterion to evaluate social practices.[20]

In political science, valuable work has been done to further our understanding of tax competition and of how it has become part of our institutional landscape without being intentionally created by anyone.[21] Yet, what tends to be lacking in the political science perspective on tax competition is a normative vantage point that would allow us to justify a political and institutional response to the phenomenon. With a handful of exceptions, the same is true for otherwise very insightful contributions from international tax law.[22]

This book brings together strands from all four of these disciplines[23] and, consequently, aims to withstand scrutiny and criticism from all four. Yet, despite this clearly interdisciplinary orientation, this work is ultimately an exercise in economic philosophy. This means that my primary interest in this book lies in the normative underpinnings that we can provide not only for the way in which we design the international tax regime and, in particular,

---

20. Hans-Werner Sinn, *The New Systems Competition*, Yrjö Jahnsson Lectures (Oxford: Blackwell, 2003).
21. To name but some examples, see Thomas Rixen, *The Political Economy of International Tax Governance* (Basingstoke: Palgrave Macmillan, 2008); Jason C. Sharman, *Havens in a Storm: The Struggle for Global Tax Regulation* (Ithaca, NY: Cornell University Press, 2006); Palan et al., *Tax Havens*; Richard Eccleston, *The Dynamics of Global Economic Governance—The Financial Crisis, the OECD, and the Politics of International Tax Cooperation* (Cheltenham: Edward Elgar, 2013).
22. See, for instance, Reuven S. Avi-Yonah, 'Globalization, Tax Competition, and the Fiscal Crisis of the Welfare State', *Harvard Law Review* 113, no. 7 (2000): 1573–676. For the rare legal scholarship on international taxation that explicitly addresses normative questions, see Nancy H. Kaufman, 'Fairness and the Taxation of International Income', *Law and Policy in International Business* 29, no. 2 (1998): 145–203; as well as Allison Christians, 'Sovereignty, Taxation, and Social Contract', *Minnesota Journal of International Law* 99 (2009): 99–153.
23. See also Peter Dietsch and Thomas Rixen, eds., *Global Tax Governance—What is Wrong With It and How to Fix It* (Colchester: ECPR Press, forthcoming).

for the regulation of tax competition, but also for the related questions of efficiency, fiscal sovereignty, and redistributive obligations between states. My goal is to provide a unified normative framework in which all of these issues can be addressed both coherently and comprehensively.

At the same time, laying the normative foundations without constructing the institutional edifice on top of them would be unsatisfactory in its own way. The book explicitly proposes to bridge the gap between normative groundwork and the concrete institutional reforms that this groundwork necessitates and calls for. In doing so, it helps to fill an important gap in our thinking about global socio-economic arrangements. Consider the following question raised by Allen Buchanan and Robert Keohane in a paper on the legitimacy of global institutions: 'What are the proper responsibilities of states in the pursuit of global justice, taking into account the proper scope of state sovereignty (because this will determine how extensive the role of global institutions should be), and what are the capabilities of various global institutions for contributing to the pursuit of global justice?'[24] Buchanan and Keohane argue that substantive answers to these questions are not yet available, in part because theorists have only recently turned their attention to them. As a consequence, Buchanan and Keohane's account of the legitimacy of global institutions holds back on substantive criteria and focuses instead on what they consider to be the epistemic virtues of global institutions.

This book goes further. Regarding the fiscal context, I offer an answer to Buchanan and Keohane's questions. Based on a normative framework that allows me to take a position on the privileges

---

24. Allen Buchanan and Robert O. Keohane, 'The Legitimacy of Global Governance Institutions', *Ethics & International Affairs* 20, no. 4 (2006): 418.

and responsibilities of states, as well as on questions of global justice, I advance a regulatory framework for tax competition. The proposed framework will no doubt be controversial, but I unsurprisingly agree with Buchanan and Keohane that this is exactly the type of thinking on global institutions that we need more of. One important characteristic of this kind of theorizing is that it combines work at different levels of abstraction. Being alert to feasibility constraints is very important in this context. Ideal normative principles are of little use if they fall before the hurdle of moral or political feasibility.

Before moving on to a short primer on taxation, it is worth pausing to ask why questions of international taxation and of tax competition have not been on the radar of political philosophers. Traditionally, taxation has played an important role in the context of theories of distributive justice. Most of these theories appeal to redistributive tax-and-transfer regimes when it comes to implementing their ideal of a just society. The theories of John Rawls and Ronald Dworkin are paradigm examples of this kind of approach.[25]

The shift in the distributive justice literature from domestic justice to global justice that has taken place over the last twenty years has failed to pick up on the fact that the interactions between different tax systems have dynamics all their own. As we shall see in detail in chapter 1, tax competition between states tends to exacerbate income inequalities both within countries and between them, and thus poses questions of domestic, as well as global, justice. In other words, political philosophers concerned with questions about distributive justice both at the domestic and at the

---

25. See John Rawls, *A Theory of Justice*, 2nd ed. (Cambridge, MA: Belknap Press, 1999), 242–50; Ronald Dworkin, *Sovereign Virtue: The Theory and Practice of Equality* (Cambridge, MA: Harvard University Press, 2000), chap. 2.

global level must keep the dynamics of international taxation in mind. Taxation is not only the *instrument* of redistribution but also, at times, the *source* that gives rise to the obligation to redistribute in the first place. Indeed, recognizing this has been one of the main motivations behind my writing this book. This insight shifts our attention from the remedial approach via redistribution that has traditionally been favoured by theorists of justice to the question of how to rewrite the rules of the game in international taxation.

2. A PRIMER ON TAXATION

Some general background on fiscal policy is not only necessary to situate the argument of this book properly but also useful to identify some debates that I deliberately choose to steer clear of in order to avoid unnecessary controversy. These preliminary remarks about taxation are not specific to either the domestic or the international context. They can be grouped into three central questions: Why do we tax? What do we tax? And who taxes?[26]

Regarding the first question, three central goals of taxation have been distinguished. First, taxes raise revenue to finance government spending. This spending serves an *allocative* function predominantly focused on those areas where market allocation does not lead to efficient results, including the provision of public goods, addressing externalities, competition policy, encouraging or discouraging certain kinds of economic behaviour, and so on.[27]

---

26. This section borrows from Peter Dietsch and Thomas Rixen, 'Redistribution, Globalisation, and Multi-Level Governance', *Moral Philosophy and Politics* 1, no. 1 (2014): 61–81.

27. Note that this allocative function includes the provision of the necessary legal infrastructure of markets (property rights, judicial review, etc.), which can itself be understood as a public good. See Douglass C. North, *Structure and Change in Economic History* (New York: Norton, 1981).

Of course, how far government intervention actually serves these purposes will often be controversial. That is why decisions about it ought to be reached democratically. Second, taxes represent an instrument to *redistribute* income and wealth to promote the conception of social justice that has been chosen through the democratic process. Note that both revenue and spending contribute to redistribution. Hence, the progressivity or regressivity of a fiscal regime can only be evaluated by taking both into account. Third, fiscal policy is traditionally used to *stabilize* and smooth the business cycle by tightening policy during boom years and pursuing expansionary policies during economic busts.[28]

I should emphasize that nothing I say in this book commits me to a substantive position on any of the three functions of taxation discussed in the previous paragraph. My argument does not favour any particular role of the government in the economy, nor does it advocate any particular level of redistribution. This is not a book that calls for higher or lower taxes. On the contrary, within a set of rather limited constraints, I explicitly defer these decisions to the democratic process, and I argue that tax competition is problematic because it undermines democratic choices. The importance of this point can hardly be overstated.

What do we tax? The elements of the modern tax base can be described in different ways. For the purposes of this book, the most relevant distinction is the one between mobile factors— mainly capital—and relatively immobile factors such as labour, consumption, or land. Tax competition focuses on the mobile factor of capital. This book does not contain a substantive position on what should be taxed, and once again defers these choices to

---

28. See Richard A. Musgrave and Peggy B. Musgrave, *Public Finance in Theory and Practice,* 5th ed. (New York: McGraw-Hill, 1989).

the democratic process. If citizens wish to tax capital, they should be able to do so. Having said that, it is worth pointing out that a broad tax base, one which does not put all its eggs in one basket, tends to reduce incentives for evasion.[29]

Finally, the objectives of taxation can be pursued at different levels of governance, which brings us to the question of who should tax. The power to tax should ideally be situated at the level of government that best reflects the reach of the benefits provided and the burdens imposed. This 'principle of fiscal equivalence' requires that all beneficiaries of certain government activities share their costs.[30] One rationale for this principle is the basic requirement of legitimacy, namely that those who are subject to the rules should also be their authors. In turn, the question of who needs to be subjected to the rules depends on the phenomenon at hand. While it makes sense to finance garbage collection through municipal taxes, for instance, activities that generate externalities such as pollution call for the power to tax to be shifted to a higher level of governance. In other words, the power to tax is subject to the *principle of subsidiarity*, which requires that government functions be located at the lowest possible level that includes both the beneficiaries and the cost bearers. In the case of tax competition, I shall argue that while the principle of fiscal equivalence does not call for supra-national taxation as such, it does require a certain level of tax coordination between states in order to close the door to evasion and avoidance.

Note that fiscal coordination of this type exists already in some closely related areas. Most prominently, the World Trade Organization (WTO) rules out most national subsidies to industries

29. See Reuven S. Avi-Yonah, 'The Three Goals of Taxation', *Tax Law Review* 60 (2006): 8.
30. See Mancur Olson, 'The Principle of 'Fiscal Equivalence': The Division of Responsibilities among Different Levels of Government', *American Economic Review* 59, no. 2 (1969): 479–87.

because they undermine a level playing field for competitors from different countries. Economically speaking, subsidies are simply the flip side of taxes. If the international regulatory regime were consistent, it would have to either permit both or prohibit both, at least in principle, and allow only certain, clearly defined and well-justified exceptions. Given my evaluation of tax competition in this book, prohibiting both would be more plausible.

3. WHAT IS AT STAKE

At first sight, the failure of states to catch capital under tax competition is an entirely fiscal phenomenon. Its fiscal impact is indeed significant and lies at the heart of this book. Yet, on closer inspection, it turns out that tax competition forms part of an even more fundamental socio-economic trend. Tax competition is but one important facet of a development that draws into question the functioning of political economic life as we know it.[31]

To identify the trend in question, start by considering the 'golden age' postwar economy of the 1950s and 1960s. Granted, the growth rates experienced during this period included the reconstruction effort and recovery from World War II, and one should not assume that they would have been sustainable over longer periods. However, the remarkable feature of these years was that the spoils of economic growth were widely shared. Both real wages and returns on capital increased. John F. Kennedy's expression that 'a rising tide lifts all boats' was an appropriate metaphor to describe economic development. Given the level of economic growth, distributive conflict between labour and capital was minimal.

---

31. I would like to thank Alex Anderson for encouraging me to develop this point further.

This changed with the oil shocks and ensuing stagflation of the 1970s. During the economic downturn, it was clear that earnings expectations on behalf of both labour and capital that extrapolated from previous years were going to be frustrated. Unsurprisingly, distributive conflict followed. Common sense would suggest that both sides have to make compromises in such a conflict unless their bargaining positions turn out to be unequal.

Usually, the dénouement of this distributive conflict is told as follows. Unions in industrialized countries refused to revise their wage expectations downwards, and as long as they succeeded to have their demands met through strike-action, they contributed to the inflationary pressures of the late 1970s. In the early 1980s, the Reagan administration in the United States and the Thatcher government in the UK, through their combination of breaking up the unions and pursuing a shock therapy of contractionary monetary policy, managed to adjust the wage expectations of labour downward. Ever since, the imperative of competitiveness has been very successful in keeping wages in check. Real wages have stagnated. 'In the USA the median wage, that is a wage half-way up the pay distribution, was $13.62 in 2003; in 1979 it was $12.36 reckoned at 2003 prices.'[32] Looking at median wages is a more reliable indicator than averages, because the latter include the wages of top earners, which have increased substantially. For instance, in the first three years of the recovery since the onset of the financial crisis in 2008, 95 percent of the income gains of the American workforce have gone to the top 1 percent of its earners.[33]

---

32. Andrew Glyn, *Capitalism Unleashed: Finance, Globalization, and Welfare* (Oxford: Oxford University Press, 2007), 116.
33. Emmanuel Saez, 'Striking it Richer: The Evolution of Top Incomes in the United States', 3 September 2013, accessed 21 March 2014, <http://elsa.berkeley.edu/users/saez/saez-UStopincomes-2012.pdf>.

Why has labour fared so badly in the distributive conflict with capital over the last thirty-five-odd years? Has their bargaining position deteriorated and, if so, why? An important element in the response to these questions lies in the part of the story that is much less frequently told, namely how well capital has done in the distributive conflict since the early 1980s.

It is common knowledge that the bargaining position of capital has improved markedly thanks to various aspects of deregulation over the last decades. Capital controls have largely disappeared, labour markets have become more 'flexible,' and favourable changes were introduced on financial markets; to name just a few examples, think of lower reserve requirements for banks, the fading of the line between commercial and investment banks, growth in the market for derivatives, the increasing role of shadow banks, securitization, and so on. More often than not, these changes are ascribed entirely to the tenets of neoliberal economic theory, but this would be missing part of the story. Running parallel to the waves of labour strikes in the 1970s and 1980s, capital has also played an active role in protecting its earning expectations.[34] Capital, too, can go on strike. Capital owners, when unsatisfied with their expected return on capital, can go on an 'investment strike.'[35] During the golden years of the 1950 and 1960, resorting to this strategy was neither necessary nor, for that matter, possible because capital controls meant that an investment strike would not have been a credible threat. In today's world of capital mobility, by contrast, investment strikes have become a common occurrence.

---

34. Some commentators might argue neoliberal economic policy is nothing other than the ideological and theoretical packaging of capital interests, but I do not have to go that far to make my argument here.

35. See Wolfgang Streeck, *Gekaufte Zeit—Die vertagte Krise des demokratischen Kapitalismus* (Berlin: Suhrkamp, 2013), 46ff., for a discussion of the notion of an investment strike. The English translation of Streeck's book appeared with Verso Books in 2014 under the title *Buying Time – The Delayed Crisis of Democratic Capitalism.*

Consider the following examples. The first kind of investment strike is employed in the ongoing distributive conflict with labour. Hardly a week goes by these days without a story in the papers about an MNE pressuring its workers to accept a wage cut or a drop in pensions or other benefits. These measures are necessary to stay competitive, so the argument usually runs, and refusing to accept them will lead to a loss of jobs and, in the extreme, to moving abroad the entire economic activity in question. A particularly striking example of this dynamic is Boeing's conflict with the workers at its assembly plant in Seattle in late 2013. A company whose stock hit record highs and whose CEO had received a 20 percent pay increase to $27.5 million in the previous year wanted its union to make concessions in pay negotiations.[36] As if this were not reckless enough, consider that Boeing made this move after having been granted the 'largest single state-tax giveaway in the nation's history' with a subsidy of $8.7 billion.[37] Moreover, Boeing was one of twenty-six Fortune 500 companies that were profitable in every year in the period 2008–2012 without paying a cent (!) of federal tax for that same period.[38]

These last two figures show that Boeing's strike threat was not only directed at its own workers but also at the state. Without a guarantee that the company would be exempt from contributing its share to the public purse, Boeing vowed to pack up and set up shop elsewhere; in this case, the tax competition was mainly between U.S. states, with Texas and Wisconsin immediately on hand to offer subsidies of their own. In the end, Boeing's investment strike worked on both fronts. After initially refusing the deal, the unions made considerable concessions, and both Washington

36. See Timothy Egan, 'Under My Thumb', *New York Times*, 14 November 2013.
37. Egan, 'Under My Thumb'.
38. McIntyre, 'The Sorry State of Corporate Taxes'.

State and Washington, D.C., continue to subsidize Boeing without making them pay the taxes they owe.

Arguably, a more general kind of investment strike on a much larger scale than that of individual companies has emerged in recent years. Think of what has happened since 2008 to the bond spreads of Mediterranean countries—the premium they pay over bonds that are considered less risky investments. Whenever there is a chance of a heavily indebted state without an independent central bank of its own—Greece, Italy, Portugal, or Spain, for example—considering a policy that could weaken the position of its creditors, the punishment of the markets in terms of rising bond spreads is immediate. Even in countries with an independent central bank—such as the United States, the UK, or Canada—the constraint of not upsetting the markets weighs heavily on their monetary policy. What are the wider political implications of this dependence on the verdict of financial markets? As Wolfgang Streeck has poignantly expressed it, the indebted state of the twenty-first century in effect faces two constituencies.[39] On the one hand, it serves its traditional constituency of citizens, who exercise their political rights through regular elections; on the other hand, when the tax revenues from its citizens no longer suffice to cover its budget, it enters private financial obligations towards creditors in bond markets. This latter constituency in effect represents the interests of capital.

When a distributive conflict arises between these two constituencies—for instance, if a choice has to be made between increasing the national debt versus cutting pension benefits—it turns out that the constituency of capital has a structural advantage. Thanks once again to its mobility, capital can make a credible threat to

---

39. See Streeck, *Gekaufte Zeit*, especially 117ff.

leave—that is, to stop refinancing the debts of the state at a reasonable rate of return if its interests are not prioritized over those of the regular citizens. This shows just how asymmetrical the bargaining positions of capital and labour have become over the last decades. Not only does capital have the advantage over labour, but it also has leverage over the traditional arbitrator in the distributive conflict, namely the state. If a government today attempted to take on capital and try to readjust its earnings expectations as Reagan and Thatcher did with labour in the 1980s, it would fail. Governments have lost the power to unilaterally contain investment strikes.

The bargaining positions of capital and labour have become asymmetrical indeed. It is no longer true in today's economy that a rising tide lifts all boats. Today's rising tide lifts the yachts of capital owners, while the dumb barges of workers bob up and down in stagnating water. The distributive consequences of this trend are plainly visible. While the statistics of global inequality show a slight decrease of late owing to the rise of average incomes in China and India, inequality *within* countries has increased in the vast majority of countries in recent years.[40]

In a nutshell, it is no exaggeration to describe the fundamental trend I have been sketching in this section as the de-democratization of capitalism.[41] The mobility of capital in an environment of deregulated markets has allowed capital to extricate itself from the implicit social contract with labour that characterized the postwar period. It has become too easy for capital to go on investment strikes. Capital no longer expresses its interest through the channels of democratic decision making but, rather, in parallel and often contrary to them.

40. See Branko Milanovic, *Worlds Apart: Measuring International and Global Inequality* (Princeton, NJ: Princeton University Press, 2005) for a comprehensive survey of these trends.
41. See Streeck, *Gekaufte Zeit*.

It is easy to see that tax competition is a constitutive element of this process. As chapter 1 will document in detail, tax competition ensures that capital indeed falls outside the fiscal reach of modern democracies.

In principle, there are two ways to counter the de-democratization of capitalism. One is to enlarge the democratic tent and, in the extreme, to go for global democracy. Suggestions along these lines are in my view utopian and hence unhelpful, if not counterproductive. The alternative, which I adopt in this book, is to promote reforms that would bring all stakeholders of capitalism back under the control of democratic decision making. A renewed and sustainable social contract will only be possible if the bargaining positions of labour and capital at the negotiating table become once again symmetrical. While many of the arguments and assertions in this short section of the introduction need fleshing out, I hope to have convinced the reader that the stakes involved in addressing the challenge of tax competition are much higher than an exclusively fiscal perspective might suggest.

4. TAX COMPETITION AND THE FINANCIAL CRISIS

The phenomenon of tax competition existed long before the financial crisis triggered by the fall of Lehman Brothers in September 2008. However, it can be argued that tax competition, while not a direct cause of the crisis, has at least had an aggravating effect. A brief discussion of the relation between the crisis and tax competition will bring into sharper relief the importance of reform. Furthermore, from a feasibility perspective, the crisis offers a unique opportunity for reform whose window might close rapidly once the painful effects of the crisis have passed.

The financial crisis took place in two successive and then parallel waves, namely the banking crisis and the sovereign debt crisis. The banking crisis had its origins in the real estate market. A lack of regulatory oversight as regards the securitization of mortgages—which, to some extent, was also the result of competitive pressures for light regulation—forced banks into writing off significant assets when the real estate bubble burst. With the exception of Lehman Brothers, states came to the rescue with bailouts because they feared that most banks were too big to fail without unleashing contagion in the financial markets.

The link between the banking crisis and tax competition is twofold. First, tax competition contributed to the credit bubble that fuelled the banking crisis—for instance, through the race to offer fiscal privileges to debt over equity. Second, tax competition for paper profits allowed multinational financial firms to relocate their profits to low-tax jurisdictions. By contrast, when the crisis struck, the resulting losses were socialized through the bailout packages. Most of the solutions that have been implemented or proposed thus far—de-leveraging by the banks themselves, raising their capital requirements, separating retail and investment banking as had been the case in the United States under the Glass-Steagall Act,[42] or instituting a financial transactions tax—while representing necessary steps to overcome the crisis in the short term, do not address these structural deficiencies of the financial system that are linked to tax competition.

The second component, the sovereign debt crisis in the European Union, has multiple causes of which here I will single out four.

42. The Glass-Steagall Act refers to those sections of the U.S. Banking Act of 1933 that limited financial banks' securities activities. It was partly repealed in 1999 through the Gramm-Leach-Bliley Act. For an overview, see, e.g., James R. Barth et al., 'Policy Watch: The Repeal of Glass-Steagall and the Advent of Broad Banking', *Journal of Economic Perspectives* 14, no. 2 (2000): 191–204.

First, and most important, in a heterogeneous currency union, the fact of giving up one's independence to conduct monetary policy comes at a high cost in times of crisis.[43] For example, Spain's debt to Gross Domestic Product (GDP) ratio at the beginning of the crisis, 40.2 percent, was considerably lower than that of the UK, 52.3 percent.[44] And yet, because Spain's hands in monetary policy are tied to those of the European Central Bank, the pressure of the financial markets is on Spain and not on the UK. Second, fiscal profligacy played a role in contributing to the sovereign debt crisis. Benefiting from the low interest rates in the eurozone, countries such as Greece, Portugal, Ireland, and Italy took on imprudently high levels of debt. Third, bailing out the banks weighed heavily on public balance sheets. In this sense, the banking crisis partially caused the sovereign debt crisis. Fourth, the crisis happened in part because the discrepancy between national fiscal and regulatory policies, on the one hand, and cross-border capital flows, on the other, meant that individual states were unable to respond to the crisis effectively.

The link between the sovereign debt crisis and tax competition is once again twofold. First, as chapter 1 will demonstrate in detail, tax competition puts pressure on government revenues, and this has aggravated the crisis. One indicator of this effect is the so-called tax gap, which measures the difference between the revenues a government should receive given its fiscal policy and the actual revenues it does receive. The difference is due to various forms of tax evasion and tax avoidance—schemes that tend to prosper under tax competition. The UK, one of the few states

43. See Paul de Grauwe, *The Economics of Monetary Union* (Oxford and New York: Oxford University Press, 2003), part 2.
44. These are the consolidated gross debt rates for the year 2008 as provided by Eurostat. See Eurostat website, accessed 19 February 2015, http://ec.europa.eu/eurostat.

that actually calculate the tax gap, estimates it at £35 billion for 2009–10, around 8 percent of the total tax liability for this time period.[45]

The second connection between tax competition and the sovereign debt crisis concerns the potential policy responses to the latter. When running a deficit, the two possible fiscal responses are either to reduce spending or to increase taxes. Thus far, the crisis management of the eurozone has almost exclusively relied on the former. Arguably, the reason lies not merely in the unpopularity of raising taxes but also in the fact that, at least as far as taxation on capital is concerned, tax competition imposes considerable constraints. There is a real possibility that the capital outflow caused by a rate increase in capital taxation is significant enough to cancel out the revenue effect. In short, under tax competition, the fiscal responses to the crisis are more limited. Just like in the case of the banking crisis, most of the political remedies for the sovereign debt crisis that have been implemented or proposed thus far—austerity measures, liquidity injections by the ECB, euro bonds—do not address these structural fiscal questions. A potential fiscal union is the exception here, but scepticism is justified as to whether it would be far reaching enough and, for those institutional designs that are, whether they would be politically feasible.

My book does not suggest that regulating tax competition is a panacea for overcoming the financial crisis. What I do claim is that the political response to the crisis so far has concentrated far too much on alleviating its symptoms rather than on the structural deficiencies of our financial infrastructure.[46] We need to do more

45. See HM Revenue and Customs, *Measuring Tax Gaps 2011* (London: HM Revenue and Customs, 2011), 5, accessed 11 December 2012, <http://www.hmrc.gov.uk/statistics/tax-gaps/mtg-2011.pdf>.
46. For a similar argument see Palan et al., *Tax Havens*, introduction.

than merely muddle through this crisis. We need to significantly reduce the probability of future crises. I believe that regulating tax competition represents one important step among many in this direction.

Given the urgency of the fiscal situation in many European countries, given the recurring prospect of the United States falling off the 'fiscal cliff,' and given the popular awareness of the injustice of the status quo as emphasized for example by the Occupy movement, the political preconditions for change are in place. The objective of this book is to engage in the normative reflexion necessary to decide which form this change should take and why.

5. A SHORT OUTLINE OF THE BOOK

My argument aims to reach an audience beyond the community of political philosophers. As I have underscored already, a normative assessment of tax competition is by necessity an interdisciplinary undertaking. The book is addressed to theorists from philosophy, economics, political science, and law who are interested in taxation. Moreover, it will be of interest to policymakers and members of international and nongovernmental organizations. To make it a more accessible read for nonacademics, I have attempted to avoid academic jargon as much as possible. Anyone who understands an article on international taxation in a leading newspaper should be able to follow my argument. References to debates in the academic literature have, for the most part, been relegated to the footnotes.

In a nutshell, part I of the book asks what is wrong with tax competition from an ethical perspective and what we should do about it. Chapter 1 presents the idea of fiscal autonomy as the normative bedrock on which my argument rests. It then shows how tax competition works and how it undermines this autonomy. This analysis is complemented with a section on the incentive structures facing different types of states under tax competition, which is key to formulating an appropriate regulatory response.

The fleshing out of this response lies at the heart of chapter 2. Having discussed a number of existing reform proposals and their shortcomings, I put forward two regulatory principles for tax competition: the *membership principle* and the *fiscal policy constraint*. A summary statement of these principles can be found just before section 2.1 of that chapter. This regulatory framework is based on joint work with my colleague Thomas Rixen. The bulk of the chapter is dedicated to providing a normative justification of these principles and to spelling out the institutional structure they require to be effectively implemented. It also contains an assessment of recent policy initiatives by the Organization for Economic Cooperation and Development (OECD) and the European Union (EU) to combat tax evasion and tax avoidance.

Part II addresses a series of challenges and objections that a regulation of tax competition of the type laid out in part I faces. Most important, opponents to any form of tax cooperation, including the specific version of it defended here, will argue that it entails economic inefficiencies. Chapter 3 analyses the various formulations this claim can take, and comes to the conclusion that it is unfounded. Not only does the efficiency objection to regulating tax competition fail, but I also show that efficiency arguments in the optimal tax literature are often applied clumsily, in a way that camouflages the problems posed by tax competition.

Chapter 4 focuses on the concept of sovereignty in the fiscal context. Could current beneficiaries of tax competition claim that the demands tax cooperation puts on them represent an infringement of their sovereignty? I reject this possibility and conclude that tax cooperation, and regulating tax competition in particular, rather than being a constraint *on* sovereignty, should be viewed as a requirement *of* sovereignty that is necessary for states to set effective fiscal policy.

The ethical questions relating to tax competition are not limited to identifying an appropriate normative and institutional framework for regulation. How should we evaluate the actions of states prior to reform—that is, under the system of tax competition as it operates today? More specifically, do the winners of tax competition have any moral obligations towards the losers? Should tax competition from low-income countries be tolerated as a policy tool for economic development? Similarly complex questions will arise once the regulation of tax competition actually sees the light of day. For instance, might shutting down a tax haven require the international community to compensate some of its individual citizens who suffer from the resulting economic downturn? Chapter 5 discusses these kinds of questions under the heading of 'transitional justice.'

PART I

Chapter 1

Fiscal autonomy and tax competition

1. FRAMING THE QUESTION AS ONE OF AUTONOMY

What is the good that is endangered by tax competition? Why should we be worried about this practice? The short answer, which I will develop in detail in section 3 of this chapter, has two components. First and foremost, and this is the core claim of this book, tax competition undermines fiscal self-determination. Second, tax competition tends to widen the income gap both between capital owners and everyone else, and between rich and poor countries. As we shall see later, the exception to the latter rule are situations where small, poor countries manage to use tax competition to improve their lot.

The present section focuses on the first component. An evaluation of tax competition and its impact on fiscal self-determination can be conducted at different levels of abstraction. Starting at a relatively high level of abstraction, the instinct of political philosophers would be to provide a normative foundation for the desirability of the (fiscal) self-determination of states in the first place. Why is a world of states with a certain level of autonomy desirable? In answering this question, the ideal of giving individuals a say in the decisions that affect their lives will have to be weighed against the potential injustices involved in granting a community the right to make autonomous decisions without taking into account the situation of nonmembers. The outcome of a reflection of this kind might conceivably be that we should abolish the state structure in which tax competition happens in the first place in favour of some type of world government. Or we might conclude, more plausibly in my opinion, that a convincing justification for the state structure can in fact be formulated.[1] In either case, there will be considerable philosophical disagreement before we even get to the question of tax competition.

Alternatively, and starting at a lower level of abstraction, we can take a number of features of the world today as parameters rather than as variables of our normative reflection.[2] In the context of tax competition, the existence of states as political units with a considerable level of autonomy is an obvious candidate for a parameter of this sort. My book adopts this second, pragmatic approach. Even if, and this is an open question, a world carved up into states turns out to be a second-best world from a normative viewpoint, states will not disappear in the near future. From this perspective, a philosophical reflection that analyses a world without states would at best be practically irrelevant. Worse, as Aaron James puts it, 'abstracting away from the embedding international form of the global economy'

1. I propose such a normative justification of the state in Peter Dietsch, 'The State and Tax Competition–A Normative Perspective', in *Political Philosophy and Taxation*, ed. Martin O'Neill and Shepley Orr (Oxford: Oxford University Press, forthcoming). Cf. also Simon Caney, 'Cosmopolitan Justice and Institutional Design: An Egalitarian Liberal Conception of Global Governance', *Social Theory and Practice* 32, no. 4 (2006): 725.

2. Daniel Weinstock's way of approaching ethical questions in this way has had an important influence on me over the years. In fact, any ethical evaluation takes for granted some features of the world; the only question is how fundamental the assumed features are. For example, in imagining a world without borders, one would still rely on a battery of assumptions about human motivation and their impact on the feasibility of alternative institutional arrangements.

might 'obscure the question of how a distinctive class of fairness responsibilities could emerge from that kind of social relationship.'[3] The goal of this book is to identify this distinctive class of fairness responsibilities in the context of international tax governance.

One might object to this framing of the normative question that it is philosophically unsatisfying not to push for the 'ultimate' normative justification of one's position. Yet, this objection misses the point. The question 'How should we design our fiscal institutions in an international context?' is underdetermined. If the question refers to a scenario where we are setting up the institutional framework from scratch, then it would indeed be philosophically unsatisfying to take states as given. However, if the question refers to our world today, then it might on the contrary be counterproductive to draw the existence of states into question. Both of these projects are worth pursuing, but they are fundamentally different projects and this book is engaged in the latter.[4]

Having said that, taking states as political units with a considerable level of autonomy as given does not imply writing them a blank cheque as to how they exercise this autonomy. First, states and their citizens may well have obligations of justice or of assistance towards others that trump their right to self-determination.[5] For example, one might think that duties of humanitarian assistance trump the right to self-determination. This is an important qualification to self-determination, but one that I set aside for the purposes of this book.

3. Aaron James, *Fairness in Practice* (Oxford: Oxford University Press, 2012), 13.

4. I purposefully avoid the terminology of ideal versus non-ideal theory here because I agree with Laura Valentini that it needs to be specified further to be useful. See Laura Valentini, 'Ideal vs. Non-ideal Theory: A Conceptual Map', *Philosophical Compass* 7, no. 9 (2012): 654–64.

5. Considering that self-determination reigns supreme opens one up to what Simon Caney calls the 'wrong priorities objection', which holds that a polity cannot reasonably ignore what is going on beyond its borders. See Caney, 'Cosmopolitan Justice', 732.

Second, taking for granted the autonomy of states without looking into the forms through which this autonomy manifests itself would indeed be unsatisfactory from a philosophical perspective. It does matter who exercises the (fiscal) autonomy of the state. More specifically, it makes a difference whether fiscal policy reflects the democratic preferences of the citizens of a country as opposed to being imposed upon them by a ruling elite. Even without delving into the normative foundations of the idea, the whole point of *self*-determination is to give people a say over the decisions that affect them. Democratic institutions, while imperfect, represent the best framework available to achieve this goal.

At least for part I of this book, I will therefore make the idealizing assumption that governments track their citizens' democratic preferences.[6] I acknowledge that this is an unrealistic assumption, since government actions often are the result of rather messy and contentious political processes, in which different groups of citizens pursue different interests. It is, in reality, not necessarily true that differences in political preferences *within* the polity of a state are less important than differences *between* polities.

What is more, someone might observe that this is an odd assumption to make for someone like me, who aims at normative reflection with practical relevance. Am I limiting my analysis to countries with democratically elected governments? Could a partial regulation of tax competition between such countries ever be effective if big economies such as China are not on board? These are legitimate questions, and chapter 4 will take them up by relaxing the idealizing assumption made here. However, not making

---

6. For a discussion of the problems associated with this assumption, see Alexander Cappelen, 'Responsibility and International Distributive Justice', in *Real World Justice*, ed. Thomas Pogge and Andreas Follesdal (Dordrecht: Springer, 2005), 220–22.

this assumption at the outset would render self-determination too weak a foundation to carry the normative weight of the regulation of tax competition I will defend.

To sum up, the scope of the normative evaluation of tax competition I will develop here is limited in two ways. First, it will take for granted the organization of the world into states with a considerable level of autonomy; second, I will assume that this autonomy is exercised through democratic decision making, an assumption that will only be relaxed in a later chapter. The regulation of tax competition I will defend is one that applies to democratic states in the first instance, but that can be extended to include non-democratic ones.

So, if we accept the existence of states as political units with a considerable level of autonomy, what exactly does this mean in the fiscal context? What is the content of fiscal self-determination that tax competition poses a threat to?

In the public finance literature, a stylized definition of fiscal self-determination covers two basic choices regarding the size of the public budget (the level of revenues and expenditures relative to GDP) and the question of relative benefits and burdens (the level of redistribution).[7] Call these choices the *autonomy prerogative*. Importantly, they extend to the means selected to realize them, as for instance the calibration of the tax mix between direct and indirect taxes. The two elements of the autonomy prerogative will play a key role in my argument.

Before demonstrating how tax competition undermines the autonomy prerogative thus defined, I shall now turn to a more detailed description of the various forms that tax competition can take.

7. See, for instance, Avi-Yonah, 'Globalization'.

2. UNDERSTANDING TAX COMPETITION . . .

To assess its impact, it is imperative to understand how tax competition actually works.[8] In the introduction, I defined tax competition as the interactive tax setting by independent governments in a noncooperative, strategic way. For tax competition to exist there must be *fiscal interdependence*. This condition holds when the fiscal policy of one jurisdiction creates externalities for other jurisdictions in the sense that it affects their tax bases. While tax competition occurs at all levels of government, from competition between municipalities to competition between states, this book focuses on the latter. Tax competition takes a variety of forms. It operates not only through lower rates but also through the definition of the tax base, preferential tax regimes for foreigners, loopholes, or other regulative measures such as bank secrecy. Owing to its mobility, capital is the prime target of tax competition.[9] Three types of capital can be distinguished to illustrate different aspects of tax competition.

First, states compete for *portfolio capital*. Investors have an incentive to shift their cash, security, and equity holdings to

8. Sections 2 and 3 of this chapter are based on Peter Dietsch and Thomas Rixen, 'Tax Competition and Global Background Justice', *Journal of Political Philosophy* 22, no. 2 (2014): 150–57. However, to ensure a consistent style throughout the book, I here speak in the first person singular even in co-authored passages. For comprehensive overviews of how tax competition works, see Avi-Yonah, 'Globalization'; and Rixen, *The Political Economy of International Tax Governance*. Palan et al., *Tax Havens*, offers a wealth of insights on the workings of tax competition and provides data to illustrate them. As for models of tax competition in the economics literature, chapter 3 of this book will provide a detailed review.

9. States may, in theory, also compete to attract mobile individuals via taxes on labour income. Empirically, while there is some competition for individuals in very high income brackets, labour tax competition is insignificant; cf. Peter Schwarz, 'Does Capital Mobility Reduce the Corporate-Labor Tax Ratio?', *Public Choice* 130, no. 3 (2007): 363–80.

countries where tax rates on their earnings are lowest.[10] Doing so has not always been both possible and a financially attractive thing to do. Until the early 1980s, exchange controls were in place in many developed economies, limiting the ability of their citizens to shift their wealth to other countries. Moreover, withholding taxes used to be common, meaning that one's tax burden did not necessarily fall when moving assets abroad. However, after a unilateral move by the United States to abolish withholding taxes in 1984 triggered a huge flow of portfolio investment into the United States, the governments of other developed nations were forced to follow suit and withholding taxes became unpopular.[11]

Tax havens target individual and corporate portfolio capital through a combination of low or even zero rates with legal provisions such as bank secrecy or trusts that obscure the ownership of capital holdings. Often, this involves the setting up of a number of shell companies to make life difficult for fiscal forensics teams.[12] Now, if you are a 'respectable' person and you do not want to set up your tax avoidance structure on some little island, an innovative study by Jason Sharman has shown that a more comfortable and

---

10. For a more detailed account of the various assets that fall into the category of portfolio capital, see Tax Justice Network, *Tax Us if You Can*, 12–13.

11. See Avi-Yonah, 'Globalization', 1579.

12. Nicholas Shaxson provides a nice illustration of this kind of structure: 'A Mexican drug dealer may have $20 million, say, in a Panama bank account. The account is not in his name but is instead under a trust set up in the Bahamas. The trustees may live in Guernsey, and the trust beneficiary could be a Wyoming corporation. Even if you can find the names of that company's directors, and even get photocopies of their passports—that gets you no closer: These directors will be professional nominees who direct hundreds of similar companies. They are linked to the next rung of the ladder through a company lawyer, who is prevented by attorney-client privilege from giving out any details. Even if you break through *that* barrier you may find that the corporation is held by a Turks and Caicos trust with a flee clause: The moment an inquiry is detected, the structure flits to another secrecy jurisdiction'. Nicholas Shaxson, *Treasure Islands—Uncovering the Damage of Offshore Banking and Tax Havens* (Basingstoke: Palgrave Macmillan, 2011), 27.

even less risky alternative is available.[13] In the wake of the crackdown on money laundering, corruption, and tax evasion by international organizations over the last decade, Sharman set out to test how effective the adopted measures were. Contacting fifty-four financial service providers in twenty-two countries, he attempted to 'found anonymous corporate vehicles without proof of identity and then to establish corporate bank accounts for these vehicles.'[14] Out of the seventeen providers who offered step 1, thirteen were firms not in a remote island tax haven but, rather, in OECD countries. As Sharman points out, the United States and Britain are among the countries that have chosen to leave their financial service providers unregulated, while imposing strict standards on so-called tax havens. While only five providers out of the whole sample offered step 2—the corporate bank account—this is still one in ten for a practice that is supposed to be strictly prohibited. All of these practices make it impossible for the revenue agencies entitled to tax the capital in question to trace it.

Tax evasion of this kind is obviously illegal, which makes it hard to come up with reliable estimates of the magnitude of these activities. However, the figures that do exist suggest that it is significant. Estimates for the annual revenue loss to governments from this kind of tax competition range between US$155 and US$255 billion.[15] To add insult to injury, some of the wealth parked offshore in this way is subsequently reinvested in the home country

13. Jason C. Sharman, 'Shopping for Anonymous Shell Companies: An Audit Study of Anonymity and Crime in the International Financial System', *Journal of Economic Perspectives* 24, no. 4 (2010): 127–40; and Jason C. Sharman, 'Testing the Global Financial Transparency Regime', *International Studies Quarterly* 55 (2011): 981–1001.
14. Sharman, 'Shopping for Anonymous Shell Companies', 129.
15. See Jeffrey Owens, 'Written Testimony of Jeffrey Owens, Director, OECD Center for Tax Policy and Administration before Senate Finance Committee on Offshore Tax Evasion, 3 May 2007', accessed 9 December 2011, <http://finance.senate.gov/imo/media/doc/050307testjo1.pdf>; Tax Justice Network, *Tax Us if You Can*.

of the tax evader as foreign portfolio investment (FPI). This phenomenon is called 'round-tripping' and has to be distinguished from tax havens acting as conduits for legal forms of corporate tax avoidance. Recent empirical studies suggest that round-tripping is an important phenomenon. In one of the first estimates of the effect of tax evasion by investors on cross-border investment in debt and securities, in this case for the United States, Hanlon et al. report two revealing findings. First, they 'estimate that a 1% increase in the top U.S. ordinary tax rate results in an approximate 2.1% to 2.8% increase in inbound equity FPI from tax havens relative to non-havens.'[16] Second, they show that the signing of TIEAs (tax information exchange agreements) with tax havens results in a decrease of FPI of up to a third from these countries.[17] In developing countries, where the proportion of wealth held offshore sometimes exceeds 50 percent,[18] one would suspect round-tripping to be even more prevalent.

To complete the picture of tax-avoiding strategies for portfolio capital, another practice has to be mentioned, even though it falls outside the remit of *international* tax competition. The fiscal systems of several countries offer internal, and legal, loopholes for individuals to reduce their tax bills. They have recreated at home many of the opportunities of tax evasion that exist internationally, but in ways that are legal and therefore give the practices a veneer of legitimacy. A striking example of this is the trust industry in the United States. As documented by the 'Artful Dodgers'[19] series on bloomberg.com, the ways in which several U.S. states jostle

16. Michelle Hanlon et al., 'Taking the Long Way Home: U.S. Tax Evasion and Offshore Investments in U.S. Equity and Debt Markets', *Journal of Finance* 70, no. 1 (2015): 259.

17. See Hanlon, 'Taking the Long Way Home', 260.

18. See Tax Justice Network, *Tax Us if You Can*, 3.

19. Bloomberg News, 'Artful Dodgers', accessed 6 February 2014, <http://topics.bloomberg.com/artful-dodgers/>.

for out-of-state wealth are multiplying, attracting vast sums of capital and seriously denting fiscal revenues in other states and at the federal level. For example, by using incomplete non-grantor trusts possible in Delaware or Nevada, residents of states with a relatively high state income tax, such as California or New York (13.3% and 12.7% marginal tax rate, respectively, on taxable income exceeding $1 million), can avoid these levies altogether because Nevada does not have a state income tax and Delaware's income tax only applies to state residents.[20] Another striking example are so-called dynasty trusts set up in South Dakota that allow rich Americans to shield, for generations to come, some of their wealth from the federal estate tax of 40 percent.[21] Now, these are forms of intra-country tax competition, which is not the focus of this book. However, it is plausible to think that states will be more tolerant towards this kind of tax avoidance in a situation where the alternative is to see capital flow into tax shelters abroad. If the latter issue were addressed, pressure to tighten regulation of intra-country tax competition would likely mount, too.

Second, there is competition for so-called *paper profits*. Multinationals are able to shift profits from high-tax jurisdictions to low-tax jurisdictions by using a number of techniques.[22] Here, I will name but two examples. The first of these is transfer pricing. Under a transfer-pricing arrangement, one subsidiary of a company sells products or

20. See Richard Rubin, 'Wealthy N.Y. Residents Escape Tax with Trusts in Nevada', *Bloomberg News*, accessed 6 February 2014, <http://www.bloomberg.com/news/articles/2013-12-18/wealthy-n-y-residents-escape-tax-with-trusts-in-nevada>.

21. See Zachary R. Mider, 'Moguls Rent South Dakota Addresses to Shelter Wealth Forever', *Bloomberg News*, accessed 6 February 2014, <http://www.bloomberg.com/news/articles/2013-12-27/moguls-rent-south-dakota-addresses-to-dodge-taxes-forever>.

22. For a survey, see Michael P. Devereux, 'The Impact of Taxation on the Location of Capital, Firms and Profit: A Survey of Empirical Evidence (with Data Appendix by Giorgia Maffini)' Oxford University Centre for Business Taxation, working paper 07/02, April 2006.

services to another of its subsidiaries. Such transactions should respect the arms-length standard (ALS) for intra-firm trading, namely the principle that the transaction be conducted at market prices. However, in violation of this principle, the traded commodities are often not sold at market prices but, rather, at prices designed to minimize the tax burden. For example, the high-profit U.S. subsidiary of a firm buys 10,000 pencils at $50 a piece from its subsidiary in a low-tax jurisdiction such as Luxembourg or Malaysia. International bodies have developed guidelines to limit such blatant abuse of transfer pricing.[23] However, this has not solved the problem; it has merely shifted it to commodities that are much harder to police, as for instance the internal trading of services or intellectual property rights. A second tool employed by multinationals to minimize their tax burden in high-tax constituencies is a technique called 'thin capitalization' or 'earnings-stripping.' This practice consists of a shift from equity to debt finance. Instead of issuing shares, the high-profit subsidiary of a multinational will take a loan from another of its subsidiaries that is located in a low-tax jurisdiction. The high-profit subsidiary will then be able to write off the interest it has to pay on the loan from its tax bill, whereas the interest earned on the loan in the other subsidiary will be subject to a very low tax or even none at all.

Through these various techniques—corporate inversions or hybrid mismatch arrangements using the Double Irish or other tax structures are additional examples—MNEs can assign profits made in high-tax countries to their subsidiaries in low-tax countries without relocating real business activity. Such 'tax planning' activity of

---

23. See, for instance, Organization for Economic Co-operation and Development (OECD), *OECD Transfer Pricing Guidelines for Multinational Enterprises and Tax Administrations 2010* (Paris: OECD Publishing, 2010); or World Trade Organization, *Agreement on Implementation of Article VII of GATT 1994 ('The Customs Valuation Agreement')*, 1994, accessed 4 June 2013, <http://www.wto.org/english/docs_e/legal_e/20-val.pdf>.

MNEs is not necessarily illegal; it constitutes (legal) tax avoidance.[24] It is also noteworthy to what extent several governments have colluded with MNEs to see profits shift to their jursidiction. The latest example of this kind is Luxembourg. As revealed by The International Consortium of Investigative Journalists (ICIJ), the government of the Grand duchy struck numerous favourable tax deals with MNEs, cutting the latter's tax bills in other countries by billions of dollars.[25] The fact that the current president of the European Commission, Jean-Claude Juncker, was prime minister of Luxembourg when these arrangements were made renders the situation particularly delicate.

Despite different approaches, all empirical investigations into the issue of profit shifting come to the same conclusion: the transfer of taxable profits is very sensitive to taxation, and companies make ample use of these possibilities. The decisive factor to attract mobile profits is the nominal tax rate, because companies shift only those profits that cannot be offset against depreciation and other tax benefits.[26] Again, governments may also decide to compete via specially designed regimes to attract paper profits. For example, the regime of special financial institutions (SFIs) in the Netherlands allows foreign companies to channel capital through them in order to realize tax benefits. Estimates for the magnitude of this type of

---

24. It has famously been said by former British Chancellor Denis Healey that the difference between avoidance and evasion is the 'thickness of a prison wall'. For a description of these and other techniques of shifting paper profits, see, e.g., Brian J. Arnold and Michael J. McIntyre, *International Tax Primer* (The Hague: Kluwer Law International, 1995), 8–17.

25. See The International Consortium of Investigative Journalists (ICIJ), "Luxembourg Leaks: Global Companies' Secrets Exposed". ICIJ website, accessed 24 February 2015, <http://www.icij.org/project/luxembourg-leaks>.

26. Ruud A. de Mooij and Sjef Ederveen, 'Corporate Tax Elasticities: A Reader's Guide to Empirical Findings', *Oxford Review of Economic Policy* 24, no. 4 (2008): 680–97. The fact that profit shifting is possible may explain the weaker effect of tax policies on FDI. As long as MNEs can realize tax savings without business relocations, the competition for FDI and paper profits is in a substitutive relationship.

tax competition are hard to come by, but the fact that 60 percent of international trade is intra-firm suggests that it is significant.[27]

Third and finally, governments use their fiscal policy to attract *real investment* from multinationals. This can be done either through a low corporate tax rate or by creating so-called preferential regimes for foreign corporations ('ring-fencing'), which has the advantage of protecting the revenue stream from domestic firms. Ireland is a classic example of a country that had a preferential tax regime for a long time, and as a result benefited from a large inflow of foreign direct investment.[28] Foreign direct investment obviously depends on a number of other factors, too, including the quality of infrastructure and of human capital. Yet, empirical studies confirm that fiscal policy plays an important role. In practice, multinationals frequently 'shop around' for a favourable tax arrangement among a number of potential locations that suit their business needs.[29] They will identify a number of locations that equally satisfy their general business needs and then play the different jurisdictions against each other to negotiate the best deal.[30] Empirical studies come to the conclusion that raising taxes

27. This statistic is provided by the Organization for Economic Co-operation and Development (OECD), 'Intra-industry and Intra-firm Trade and the Internationalisation of Production', special chapter of the *OECD Economic Outlook 71* (Paris: OECD Publishing, 2002), accessed 9 December 2011, <http://www.oecd.org/dataoecd/6/18/2752923.pdf>.

28. See, for instance, *The Economist*, 'A Survey of Ireland'.

29. See Palan, 'Tax Havens and the Commercialization of State Sovereignty'.

30. See Louise Story, 'As Companies Seek Tax Deals, Governments Pay High Price', *New York Times*, 1 December 2012, for an insightful survey of this phenomenon in the United States. For an extreme case of tax break or subsidy shopping, consider the move by Nokia from Bochum in Germany in 2008—after it had received 60 million euros in subsidies the year before, with the understanding that its factory would operate for eleven years—to first Romania, where the Romanian state contributed another 37 million euros, and then to China in 2011. See Hugh Williamson, 'German Protests Grow over Nokia Relocation', *Financial Times*, 19 January 2008; as well as Nick Thorpe, 'Romania's "Nokia City" Hopes Dashed', *BBC News*, accessed 6 February 2014, <http://www.bbc.co.uk/news/world-europe-16290078>.

decreases the inflow of FDI. However, the direction and strength of the correlation is strongly affected by the method of measurement and the kinds of tax rates investigated.[31]

Tax competition for FDI differs from the first two kinds of tax competition in one important respect. When a country attracts portfolio capital or paper profits, the individual or corporate owner of this capital does not follow her holdings but, rather, stays abroad. These forms of tax competition have been labeled 'poaching' by the OECD,[32] reflecting the intrusion or free-riding on someone else's fiscal territory. Tax competition for FDI, by contrast, invites the owner of the capital to migrate with the capital in question. It does not 'poach' foreign tax bases but, instead, 'lures' capital to become part of its domestic tax base. Intuitively, this might seem less objectionable than poaching; and indeed, as we shall see in chapter 3, this difference does warrant a differentiated regulatory response to the various forms of tax competition.

In some cases, both poaching and luring practices are made more attractive by the fiscal stance of other states. For instance, consider the deferral rules laid out in Subpart F of the U.S. Internal Revenue Code, which state that 'U.S. taxation on foreign income [is deferred] until it is repatriated, for example, as a dividend.'[33] Initially intended to *curtail* tax avoidance schemes—the Kennedy administration had proposed to end all deferral of foreign income in 1961, before Congress watered down the legislation, probably fearing for the competitiveness of U.S. corporations abroad—the deferral opportunities

31. de Mooij and Ederveen, 'Corporate Tax Elasticities'.
32. Organization for Economic Co-operation and Development (OECD), *Harmful Tax Competition—An Emerging Global Issue* (Paris: OECD Publications, 1998), 16, accessed 11 June 2013, <http://www.oecd.org/tax/transparency/44430243.pdf>.
33. U.S. Office of Tax Policy at the Department of Treasury, 'The Deferral of Income Earned Through U.S. Controlled Foreign Corporations, 2000', ix, accessed 6 February 2014, <http://www.treasury.gov/resource-center/tax-policy/Documents/subpartf.pdf>. Most of the factual information in this paragraph is drawn from this document.

that Subpart F leaves intact are considerable and extensively used by U.S. multinationals today. This in turn has a significant impact on the incentive structure for capital-importing countries to set their tax rates. Normally, against the background of the general principle of taxation of worldwide income, they would expect the United States to tax U.S. multinationals' incomes in their jurisdictions if they as the source country do not. After all, while taxation at source is the norm for the taxation of multinationals, residence countries do retain a right to tax if the source country does not. If the United States exercised this right, there would be no incentive for the capital-importing countries either to poach some of the United States' tax base or to lure in foreign direct investment. In short, U.S. deferral rules *encourage* tax competition practices by other countries. The United States plays the role of a 'pusher' of international tax competition.[34]

The same is true for countries using an exemption rather than a deferral system, Canada being one example. Provided Canada has signed a tax treaty with another state, Canada will not tax the foreign income of affiliates of Canadian companies in that other state regardless of whether this income is repatriated or not—this is what distinguishes exemption from deferral, where a tax is due if and when the income is repatriated. Initially, when tax treaties were signed with the objective of avoiding double taxation, exemption was granted on the assumption that the other state was taxing the income in question. Today, with a proliferation of tax treaties being signed with tax havens, this assumption no longer holds. As in the case of deferral, granting exemption encourages other countries to compete for tax bases.

34. I owe this term to Allison Christians, who drew my attention to the phenomenon described in this paragraph and the next. See also Allison Christians, 'Drawing the Boundaries of Tax Justice', in *The Quest for Tax Reform Continues: The Royal Commission on Taxation Fifty Years Later*, ed. Kim Brooks (Toronto: Carswell, 2013), esp. secs. II and III.

More generally, when capital-exporting countries that tend to be rich set the floor for capital taxation abroad at zero, they push poorer capital-importing countries into the competition to attract capital. By contrast, if all countries operated a credit system without deferral or exemption, then tax competition among source countries would be dampened.[35] These observations add another twist to the dynamics of international tax competition. As chapter 2 will show, this twist has given rise to a separate reform proposal on how to address tax competition.

To round out this taxonomy of tax competition, let me add one general remark that holds for all kinds of tax competition. There is an important first-mover advantage in tax competition. Consider again the example of Ireland. Lowering its corporate tax rate below the rates of other European countries allowed the country to attract an unprecedented inflow of foreign direct investment (FDI). Being the first EU country to offer such a low corporate tax rate paid off for Ireland. Moreover, the beneficial effect of being the first mover is more than just temporary. Once a company such as Intel has sunk millions into building a manufacturing facility in Ireland, a slightly lower corporate tax rate elsewhere might not be enough incentive to justify relocating again.

3. . . . AND ITS CORROSIVE IMPACT

So much for an overview of how tax competition works. The phenomenon could be discussed in more intricate detail, but the above characterization will suffice for our purposes here. I will now show

---

35. See, e.g., George R. Zodrow, 'Capital Mobility and Source-based Taxation of Capital Income in Small Open Economies', *International Tax and Public Finance* 13 (2006): 269–94.

how the practice of tax competition undermines both aspects of the autonomy prerogative introduced in section 1 of this chapter. In a nutshell, it puts downward pressure on tax rates on mobile capital, thereby squeezing *government revenues,*[36] and it tends to result in more regressive fiscal regimes, which are not necessarily in line with citizens' democratic preferences concerning *the level of redistribution.* In addition, we shall see that tax competition tends to exacerbate income differentials between rich and poor countries. Let us run through the empirical data to substantiate these claims one by one.

The impact of tax competition on the *autonomy prerogative* is both predicted by economic theory and corroborated by economic practice. Economic theory predicts a so-called race to the bottom in capital taxation and, as a consequence, the underprovision of public goods in all jurisdictions.[37] Yet, while both corporate tax rates and rates for the top income tax brackets have fallen across OECD countries over the last thirty years,[38] they have clearly not hit rock bottom. The explanation for this discrepancy from the predictions of economic theory lies in the way these countries have reacted to tax competition.

They have broadened the tax base, mainly by shifting the burden to the relatively immobile factors of consumption and labour, and

---

36. As Rixen points out, the rules of today's international double-tax treaty regime— originally designed to avoid double taxation—are central in facilitating tax competition and in undermining fiscal autonomy. See Thomas Rixen, 'From Double Tax Avoidance to Tax Competition: Explaining the Institutional Trajectory of International Tax Governance', *Review of International Political Economy* 18, no. 2 (2010): 197–227.

37. See, e.g., John D. Wilson and David E. Wildasin, 'Capital Tax Competition: Bane or Boon', *Journal of Public Economics* 88, no. 6 (2004): 1069–70; as well as George R. Zodrow and Peter Mieszkowski, 'Pigou, Tiebout, Property Taxation, and the Underprovision of Local Public Goods', *Journal of Urban Economics* 19, no. 3 (1986): 356–70.

38. In OECD countries, nominal corporate tax rates have fallen from an average of around 50% in 1975 to an average below 30% in 2005. Over the same period, nominal top income tax rates have fallen from around 70% to well below 50%.

have thus been able to prevent a significant loss of revenue.[39] However, this fiscal policy response has a regressive effect. It shifts the tax burden from capital to labour, from direct taxation on revenue to indirect taxation on consumption, and from high incomes to low incomes. The renewed surge in inequality in OECD countries, while certainly due to a multitude of factors, corroborates this analysis.[40] One way to assess this development, then, is to say that OECD countries have bought fiscal stability in terms of revenue at the cost of a less redistributive system.[41] In other words, they have bought the first element of their autonomy prerogative (the size of the public budget) at the price of the second (the level of redistribution).

Note that the situation in developing countries differs in an important respect. While the pressures tax competition exercises on the public purse are parallel to those in developed countries, developing countries usually do not have the administrative resources to stabilize their revenues by broadening their tax bases. As a result, what we observe in developing countries is closer to the economic prediction of a race to the bottom.[42] Here, tax competition

39. For an assessment of the German tax cut cum broadening of the corporate tax base, see, for instance, Katharine Finke et al., *Impact of Tax Rate Cut cum Base Broadening Reforms on Heterogeneous Firm's – Learning from the German Tax Reform 2008*, ZEW Discussion Paper 10–036 (Mannheim: Zentrum für Europäische Wirtschaftsforschung, 2010).

40. Organization for Economic Co-operation and Development (OECD), *Divided We Stand: Why Inequality Keeps Rising* (Paris: OECD Publishing, 2011), accessed 10 June 2013, <http://www.oecd.org/els/soc/dividedwestandwhyinequalitykeepsrising.htm>.

41. On this point, Bjorvatn and Cappelen make the interesting observation that tax competition, perhaps counterintuitively, poses more of a problem for states with an unequal pre-tax income distribution they want to correct for than for countries where the pre-tax income distribution is more egalitarian to start with. See Kjetil Bjorvatn and Alexander W. Cappelen, 'Income Distribution and Tax Competition' (Norwegian School of Economics and Business Administration working paper 29/01 [2001]), accessed 14 May 2014, <http://www.nhh.no/Files/Filer/institutter/sam/Discussion%20papers/2001/dp29.pdf>.

42. See, for instance, Christian Aid, 'Death and Taxes: The True Toll of Tax Dodging' (report, 2008), accessed 9 December 2011, <http://www.christianaid.org.uk/images/deathandtaxes.pdf>.

undercuts both elements of the autonomy prerogative. By putting downward pressure on rates for mobile capital, it dents revenues. Meanwhile, the feeble attempt to shore up government finances usually falls to the poor through regressive taxes on consumption or labour. The public budget shrinks and the level of redistribution is reduced.

Brazil provides a good case study to illustrate some of these trends. Between 1985 and 1997, the top personal income tax rate fell from 60 percent to 25 percent, while the lowest rate increased from zero to 15 percent.[43] The headline tax for corporate profits has fallen from 50 percent in 1985–86 to 15 percent today.[44] During the presidency of Fernando Henrique Cardoso from 1995 to 2001,

the employee's income tax rate rose by 14% and social security contributions by 75%. Taxes on profits, however, were reduced by 8% over the same period. The regressive nature of Brazil's tax regime has been magnified by a value-added tax regime that biases the tax burden towards lower income households, which pay approximately 26.5% of their disposable income on VAT whilst high income households pay 7.3% of their disposable income on VAT.[45]

43. See Parthasarathi Shome, 'Taxation in Latin America: Structural Trends and Impact of Administration' (IMF working paper 99/19 [1999]), 5.
44. See Shome, 'Taxation in Latin America', 8; and World Bank, *World Development Indicators 2007* (Washington, DC: World Bank, 2007), 284.
45. John Christensen and Sony Kapoor, 'Tax Avoidance, Tax Competition and Globalization: Making Tax Justice a Focus for Global Activism', *Accountancy Business and the Public Interest* 3, no. 2 (2004): 7. Studies on Argentina (Eduardo Engel et al., 'Taxes and Income Distribution in Chile: Some Unpleasant Redistributive Arithmetic', *Journal of Development Economics* 59, no. 1 [1999]: 155–92) and Chile (Gómez Sabaini et al., *La equidad distributiva y el sistema tributario: un análisis para el caso argentino, Serie Gestión Pública* [Santiago de Chile: Comisión Económica para América Latina, 2002]) also identify a trend towards more regressive tax systems.

While developed countries typically receive the lion's share of their tax revenue from direct taxes such as income taxes, this pattern is reversed in Brazil, where 70 percent of tax revenue comes from indirect taxes such as value-added taxes.[46] Since direct taxes are usually more progressive than indirect taxes, this feature of the Brazilian tax mix in no way helps to reduce poverty and inequalities. With poverty still widespread, and with Brazil scoring 0.58 on the Gini index for income inequality in 2003, this is all the more troubling.[47] These inequalities are perpetuated by substantial capital flight. 'Over 50% of the total holdings of cash and listed securities of rich individuals in Latin America is reckoned to be held offshore.'[48] It would be surprising if the figure for Brazil lay far below average.

Note that the asymmetric effect tax competition has on the developed versus the developing world shows that tax competition is problematic in ways above and beyond its impact on self-determination. By depriving the governments of developing countries of vital resources in their fight against poverty,[49] tax competition tends to widen the income gap between the global

46. See James Edwin Kee, 'Fiscal Decentralization: Theory as Reform', 5 (paper presented at the VIII Congreso Internacional del CLAD sobre la Reforma del Estado y de la Administración Pública, Panamá, 28–31 October 2003). The heavy reliance on indirect taxes is a common feature of most if not all developing countries. For data on the tax mix of various countries, see Alex Cobham, 'Tax Evasion, Tax Avoidance and Development Finance' (QEH Working Paper Series 129 [2005]), <http://www3.qeh.ox.ac.uk/pdf/qehwp/qehwps129.pdf>; and Alex Cobham, *Taxation Policy and Development*, OCCG Economy Analysis 2 (Oxford: Oxford Council on Good Governance, 2005), accessed 10 June 2013, <http://www.ocgg.org/fileadmin/Publications/EY002.pdf>.

47. United Nations Development Programme, *Human Development Report 2006: Beyond Scarcity-Power, Poverty and the Global Water Crisis* (Basingstoke: Palgrave Macmillan, 2006), 292 and 336.

48. Tax Justice Network, *Tax Us if You Can*, 4.

49. It is another, and important, question whether the governments of developing countries *actually* use their public funds to this end. Here, I limit myself to the claim that tax competition partially deprives them of the *capacity* to do so.

poor and the global rich.[50] Now, I have made it clear that my argument in this book does not rely on any particular theory of either domestic or global justice. Therefore, I cannot appeal to some independent standard of justice to claim that the inegalitarian impact of tax competition is unjust. While in the domestic context I am deferring this judgement to the democratic exercise of the autonomy prerogative, there is no global polity to make a parallel judgement here. Nevertheless, it is worth pointing out that the political declarations of both national politicians and the heads of international organizations confirm the sense that growing global income inequalities are problematic indeed. Given the fact, pointed out by the Secretary-General of the OECD, Angel Gurria, that '[d]eveloping countries are estimated to lose to tax havens almost three times what they get from developed countries in aid,'[51] anyone who worries about the income gap between rich countries and poor countries has to be troubled by tax competition.

The losses tax competition imposes on some members of society, mostly on those who do not own capital, cannot be captured by income considerations alone. Both in the developed and in the developing world, the effect of shifting the tax burden away from mobile factors such as capital to relatively immobile factors such as labour and consumption also has implications in other dimensions of social justice. Two of these are worth highlighting.

50. For an analysis of the impact of tax competition on inequality, see Peter Dietsch, 'Tax Competition and its Effects on Domestic and Global Justice', in *Social Justice, Global Dynamics: Theoretical and Empirical Perspectives*, ed. Ayelet Banai et al. (London: Routledge, 2011), 95–144; as well as Thomas Rixen, 'Tax Competition and Inequality: The Case for Global Tax Governance', *Global Governance: A Review of Multilateralism and International Organizations* 17, no. 4 (2011): 447–67.
51. Angel Gurria, 'The Global Dodgers', *The Guardian*, 27 November 2008.

First, tax competition not only has a direct effect on the income distribution via its tendency to usher in more regressive fiscal policies, but it also has an indirect effect via the pressure it puts on government expenditure. To the extent that governments suffer revenue losses—and the above analysis has shown that this is more likely to be true in developing countries—cutbacks in government programmes will affect the opportunity sets that different members of society face. In particular, if the equalizing effect of spending on health and education is compromised, this not only has knock-on effects for the distribution of income but, more importantly, it constitutes an injustice in its own right. To some people, especially to those who refuse to accept an outcome-oriented criterion to decide which inequalities of income are unjust, respecting a procedural conception of equality of opportunity may even be more fundamental than focusing on the direct monetary consequences of tax competition. Note that equality of opportunity in this sense covers not only spending on health and education; it also extends to social insurance schemes that help to protect individuals against the increasing income insecurity and income volatility of contemporary economies. Insuring individuals against these risks is part and parcel of ensuring equal opportunity to participate in the labour market. Pressure on government finances may compromise the scope of such programmes.

Second, tax competition affects the distribution of employment, another important dimension of social justice. In contemporary society, having a job is not merely a means to earn an income; it is also an important source of self-respect. While the first two kinds of tax competition have indirect employment effects, competition for FDI has a direct and potentially significant impact. For example, it is widely recognized that one factor behind the remarkable economic growth of Ireland in the 1990s and early 2000s was its low tax rate on foreign corporations. The employment this economic boom generated in Ireland came, to some extent at least, at the expense of growth elsewhere.[52]

Portraying the distribution of jobs as a dimension of social justice may be controversial. Economists might object that jobs are not to be considered a social advantage that governments should 'distribute' as if it were manna from heaven. Instead, the forces of supply and demand should be left to create jobs where they are most profitable.

I agree. In fact, this is precisely the point. Tax competition distorts market forces by influencing the profitability of investments and thereby of creating jobs. In many cases, government decisions to compete on tax rates are quite clearly motivated by the prospect of either creating employment or of losing jobs to lower-tax jurisdictions. In this environment, the market no longer resembles a level playing field, and the project of evaluating 'where jobs fall' from a normative perspective becomes not only a possibility but also a necessity.

I should add an important qualifier concerning all three kinds of social advantage just outlined. Variations in the distribution of income, opportunities, and jobs are of course not necessarily the result of tax competition alone. Other causes are at work at the same time. Isolating the causal link between tax competition and the distribution of these forms of social advantage is notoriously difficult. However, this is no excuse to neglect it.

The principal upshot of the analysis of this section is that tax competition undermines both aspects of the autonomy prerogative. In developing countries in particular, it makes states less

52. The qualifier 'to some extent' is needed here because the lower tax rate in Ireland plausibly has the effect of generating more private investment globally. That said, it is an open question whether the welfare benefits of this increase in global private investment will be outweighed by the simultaneous welfare losses due to lower tax rates and lower global tax revenues.

responsive to the democratic judgements of its citizens in terms of the size of the public budget and the desired level of redistribution. Developed countries, by contrast, have managed to protect the level of their revenues, but only by shifting to a more regressive tax system and by paying the price in terms of increasing inequality domestically.

4. STATE INCENTIVES UNDER TAX COMPETITION

Important insights into the potential solutions to the problem of tax competition can be gleaned from a closer look at the strategic landscape that states face under conditions of tax competition. This analysis reveals that while tax competition represents a more complex problem than frequently assumed, it is not intractable.

Economists and political scientists have used game theoretic tools to analyse the incentive structures of states under tax competition.[53] While it abstracts away some relevant complexities of tax competition—for instance, by treating states as unitary actors— game theory can serve as a useful heuristic to better understand the dynamics of international fiscal policy.[54] In this section, I will present and comment on some of its central findings with respect to tax competition. In doing so, we can look at tax competition generally without distinguishing between the three forms of tax competition introduced in section 2.

My description of the phenomenon of tax competition thus far might suggest that state attempts to attract capital from abroad are

---

53. I thank an anonymous referee for pushing me to say more on this point.
54. Cf. Rixen, *The Political Economy of International Tax Governance*, 14.

individually rational but collectively suboptimal. And indeed, several if not most game-theoretic analyses have presented tax competition as a game of prisoner's dilemma.

In a symmetric case as depicted in table 1.1, this analysis is convincing. Independently of the other country's fiscal policy, each country has an incentive to defect—that is, to lower its tax rates in order to poach or lure tax base from its neighbour. Despite the fact that the Pareto-optimal outcome is the cooperative one, where the two countries do not compete on taxes, the suboptimal Nash equilibrium where they will end up is that of tax competition.[55]

However, the symmetric case does not adequately represent what is going on in the real world. More realistically, when one allows for countries of different sizes, the situation and the conclusions of the model change significantly. As Bucovetsky first pointed out, under tax competition, small countries have an

Table 1.1 PAYOFFS UNDER SYMMETRIC TAX COMPETITION

Country A \ Country B	Tax	Under-tax
Tax	0; 0	–10; 5
Under-tax	5; –10	–4; –4 (Nash eq.)

55. Analyses that see tax competition as a problem of this sort include Eckhard Janeba and Wolfgang Peters, 'Tax Evasion, Tax Competition and Gains from Nondiscrimination: The Case of Interest Taxation in Europe', *Economic Journal* 109, no. 452 (1999): 93–101; Mark Hallerberg and Scott Basinger, 'Internationalization and Changes in Tax Policy in OECD Countries. The Importance of Domestic Veto Players', *Comparative Political Studies* 31, no. 3 (1998): 321–52. The model that has become the *baseline model* of tax competition in the economics literature, while not using the language of the prisoner's dilemma, comes to the same conclusion. See Zodrow and Mieszkowski, 'Pigou, Tiebout, Property Taxation'. We shall look at this model in more detail in chapter 3.

Table 1.2 PAYOFFS UNDER ASYMMETRIC TAX COMPETITION

Big country \ Small country	Tax	Under-tax
Tax	0; 0	−10; 5
Under-tax	3; −8	−5; 3 (Nash eq.)

advantage over large ones.[56] In this case, the payoff structure of the two countries looks as shown in table 1.2.

While it is true that the Nash equilibrium is still the collectively suboptimal scenario of tax competition, it is no longer true that both countries prefer the cooperative outcome to the Nash equilibrium of tax competition. Why is this so? What explains the bias that size introduces into the payoffs from tax competition? The answer to this question lies in the interaction of two different effects.[57] First, the *tax rate effect*: when a country lowers one of its tax rates, it will collect less revenue *ceteris paribus*, in this case given the same tax base. Second, the *tax base effect*: when a country lowers its tax rate, the resulting capital inflows will add to its tax base and thus its revenue. Which of the two effects outweighs the other depends to a large extent on the size of the country. For large countries, the tax rate effect dominates, since they lose substantial domestic revenues while attracting relatively small capital inflows. For small countries, however, the tax base effect dominates—their gains from capital inflows tend to more than compensate for the

56. See Bucovetsky, 'Asymmetric Tax Competition'.
57. For the treatment of these effects, see also Vivek H. Dehejia and Philipp Genschel, 'Tax Competition in the European Union', *Politics & Society* 27 (1999): 408; as well as Rixen, *The Political Economy of International Tax Governance*, 43.

lost revenue. This explains why small countries benefit from tax competition and have no interest in shifting to a world of tax cooperation represented by the top-left of table 1.2. By definition, then, this game is no longer a prisoner's dilemma.[58]

As argued convincingly by Dehejia and Genschel,[59] it is this second game rather than the prisoner's dilemma that we should use as a heuristic to think about state incentives under tax competition. It is no coincidence that most tax havens today are small countries. And it is not surprising, either, that it is countries such as Switzerland, Luxembourg, and Singapore that are consistently blocking reforms towards more tax cooperation. While tax competition is collectively detrimental, it is beneficial for them. Dehejia and Genschel take the analysis one step further by asking why large countries do not use their geopolitical weight to bring tax havens into line.[60] The answer, they suggest, has two components. First, merely increasing the number of cooperators is not enough. As long as there is even one tax haven left, there will be massive capital outflows from the cooperating countries. This is what the authors call the 'outside world constraint.' Second, changing the payoffs of each tax haven is costly. The more of these transfer payments one makes to strengthen the coalition, the smaller the gains are to the large countries as the initiators of tax cooperation. In other words, Dehejia and Genschel conclude, tax competition poses a dilemma: 'either actors reduce intracoalition conflict by selectively excluding potential claimants on side payments, but then the outside world constraint becomes more stringent, or they

58. Rixen refers to this second game as an 'asymmetric prisoner's dilemma'. Yet, since he recognizes the change in incentives, the difference between his analysis and mine is merely terminological. Rixen, *The Political Economy of International Tax Governance*, 45.
59. See Dehejia and Genschel, 'Tax Competition in the European Union'.
60. Dehejia and Genschel, 'Tax Competition in the European Union', sec. 4.

mitigate this constraint by extending the coalition to outsiders, but then any potential gains are eroded by intracoalition transactions costs needed to ensure these gains.'[61]

This model allows us to refine our understanding of tax competition. In particular, the insights it offers into the incentives of various types of countries will be useful to assess the feasibility of various reform proposals. Let us look at some of the conclusions we should draw from this analysis.

First, it is useful to highlight that the distinction with respect to the different incentive structures of small versus large countries cuts across the distinction between the effects that tax competition has on developed versus developing countries. This leaves us with a typology of four different categories of countries, shown in table 1.3.

Table 1.3 THE EFFECT OF TAX COMPETITION ON DIFFERENT TYPES OF COUNTRIES

Country size (population) / Level of development	Large	Small
High-income	France, Germany, Japan, United States, etc.	Ireland, Luxembourg, Singapore, Switzerland, etc.
Low-income	Argentina, Brazil, India, Mexico, etc.	Cambodia, Haiti, Namibia, Panama, etc.

61. Dehejia and Genschel, 'Tax Competition in the European Union', 426.

Note first what table 1.3 does *not* tell us. It does not allow us to say that tax havens only occur in a particular subset of the four different categories. While small countries have the structural advantage described above, large countries are doing everything they can to level the playing field in the game of tax competition. The United States, Germany, or Japan are perhaps not the first countries that come to mind when one thinks about tax havens, but they have managed to create niche loopholes to stem the tide of capital outflows to smaller countries. All of the three countries just mentioned rank in the top ten of the 'Financial Secrecy Index' constructed by the NGO Tax Justice Network, which has been developed as a 'tool for understanding global financial secrecy, tax havens or secrecy jurisdictions, and illicit financial flows.'[62]

What table 1.3 *does* allow us to do is to refine our understanding of the winners and losers from tax competition in a way that matters for the regulatory response. *Large low-income countries* lose out under tax competition; as the last section showed, both aspects of their autonomy prerogative—size of the public budget relative to GDP and level of redistribution—are violated. *Large high-income countries* are often able to protect the level of their revenues. They still tend to lose out under tax competition by paying the price of higher inequality. What is more, table 1.3 allows a more nuanced perspective on small countries. On the one hand, *small high-income countries* are clear winners from tax competition, and condemning their role in the international fiscal system appears to be the most straightforward case, ethically speaking. The case of *small low-income countries*, on the other hand, is more complex. There are some small low-income countries—from the ones named in table 1.3, Panama is

---

62. See Tax Justice Network, 'Financial Secrecy Index', accessed 17 February 2014, <http://www.financialsecrecyindex.com/>.

an example—that actively use their size advantage to compete for foreign tax base. Both for them and for larger low-income countries that attempt to do the same—albeit less successfully due to their size—a tricky question arises: Should one tolerate their tax competition practices as a way for them to pull themselves out of poverty? In other words, from a collective viewpoint, is the case for shutting down a tax haven less robust when that tax haven is a low-income country? These are questions that the regulatory response to be defended in subsequent chapters of this book will have to take into account.

Second, the game-theoretic analysis presented in this section provides an explanation for why the prediction of a race to the bottom formulated by economic theory does not hold in practice. As Dehejia and Genschel point out,[63] even for small countries, there will be a point where lowering the tax rate further will no longer be advantageous. Why? Because the lower the tax rate, the lower the positive tax base effect for small countries; at some point, it will no longer suffice to compensate the tax rate effect. 'The competition for foreign tax base is subject to diminishing returns and therefore is self-limiting.'[64]

Third, the asymmetry in incentives to compete for taxes between small and large states shows that, politically, the solution will have to come from larger states. Small states, even though they will of course pay lip service to ideas of tax justice, do not have an interest in creating a framework of tax cooperation. The importance of this point can hardly be overstated.

Fourth, and finally, the dilemma of tax cooperation formulated by Dehejia and Genschel offers a clue as to what large countries must

63. See Dehejia and Genschel, 'Tax Competition in the European Union', 409.
64. See Dehejia and Genschel, 'Tax Competition in the European Union', 409.

and can do to change the payoff structure of small countries and get them on board for reform. They argue, you recall, that tax cooperation is likely to be ineffective or at least too costly, due to the outside world constraint. As long as there is at least one destination for capital to flee to, any multilateral cooperation to raise tax rates will be futile.

However, and I take it this weakens the dilemma posed by Dehejia and Genschel somewhat, rates are only one of the fiscal parameters that tax cooperation can operate on. Indeed, given that this book is based on the idea of fiscal autonomy of states, cooperation on rates and certainly outright rate harmonization are not attractive options precisely because they would violate this autonomy. The other parameter that large states pursuing tax cooperation can work on is the tax base. Here, they have more room for manoeuvre. For instance, an important step towards changing the payoff structure of tax havens would be to stop *pushing* them into competing for mobile tax base, as capital exporters are doing today by setting the floor of tax rates on worldwide income at zero. At present, to return to an earlier example, institutional arrangements such as the deferral on foreign income of U.S. multinationals not only encourage other countries to compete for the tax base in question but also the United States de facto forfeits its residual right to tax that base if the tax haven chooses not to tax it. In other words, the United States in effect voluntarily limits the reach of its corporate tax base to its own territory—note that this does not apply to its personal income tax, whose base is worldwide income. More generally, abolishing deferral and exemption arrangements reduces the pull of tax havens because the outflowing capital would not actually escape the fiscal net. The outside world constraint is considerably weaker if the tax base is worldwide income.[65]

---

65. To avoid double taxation, a credit system could be put in place. See Rixen, *The Political Economy of International Tax Governance*, 32–43.

This last point will be particularly relevant to my later discussion of the feasibility of different reform proposals. But before asking the question of what is feasible, the next chapter will turn to the issue of what is ethically desirable. Once we know what an ethically acceptable framework for international taxation would be, we will then be in a position to analyse the feasibility of various strategies to get there.

5. CONCLUSION

This opening chapter has put in place the normative and empirical premises for regulating tax competition. Taking as a given that states are political units with a considerable amount of autonomy, I have spelt out this autonomy in the fiscal realm as a prerogative to set the size of the public budget relative to GDP, as well as to determine the level of redistribution. For now, I have assumed that the autonomy prerogative rests on democratic foundations, with governments making choices that reflect the preferences of their citizens. This assumption will be relaxed in chapter 4.

Second, the chapter has given an overview of the various types of tax competition and how they work. A distinction has been drawn between the *poaching* of foreign tax base, on the one hand, where the tax base moves from one country to another while the owner of the capital in question stays put—as in the cases of individual tax evasion, as well as profit shifting of MNEs—and the *luring* of foreign tax base, on the other hand, where owner and capital move together, as in the case of FDI.

Third, I have outlined the ways in which tax competition is problematic from an ethical perspective. Most importantly given the normative premises of this book, tax competition undermines the fiscal autonomy of states. While high-income countries suffer mostly in terms of a more regressive tax structure, low-income countries also lose out on government revenues. In addition, this asymmetry means that tax competition tends to exacerbate income differentials between rich and poor countries.

Finally, I have relied on game theory to sharpen our understanding of the incentives of states to engage in tax competition. It turns out that small countries have a structural advantage under tax competition that will make them reluctant to enter into tax cooperation. Keeping this insight in mind will be key to developing a regulatory framework for tax competition in subsequent chapters that is not only ethically sound but also feasible.

Chapter 2

Regulating tax competition

1. EXISTING REFORM PROPOSALS AND WHERE THEY FALL SHORT

Before setting out the regulation of tax competition defended in this book, I will spend some time describing alternative ways to address the problem. Assessing their respective strengths and weaknesses will allow us to further refine the list of *desiderata* that a regulatory framework for tax competition should satisfy. I should emphasize that a lot more could be said on each of the approaches discussed in this section. I deliberately concentrate on those aspects that allow me to establish a comparison with the two principles of global background tax justice that I will develop in section 2 of this chapter. Moreover, the list of reform proposals here does not claim to be exhaustive.

Even prior to discussing *institutional* alternatives, it is important to acknowledge at least one alternative *normative foundation* for thinking about tax competition. Rather than constructing one's response to tax competition on the normative premise of fiscal self-determination—as I have done in chapter 1—someone might analyse the phenomenon exclusively through a distributive lens. Starting from the observation that tax competition undermines the fiscal capacity of the state and, in particular, its capacity to redistributive income and wealth, the person might argue that this capacity should be recreated at a higher level of government. In other words, if tax competition as one of the forces of globalisation makes *national* redistribution more difficult, we should create *global* channels of redistribution to pick up the slack. Several of the increasing number of proposals for global taxes—such as the financial transactions tax (FTT) or the global resource dividend (GRD)—can be read in this light.[1] The underlying idea of this approach is to match economic globalisation with certain forms of political governance with a global reach.

Let me emphasize that, in principle, I am very sympathetic to this line of thought. However, as I have argued in more detail in a paper co-authored with Thomas Rixen,[2] I believe that this approach faces formidable feasibility constraints. First, note that it has to rely on a theory of global justice to determine what level of global redistribution is adequate. Already this first step is one that I have shied away from in this book, not because I think there are no global distributive injustices, but because the question of what theory of global justice to defend is very controversial.[3] Second, even if we could clear this first hurdle and theoretically establish the superiority of one particular theory of justice, the current

1. See, for instance, James Tobin, 'A Currency Transaction Tax, Why and How', *Open Economies Review* 7, no. 1 (1996): 493–99, for discussion of a redistributive motivation of the FTT; and Thomas Pogge, *World Poverty and Human Rights: Cosmopolitan Responsibilities and Reforms*, 2nd ed. (Cambridge: Polity Press, 2008), 202ff., for the GRD. Note that the FTT does not have to be, and indeed has not been historically, defended on redistributive grounds. Its primary rationale as originally put forward by Tobin (James Tobin, 'A Proposal for International Monetary Reform', *Eastern Economic Journal* 4, nos. 3–4 [1978]: 153–59) is financial stability; see also the discussion of capital controls below.

2. Dietsch and Rixen, 'Redistribution, Globalisation, and Multi-Level Governance'. The argument in this paragraph and the previous one relies on this paper.

3. Brian Barry and Laura Valentini, 'Egalitarian Challenges to Global Egalitarianism: A Critique', *Review of International Studies* 35, no. 3 (2009): 485–512, for an excellent survey of the literature.

world order poses important difficulties as to its implementation. Is it realistic to expect the citizens of a rich state that, according to the theory of global justice, has redistributive obligations towards the citizens of a poor state to actually respect these obligations? As long as the latter do not have a say in the political decisions on the transfer, I think the answer is no. Recall that at the beginning of chapter 1, I took the division of the world into states as given in order to ensure that my response to tax competition applies to the world as we know it today. It is for the same pragmatic reason that I set aside the idea of looking at the problem of tax competition from the perspective of global *distributive* justice. Of course, the regulation of tax competition I will defend later on will require international cooperation, and will therefore face its own feasibility constraints, but these are arguably considerably weaker than calling for direct supra-national redistribution.

1.1. Capital controls

With this clarification as to the normative premises of regulating tax competition in place, let us turn to a first potential institutional fix to address tax competition. A quick look at the history of tax competition suggests that the problem is directly connected to the gradual abolition of capital controls following the collapse of the financial architecture of Bretton Woods in the 1970s. This makes sense. For economic agents to be able to respond to the fiscal incentives set by foreign governments, they need to be able to shift their capital across borders. Capital controls limit their ability to do so. It is unsurprising, then, that tax competition has flourished since the abolition of capital controls.[4]

4. See, for instance, Avi-Yonah, 'Globalization'.

Against this background, a return to capital controls seems like a natural strategy to deal with tax competition.[5] Indeed, while the most common motivations for capital controls are the need to readjust a country's balance of payments, as well as countering the competitiveness-reducing effect of a real appreciation of the exchange rate,[6] maintaining the domestic tax base has been named as one of the reasons why governments may want to impose capital controls.[7]

Generally speaking, capital controls can be defined as taxes or restrictions on international transactions of financial assets. They operate on the items that go through the *capital* account of a country's balance of payments—as opposed to the trade in goods and services, which goes through the *current* account. Depending on the purpose of the controls, they target capital *outflows* (e.g., when aimed at correcting a balance-of-payments deficit) or capital *inflows* (e.g., when the goal is to prevent financial instability).[8] Capital controls can either prohibit or restrict certain kinds of financial transactions, or they can discourage them by imposing a tax—incidentally, an FTT represents a moderate form of capital controls in this latter sense.

Do capital controls work? Here, I will first make some remarks about capital controls in general, before dealing more specifically with the kinds of capital controls that would be needed to rein in tax competition. While capital controls had been a cornerstone

5. Thank you to Nicholas Vrousalis for encouraging me to develop this point.
6. See, for instance, Christopher J. Neely, 'An Introduction to Capital Controls', *Federal Reserve Bank of St. Louis Review* 81, no. 6 (1999): 17ff.
7. See Donald J. Mathieson and Liliana Rojas-Suarez, 'Liberalization of the Capital Account: Experience and Issues' (IMF Working Paper 92/46 [1992]); as well as Alberto Alesina et al., 'The Political Economy of Capital Controls' (NBER Working Paper 4353 [1993]), 6–7.
8. See Neely, 'An Introduction to Capital Controls', 16; as well as Kevin P. Gallagher, 'The Myth of Financial Protectionism: The New (and Old) Economics of Capital Controls' (Political Economy Research Institute Working Paper Series 278 [2012]), 3.

of the Bretton Woods system, with John Maynard Keynes as one of their most fervent advocates,[9] in the 1980s and 1990s conventional wisdom in the form of the Washington consensus held that capital controls are a bad idea. Opponents argued that they are both inefficient (they lead to a misallocation of resources between domestic and foreign investment) and ineffective (they rarely attain their declared policy objectives, largely because they can be easily circumvented). Both of these lines of attack have been put into perspective in recent years.

First, prompted by a series of financial crises starting with the Asian financial crisis of 1997–98, a number of authors including staff members of the International Monetary Fund (IMF) have argued that capital controls can in fact make resource allocation more *efficient* under certain conditions.[10] In particular, they can help to protect developing countries from financial instability. Even in these cases, however, capital controls do come at a cost.[11] Due to the restrictions, capital will often not be able to flow where it would be most productive. Moreover, the protection from market forces offered by capital controls, while a good thing in specific circumstances, creates moral-hazard problems for governments that will not push structural reform agendas as forcefully as they would have to under capital mobility.

---

9. See, for instance, the following statement by Keynes on the Bretton Woods agreement: 'Not merely as a feature of the transition, but as a permanent arrangement, the plan accords to every member government the explicit right to control all capital movements'. Donald Moggridge, ed., *Activities 1941–1946: Shaping the Post-war World, Bretton Woods and Reparations*, vol. 26 of *The Collected Writings of J. M. Keynes* (Cambridge: Cambridge University Press, 1980), 17.

10. See Barry Eichengreen, 'The Global Gamble on Financial Liberalization: Reflections on Capital Mobility, National Autonomy, and Social Justice', *Ethics & International Affairs* 13, no. 1 (1999): 205–26; Neely, 'An Introduction to Capital Controls'; Gallagher, 'The Myth of Financial Protectionism'; as well as Jonathan D. Ostry et al., 'Capital Inflows: The Role of Controls' (IMF Staff Position Note SPN/10/04 [2010]).

11. Cf. Neely, 'An Introduction to Capital Controls', 27–28, and Ostry, 'Capital Inflows'.

Second, capital controls can be *effective* depending on the circumstances. Granted, enforcement is a serious issue—for example, one classic way of circumventing capital controls is to dress up financial transactions as commercial ones through over- or underinvoicing of cross-border trade, which passes through the unrestricted current account rather than through the capital account. That said, some forms of controls tend to be more effective than others. In particular, controls of capital inflows tend to be more effective than controls of capital outflows.[12] This is plausible, since the incentives for evasion will be considerably higher among people whose capital is 'trapped' within a given economy compared to foreign investors who can always direct their capital elsewhere.[13]

This last point brings us to the specific question of capital controls as an instrument to maintain the domestic tax base. First, given that this obviously requires controls on capital *outflows*, there are serious questions about effectiveness in this context. All of the other pros and cons of capital controls just discussed apply here as well. Most importantly, however, as Razin and Sadka show, capital controls are an efficient policy tool only when governments cannot effectively tax foreign-source income.[14] True, in today's world of bank secrecy and insufficient exchange of information between fiscal authorities, this adequately describes the position of fiscal authorities. Yet, this need not, and arguably should not, be the case. Once we assume that foreign-source income can be taxed effectively, the rationale for capital controls *as a means to protect the domestic tax base* disappears—as has been shown above, there

---

12. Cf. Sebastian Edwards, 'How Effective Are Capital Controls?' (NBER Working Paper 7413 [1999]); Neely, 'An Introduction to Capital Controls'; and Ostry, 'Capital Inflows'.
13. See also Neely, 'An Introduction to Capital Controls', 26.
14. Assaf Razin and Efraim Sadka, 'Efficient Investment Incentives in the Presence of Capital Flight', *Journal of International Economics* 31 (1991): 171–81, in particular sec. 3.

may be other reasons to adopt them, but they are less relevant to the purpose of this book.

Thus, capital controls emerge as a second-best instrument to fight tax competition in circumstances where the capacity of governments to tax foreign-source income is undermined.[15] With respect to portfolio capital, the classic example for such a situation is incomplete information exchange between fiscal authorities against the background of institutions such as bank secrecy or financial trusts. With respect to the profits of MNEs, governments formally already have the capacity to tax the profits that domestically registered MNEs generate abroad, but as the section on 'pushing' in section 2 of chapter 1 has shown, they often choose not to exercise it. When this choice itself is the result of competitive pressures, which arguably is the case for developing countries in particular, one might say that the effective capacity of governments to tax foreign-source corporate income is undermined. Imagine a large developing country such as India, one of the losers in tax competition according to the analysis presented in chapter 1. In the absence of a more general framework of tax cooperation as defended in subsequent sections, capital controls may be a rational means to both boost domestic investment and protect its domestic tax base. This insight will be relevant in chapter 5.

1.2. Unilateral measures to protect one's tax base

The last section has shown that capital controls represent a useful tool when foreign-source income cannot be taxed. But can states do anything short of tax cooperation with other states to shore up their capacity to tax foreign-source income? Looked at from a different

---

15. Cf. Assaf Razin and Efraim Sadka, 'Efficient Investment Incentives'.

angle, given that competitive pressures bind their hands in terms of raising *rates* on mobile capital, are there any unilateral measures they can take to protect the foreign-source part of their tax *base*?

This section describes and comments on one recent attempt and another proposed reform, both from the United States, to do precisely that. Given the importance of the U.S. economy globally, as well as its geopolitical weight, past tax reforms in the United States have often triggered a wave of reform elsewhere, changing international tax governance in the process. I shall ask whether such a scenario is likely to repeat itself with respect to the two current reform packages.

(a) The first of the two measures is the Foreign Account Tax Compliance Act (FATCA), which 'was enacted in 2010 by Congress to target non-compliance by U.S. taxpayers using foreign accounts.'[16] In terms of the kinds of tax competition distinguished in chapter 1, FATCA targets the first kind—that is, illegal tax evasion by U.S. citizens[17] stashing their wealth in foreign accounts. The basic idea behind FATCA is to convert the financial service industry from an institution that helps tax dodgers devise new tricks for evasion into a source of information for tax authorities. The Act does so by threatening to penalize financial institutions that do not comply by imposing a withholding tax on a wide range of payments made by or to these institutions.[18]

---

16. U.S. Department of Treasury website, accessed 25 February 2014, <http://www.treasury.gov/resource-center/tax-policy/treaties/Pages/FATCA.aspx>.

17. The United States is the only country to tax on a citizenship rather than on a residence basis. This means that, in principle, its tax base of foreign-source income is bigger compared to other countries, since it includes U.S. citizens living abroad. Hence, the United States has a relatively strong incentive to shore up its capacity to tax foreign-source income.

18. See U.S. Internal Revenue Service (IRS) website for more information, accessed 25 February 2014, <http://www.irs.gov/Businesses/Corporations/Foreign-Account-Tax-Compliance-Act-(FATCA)>.

There is no conclusive evidence yet whether FATCA is effective in reducing the U.S. tax gap. However, the wider question that preoccupies us here is whether this approach could serve as a model for other countries or, even more ambitiously, whether it could be the first step towards a multilateral agreement on exchange of information between tax authorities.[19] While we shall see later in this chapter that such an agreement would indeed be desirable, there are two reasons to be pessimistic that FATCA represents a milestone on the way to bring it about.

First, in contrast to the United States, most countries, and developing ones in particular, simply do not have the necessary regulatory capacity and leverage to successfully implement a policy of this sort. While financial institutions cannot afford to lose their business in the United States, the threat of their leaving altogether is real enough to make regulatory authorities elsewhere blink first.

Second, as to the prospect of taking FATCA multilateral, talks between the United States and other states held to resolve a number of compliance issues with FATCA have shown that while the United States wants information on the accounts of its citizens abroad, there are strong domestic lobbies in the United States keen to protect the status of the United States itself as a secrecy destination.[20] In other words, the United States is trying to have its cake and eat it, too. If, as seems likely,[21] FATCA were to be extended through bilateral agreements between countries, this kind of cherry-picking by the more powerful states is highly probable. While multilateral negotiations are not immune to this danger, they get closer to the

19. Itai Grinberg, 'Taxing Capital Income in Emerging Countries: Will FATCA Open the Door?', *World Tax Journal* 5, no. 3 (2013): 325–67.
20. See Grinberg, 'Taxing Capital Income in Emerging Countries', sec. I.A.3. One prominent example cited by Grinberg are banking interests in Florida and Texas that attract substantial amounts of capital from Latin American countries in particular.
21. See Grinberg, 'Taxing Capital Income in Emerging Countries'.

idea of a level playing field by reducing the bargaining power of single nations. This is something to keep in mind.

(b) The second measure to shore up the foreign-source tax base of the United States is only at the stage of being debated at the point of this writing, but it offers interesting insights into potential developments. In November 2013, Max Baucus, then Democratic senator and chair of the Senate Finance Committee, unveiled a proposal to overhaul the way the United States taxes MNEs. At stake here are the second (profit shifting) and third (foreign direct investment) kinds of tax competition introduced in chapter 1.

The Baucus plan contains a whole list of proposed measures, but the ones of interest here are those pertaining to the taxation of the foreign income of U.S. MNEs.[22] The discussion draft considers two options here: (1) 'A minimum tax that immediately taxes all such income at [80%] of the U.S. corporate tax rate with full foreign tax credits, coupled with a full exemption for foreign earnings upon repatriation'; and (2) 'A minimum tax that immediately taxes all such income at [60%] of the U.S. corporate rate if derived from active business operations but at the full U.S. rate if not, coupled with a full exemption for foreign earnings upon repatriation.'[23] The difference between the two proposals is a slight bias in favour of active business income in the second case. Both proposals in effect call for the end of deferral in the U.S. tax code on MNEs. In addition, the Baucus plan intends to go even further

---

22. For a summary of the proposed measures, as well as for the complete text, see U.S. Senate Committee on Finance, 'Baucus Unveils Proposals for International Tax Reform' (press release), accessed 25 February 2014, <http://www.finance.senate.gov/newsroom/chairman/release/?id=f946a9f3-d296-42ad-bae4-bcf451b34b14>.

23. Max Baucus, 'Summary of Staff Discussion Draft: International Business Tax Reform', U.S. Senate Committee on Finance, 3, accessed 25 February 2014, < http://www.finance.senate.gov/imo/media/doc/Chairman%27s%20Staff%20International%20Discussion%20Draft%20Summary.pdf>. The rates are in brackets in the proposal, since they are up for discussion.

and retroactively repeal deferral by imposing a one-time 20 percent levy on all earnings from foreign subsidiaries that have not been subject to tax. On the base of these measures, the plan then proposes to lower the general corporate tax rate.

Ending deferral in this way would significantly broaden the U.S. tax base. It would also mean that the United States would no longer be 'pushing'—see chapter 1, section 2—other countries into practicing tax competition. After all, if the United States as the residence country makes it clear that it will exercise its residual right to tax foreign-source corporate income, the incentives for the source country will shift from posting a low rate to attract capital to matching the U.S. rate in order to get as large a share of the revenue as possible. In other words, ending deferral changes the payoff structure from tax competition for other states. The importance of this effect should not be underestimated. From this perspective, the Baucus plan is certainly to be welcomed. Something along its lines could well serve as a stepping-stone towards a broader, multilateral form of tax cooperation.

Having said that, let me add two reservations about the Baucus plan. First, just like with FATCA, it seems unlikely that the Baucus plan as a unilateral measure could work for other countries with less economic clout than the United States. Administrative capacity is one issue, but the more basic problem is once more capital flight to other countries. Leaving a big market such as the United States is costly, closing up shop in a small developing country much less so.

Second, from the normative stance of this book, there is a more fundamental difficulty with the Baucus plan. From the perspective of fiscal autonomy introduced in chapter 1, it should be up to each country to set its corporate tax rate, and not up to an outsider such as the United States. The Baucus plan, by setting the floor of corporate income taxation abroad at either 80 or 60 percent of the U.S. rate, violates this principle. You might quite rightly observe that this seems a minor problem compared to the broader challenges of tax competition, but it nonetheless suggests that we should keep looking for an institutional alternative that respects fiscal autonomy. This is the goal of section 2 of this chapter. Yet, just as in the case of capital controls, the measures discussed in this section will become relevant again in later chapters.

1.3. Redefining the corporate tax base

While the measures discussed thus far either restrict the mobility of the tax base or boost the state's capacity to effectively tax its foreign-source component, a third strategy to protect one's fiscal interests consists in redefining the tax base in ways that focus on its relatively immobile parts. As chapter 1 showed, OECD countries have shifted their tax burden from mobile capital to labour and consumption. However, it is precisely because such a move makes the tax structure more regressive that it tends to conflict with the autonomy prerogative.

Here, I want to look at another proposal to redefine the tax base, more specifically the part pertaining to MNEs. Corporations can shift some aspects of their business elsewhere—as we have seen, profits and production facilities are the prime factors subject to tax competition—but they cannot shift everything. Most importantly, they cannot shift their customers. Kimberly Clausing and Reuven Avi-Yonah intend to exploit this fact by placing the entire tax burden of MNEs on their sales.[24] The proposal relies on what is called a 'unitary tax with formulary apportionment' (UT + FA). In contrast to

---

24. See Kimberly A. Clausing and Reuven S. Avi-Yonah, *Reforming Corporate Taxation in a Global Economy: A Proposal to Adopt Formulary Apportionment*, Hamilton Project Discussion Paper 2007–08 (Washington, DC: Hamilton Project, Brookings Institution, 2007).

today, when the subsidiaries of MNEs file their taxes separately in different countries (separate-entity accounting), this system proposes to first calculate the worldwide profits of MNEs and then apportion each country's right to tax a part of these profits through a previously agreed formula. Clausing and Avi-Yonah suggest that the formula should look exclusively at sales. Suppose General Motors makes a $10 billion profit in a given year, and 60 percent of its sales occur in the United States, then $6 billion would be taxable there at the U.S. corporate tax rate. As Clausing and Avi-Yonah point out, given the immobility of sales, this would resolve the issue of tax competition—MNEs would no longer have fiscal incentives to shift their profits or operations abroad—and it would boost U.S. tax revenues thanks to the relative importance of the U.S. market.[25]

While I will in fact endorse a version of UT + FA myself in the coming sections, the specific sales-oriented formula proposed by Clausing and Avi-Yonah suffers from a serious flaw. It systematically favours developed countries, including the United States, with big markets for consumer goods. Imagine, for the sake of argument, that 80 percent of General Motors' production was located outside the United States, but 80 percent of its cars were sold in the United States. Under the proposal at hand, the United States would have the right to tax 80 percent of the firm's profits as they see fit. While such a reform would certainly benefit the United States, and could even be implemented unilaterally by them, it would clearly replace the biases of a system of tax competition with a different kind of bias that is no less unjust. Clausing and Avi-Yonah acknowledge that their proposal raises distributional issues.[26] Yet, they argue that developing countries would not lose

25. See Clausing and Avi-Yonah, *Reforming Corporate Taxation in a Global Economy*, sec. 3.
26. Clausing and Avi-Yonah, *Reforming Corporate Taxation in a Global Economy*, 25.

out compared to the status quo, since the ratio of MNE local sales to MNE local income is not systematically different in developing versus developed countries. This argument is flawed because, due to tax competition, the corporate income of MNEs in large developing countries is already artificially low. Hence, the benchmark proposed by Clausing and Avi-Yonah is misleading. Besides, it is clear that UT + FA based on sales alone favours developed countries when compared to a broader formula that includes other factors such as payroll and corporate assets.

One important lesson from this section is that the devil of international tax governance is in the details. A policy framework such as UT + FA that, as we shall see in subsequent sections, has a lot going for it, can be tweaked in ways that introduce important forms of bias. In any institutional reform, powerful countries will always attempt to protect their interests by introducing this kind of bias.

2. TWO PRINCIPLES OF GLOBAL TAX JUSTICE

Having presented a negative argument as to where some existing responses to tax competition fall short, I now turn to the positive normative and institutional argument of the book.[27] To set the scene, it is important to formulate clearly what we are looking for. My survey of the workings of tax competition, its impact on the autonomy prerogative, and the incentive structure it creates for states—all outlined in chapter 1—suggest that some

---

27. The remainder of this chapter—with the exception of section 2.2, parts of section 3.4, and some other, minor changes—is based on Dietsch and Rixen, 'Tax Competition and Global Background Justice'.

form of multilateral institutional reform is needed. The discussion in the previous section has supported this position by showing that the unilateral measures assessed there all lead to suboptimal outcomes.

We are looking for a framework capable of effectively protecting the autonomy prerogative. However, note an important complication. Under conditions of capital mobility, as well as diversity in terms of fiscal preferences (size of the public budget and level of desired redistribution), the autonomy prerogative of states will *always* be compromised to some extent. Consider the following example. Suppose the citizens of country A, say, Sweden, have a preference for a larger public budget with a higher level of redistribution that the citizens of country B, say, the United Kingdom. Sweden accordingly taxes both high-income earners and corporations at a higher rate than the UK does. As a consequence, there will exist an incentive for the owners of part of the Swedish tax base to shift their capital to the UK through the various mechanisms described in chapter 1, even if the UK does not actively try to poach or lure any part of the Swedish tax base. In an economically and fiscally interdependent world, such spillover effects of the fiscal policies of one country onto others are simply inevitable. If one wants to protect the autonomy prerogative of the UK as much as that of Sweden, it would seem wrong to condemn the above shift in tax base. Hence, it would seem wrong to condemn *all* types of migration of tax base between countries. The crucial question then becomes which portion of fiscal interdependence should be considered benign from a normative viewpoint, and which portion should be condemned as problematic. *Prima facie*, it is not clear that the latter category will necessarily be identical in scope to the practice of tax competition as defined above.

The analogy with individual liberty is instructive here. For example, one might take the view that individual liberty should be protected in its most extensive form whilst guaranteeing the same liberty for everyone else. This does not imply that all actions that have an effect on others are off limits. Such a demanding criterion would make life in society rather difficult. What it requires instead is a definition of where that maximum level of liberty lies that is compatible with the same liberty for others.

The challenge in the fiscal context is a parallel one. We are looking for normative principles and institutions that allow us to distinguish normatively benign fiscal interdependence from normatively problematic kinds of tax setting, where the latter will presumably include at least some forms of strategic tax setting and therefore tax competition. Note that this implies there will be *some* shifts in tax base between countries in response to differential tax rates that should count as unproblematic. *The basic challenge of this book is to identify where the boundaries of the fiscal autonomy prerogative should lie, and what institutions might serve to protect them.*

A particularly useful way of conceiving of the institutional rules invoked here is as 'standards for assessing the ground rules and practices that regulate human interactions.'[28] They are not principles that apply directly to the actions of economic or fiscal agents, but ones that should govern the fiscal structure under which these agents operate.[29] In other words, they are second-order principles

---

28. See Thomas Pogge, 'Cosmopolitanism and Sovereignty', *Ethics* 103, no. 1 (1992): 48–75, 50. Both Pogge and, more recently, Ronzoni put forward institutional or background conceptions of justice. The ultimate inspiration for both of their accounts lies in Rawls's notion of the basic structure of society. Ronzoni explicitly discusses tax competition as an example for a context where her concept of background justice is particularly relevant. See Ronzoni, 'The Global Order'.

29. Incidentally, this explains why relying on the idea of *corporate social responsibility* to address the issue of tax competition is misplaced. For a more detailed version of this argument, see Peter Dietsch, 'Asking the Fox to Guard the Henhouse: The Tax Planning Industry and Corporate Social Responsibility', *Ethical Perspectives* 18, no. 3 (2011): 341–54.

that inform the institutional design and constraints under which states set their fiscal policy and under which, ultimately, individuals or corporations face a certain set of incentives to shift their capital from one country to another.

In the course of the next three subsections, I will defend the following two principles of global tax justice. I simply state them up front in order to give the reader an idea of where the argument is heading and of how its different parts fit together.[30]

Under fiscal interdependence (given capital mobility among fiscally diverse, *democratic*[31] states) and provided *just background global governance institutions*:[32]

(1) Natural and legal persons are liable to pay tax in the state of which they are a member (the 'membership principle'). This requires transparency between taxpayers and their tax authorities, as well as between tax authorities (the 'transparency corollary').

(2) Any fiscal policy of a state is unjust and should be prohibited if it is *both* strategically motivated *and* has a negative impact on the aggregate fiscal self-determination of other states (the 'fiscal policy constraint').

2.1. The first principle: membership

Imagine you live on a street with two health clubs. One is a high-end club with expensive equipment and all kinds of freebies such as club towels and shaving equipment, and one is a less fancy club

---

30. I thank one of the anonymous referees for this useful suggestion.
31. Chapter 4, section 5, will extend the principles to apply to non-democratic states.
32. The ethical obligations of states when this idealizing condition does not hold will be discussed in chapter 5.

that lacks the rowing machines, has only three StairMasters instead of ten and no freebies. Unsurprisingly, the membership fee of the high-end club is almost three times that of its no-frills competitor. You are a member of the no-frills club. One day, you discover that your membership card actually lets you pass through the turnstile at the high-end club, too. You keep quiet and start working out there. As it turns out, quite a few members of the no-frills club frequent the fancy club. A month later, you bump into a friend in the washroom of the high-end club. 'What are you doing here?' he asks. With a sheepish look on your face, you tell him about your discovery. He is enraged. 'You guys are free-riding on our membership fees.' He informs the manager, and the next day, the high-end club starts issuing new membership cards. This reaction appears justified.

For the purposes of the present argument, the analogy between countries and health clubs is a useful one. There are places, the Scandinavian countries for example, that provide more services such as state-financed daycare, more generous unemployment insurance, and so on, but in turn also 'charge' more in terms of taxes.[33] There are others, England for example, where citizens prefer to have a leaner set of services and hence pay less. Certain forms of tax planning that involve shifting one's tax base to a low-tax jurisdiction without moving the underlying activity itself are parallel to using the high-end health club with your no-frills card. When a company uses the services of a country—that is, its infrastructure, human capital, and so on—to produce a certain commodity, but then shifts the paper profit made with this economic activity to low-tax jurisdictions

33. I put 'charge' in quotes here because I do not mean to imply adherence to the benefit principle. See also discussion below.

through practices such as transfer pricing or thin capitalization, the citizens who finance these services have a legitimate complaint. Tax evasion on portfolio capital, as suggested by its illegality, represents an even blunter form of abuse and can be likened to jumping the turnstile at the high-end health club when no one is watching.

Despite these parallels between the membership in a health club and a country, the reaction of free-riders when they are found out is rather different. Whereas it seems reasonable to expect most people to feel sheepish about free-riding at the high-end health club, the parallel practice at the level of countries is often pursued without shame and, in the case of corporate tax avoidance, even under the stamp of legality and certainly the approval of shareholders. This reaction can be explained, but not excused, by the pervasive perception of taxation as something the state takes away from us rather than as part of a social compact between citizens.[34]

We are now in a position to formulate the first principle of international taxation, the membership principle:

Natural and legal persons are liable to pay tax in the state of which they are a member.

In order to apply the principle, it is necessary to define membership. My definition is the following: individuals and companies should be viewed as members in those countries where they benefit

---

34. Liam Murphy and Thomas Nagel call this phenomenon the 'myth of ownership'. They argue that citizens do not have an entitlement to their pre-tax income but can only claim legitimate ownership to their post-tax income because the tax-financed state defines property rights in the first place (see Murphy and Nagel, *Myth of Ownership*).

from the public services and infrastructure.[35] This conception of membership is related to, but distinct from, what is called the 'benefit principle,' or the principle of 'fiscal equivalence,' in the public finance literature.[36] The *benefit principle* is usually contrasted with the *ability-to-pay principle*.[37] Whereas the latter justifies redistribution, the former does not and makes taxes strictly proportional to the individual benefits taxpayers receive in return. My conception of membership is more general and comprises both of these principles. It is compatible with what has been called 'group fiscal equivalence,'[38] which demands that the *collective* benefits of the group of citizens be proportional to the amount of taxes paid.[39] It thus allows for redistribution among individuals and corporations. As implicit in the notion of fiscal self-determination employed here, the citizens of a state may (or may not) decide that it is appropriate

35. While, as I will briefly discuss below, this definition of membership is not detailed enough to resolve all cases of ambiguous membership assignments, it does nonetheless exclude certain conceptual possibilities. It should be emphasized, for example, that my definition of membership is distinct from citizenship. Permanently nonresident citizens should not be liable for taxes in their country of citizenship. Conversely, temporary resident aliens, even though they generally do not have a democratic voice in state decisions, should be. I bracket these debates here. Finally, contrary to what Douglas Bamford claims in his discussion of the present proposal, note that my conception of membership is compatible with the idea of multiple memberships—that is, individuals or corporations being affiliated with different states to varying degrees for tax purposes. See Douglas Bamford, 'Realising International Justice: To Constrain or to Counter-Incentivise?', *Moral Philosophy and Politics* 1, no. 1 (2014): 132.

36. Mancur Olson, 'The Principle of "Fiscal Equivalence": The Division of Responsibilities Among Different Levels of Government', *American Economic Review* 59, no. 2 (1969): 479–87.

37. See, e.g., Joel Slemrod and Jon Bakija, *Taxing Ourselves. A Citizen's Guide to the Great Debate Over Tax Reform*, 3rd. ed. (Cambridge, MA: MIT Press, 2004), 61–66.

38. Ulrich Thielemann, 'Grundsätze fairen Steuerwettbewerbs - Ein wirtschaftsethisches Plädoyer für einen Steuerleistungswettbewerb', in *Regulierung oder Deregulierung der Finanzmärkte*, ed. Bernd Britzelmaier et al. (Heidelberg: Physica, 2002), 113–32.

39. The idea of self-financing constraints defended by Sinn can be interpreted as making the same point. They require that 'states agree not to subsidize capital and to finance the infrastructure investment exclusively with capital charges' (Sinn, *The New Systems Competition*, 46).

to tax higher incomes at higher rates.[40] On this issue, the above analogy between the health clubs and countries breaks down. True to its objective to re-establish the de facto sovereignty of states, the membership principle is silent on the actual tax system chosen by polities. It merely stipulates that polities should have an *effective* right to tax individuals and companies as they see fit.

The remainder of this section is dedicated to two sets of comments on the membership principle. The first concerns its relation to existing principles, rules, and practices of international taxation. The second set of comments gauges the potential impact that respecting the membership principle would have on international taxation.

My definition of membership is broad enough to encompass the major intuitions of diverse theories of international taxation. In the international tax literature, there is agreement that a nexus of some sort between taxpayer and country is required to justify taxation. Yet, there is disagreement about the proper nature of this nexus—should it be economic, social, political, or territorial allegiance, or a combination of these? The disagreement has never been fully resolved at the level of principles.[41] This is unsurprising, given that each pure solution has distributive consequences that

---

40. It has been proposed to replace the corporate income tax with user fees, which are unrelated to the profit made by the enterprise. The idea behind this is that redistributive taxation should only occur among individuals, and the distributed profit of companies would be taxable on the individual level as dividend income. Under my notion of fiscal self-determination, governments would be free to choose such a system. But they may also be of the opinion that corporations can be viewed as (legal) persons that should be incorporated in a redistributive scheme. See, e.g., Reuven S. Avi-Yonah, 'Corporations, Society, and the State: A Defense of the Corporate Tax', *Virginia Law Review* 90, no. 5 (2004): 1193–255.

41. See, e.g., Peggy Musgrave, 'Fiscal Coordination and Competition in an International Setting', in *Retrospectives on Public Finance*, ed. Lorraine Eden (Durham, NC: Duke University Press, 1991), 276–305.

favour the material revenue interests of certain groups of countries over others.[42]

Nevertheless, a working compromise has been found. According to the so-called international tax principles, *individuals* are assessed on a residence basis because residence determines where they benefit from public services and where they should therefore be counted as members. *Companies* benefit from public services and infrastructure in the country where their substantive activities take place. For this reason, the active business income of MNEs is taxed at source—that is, in those countries where the income was generated. For MNEs whose activities spread across borders, membership comes in degrees and should correspond to the distribution of its economic activities among countries. This justification for a combination of the residence and source principles of international taxation is commonly accepted. While the detailed definition of membership for particular cases remains a thorny and often controversial issue that keeps many tax experts busy, the distribution of taxing rights broadly follows this pattern, which is in line with the membership principle.

However, there are two practical problems. First, even though their underlying rationale is in line with the membership principle, the actual international tax rules, which are made up of domestic tax laws, bilateral double tax agreements (DTAs), and nonbinding model conventions of international organisations, create certain overlaps (so-called double taxation) and gaps (double non-taxation)

---

42. See, e.g., Richard A. Musgrave and Peggy Musgrave, 'Inter-Nation Equity', in *Modern Fiscal Issues: Essays in Honor of Carl S. Shoup*, ed. Richard M. Bird and John G. Head (Toronto: University of Toronto Press, 1972), 63–85; Rixen, *The Political Economy of International Tax Governance*.

in countries' taxing rights.[43] As described in chapter 1, these grey zones can be exploited by sophisticated taxpayers to minimize their tax bills, thus violating the membership principle. Second, tax arbitrage aside, the current rules are badly enforced. There is no international authority overseeing state compliance, and administrative assistance and information exchange between countries are underdeveloped. Hence, it becomes possible to pass under the radar of tax authorities, thus violating the membership principle.

This brings us to the second set of comments. How would respecting the membership principle change the international tax landscape? While the detailed answer depends on the way it is institutionalized, a general observation can be made. The membership principle ensures that tax competition is brought closer to Tiebout's idealized notion of 'voting with your feet.'[44] Tiebout's model is generally presented as a *justification for* tax competition. It is argued that competition among jurisdictions leads to an efficient allocation of public funds as individuals self-select into different jurisdictions according to the match between the various tax-expenditure packages on offer and their fiscal preferences.[45] A crucial assumption of the model is that there are neither positive nor negative externalities for other countries stemming from the provision of 'local' public goods. Yet, this assumption will generally not hold. When public goods are modeled more realistically as generating positive externalities, they will be underprovided if left to the market. Under these conditions, Hans-Werner Sinn has shown

43. For a discussion of the gaps and overlaps in the international tax regime with references to the vast legal and economic literature on the topic, see Rixen, *The Political Economy of International Tax Governance*, 66–85.

44. Charles M. Tiebout, 'A Pure Theory of Local Expenditures', *Journal of Political Economy* 64, no. 5 (1956): 416–24.

45. See, e.g., Dennis C. Mueller, 'Redistribution and Allocative Efficiency in a Mobile World Economy', *Jahrbuch für Neue Politische Ökonomie* 17 (1998): 172–90.

that tax competition is nothing other than the introduction of the market mechanism by other means and fails to produce an efficient allocation of public funds.[46]

While the costs and benefits of government action will never align perfectly in an economically interdependent world, the membership principle works to minimize the gap between them. It prohibits the hiding or shifting of part of the tax base from one's residence state in the case of individuals and from the source state in the case of MNEs. If it were implemented, two of the three kinds of tax competition, namely targeting portfolio capital and paper profits, would be eliminated altogether and free-riding would no longer be possible. Any relocation of residence in the case of individuals and of real investment in the case of companies, however, would not be problematic, because in those cases taxes are paid where the benefits from public services and infrastructure are obtained. A shift from the status quo to a world where the membership principle is respected would be a shift from a world of (merely) *virtual* tax competition for portfolio capital and paper profits to a world of *real* tax competition for FDI.

Note, however, that the membership principle not only sanctions the relocation of real investment but, by making virtual tax competition impossible, it is likely to make the competition for 'real' FDI more intense. If taxpayers can no longer realize tax advantages by shifting portfolio capital or paper profits, the incentive

---

46. Hans-Werner Sinn, 'The Selection Principle and Market Failure in Systems Competition', *Journal of Public Economics* 66, no. 2 (1997): 247–74. While Sinn and other contributors to the economic literature on tax competition frame this result in terms of welfare losses, I focus on the negative impact on fiscal self-determination (see chapter 1). Potential trade-offs between these two perspectives will take centre stage in chapter 3, which will analyse efficiency arguments in the context of international taxation.

for actual relocation increases.[47] If this is so, it becomes all the more important to determine whether real tax competition is in line with fiscal self-determination and, if so, to what extent.

While a comprehensive answer to this question will have to wait for the second principle I will introduce below, the membership principle does already impose one important constraint on real tax competition. It rules out the practice of ring-fencing—that is, discriminatory tax rates that distinguish between domestic and foreign taxpayers. As an example, think of the Irish corporate tax rate, which, until 1997, distinguished between Irish firms and foreign firms and granted the latter a preferential rate.

Why is ring-fencing problematic from the perspective of the membership principle? Recall that self-determination in the fiscal context comprises the choice of the size of the public budget, as well as the level of redistribution. Suppose the citizens of state A have a preference for a relatively large public budget with substantial redistribution from the rich to the poor. At the same time, for fear of scaring away multinational enterprises with high corporate tax rates, state A institutes a discriminatory tax rate for such enterprises that is substantially lower than the one for domestic companies. What this in effect means is that other countries, through the partial loss of their tax base, are bearing part of the costs of a large public budget with substantial redistribution in state A while seeing their own fiscal choices undermined by the outflow of corporate capital to A. Another way to make the same point is to think of a world with discriminatory tax regimes as a world in which the distribution of part of the tax base and the adjacent benefits in terms of

47. Michael Keen, 'Preferential Regimes Can Make Tax Competition Less Harmful', *National Tax Journal* 54, no. 4 (2001): 757–62; Dhammika Dharmapala, 'What Problems and Opportunities Are Created by Tax Havens?', *Oxford Review of Economic Policy* 24, no. 4 (2008): 671–76.

job creation is a zero-sum game. The winners in this game—that is, those who institute discriminatory tax regimes—are playing a strategy that does not respect the fiscal choices of other countries.

2.2. Transparency as a corollary of membership

For the membership principle to be operational, states need to have access to the income information of their members, including their foreign-source income. When individuals can hide their capital in foreign accounts behind the veil of bank secrecy, and when MNEs use opaque mechanisms to shift profit to low-tax jurisdictions, the membership principle is undermined. Transparency, therefore, emerges as a corollary of the membership principle.

Two central questions arise in this context. First, can transparency be justified from an ethical perspective? Second, what specific form of transparency are we talking about here? Starting with the first question, let us look at the case against transparency. In contemporary liberal societies, a basic distinction has taken hold between the private and the public spheres.[48] Setting aside a more fundamental discussion about the merits of this distinction, it states that some aspects of the life of individuals—and we can include corporate persons here—should be protected from public scrutiny. For example, liberals argue that one's religious beliefs, sexual relations, or consumption patterns all fall into this category. In the same vein, someone might argue 'This is my money. What I do with it, and the returns I earn on it, are a private matter. Transparency of incomes as required by the membership principle is a violation of liberal commitments.'

---

48. For a panorama of the discussion, cf. Jeff Weintraub and Krishan Kumar, *Public and Private in Thought and Practice: Perspectives on a Grand Dichotomy* (Chicago: Chicago University Press, 1997).

Arguments along these lines are not uncommon, yet they are fundamentally flawed. While the question of how one *spends* one's income might indeed be a private matter, I shall argue that the issue of how one *receives* one's income falls squarely on the public side of the liberal divide sketched above. Any labour or capital income one receives reflects a contribution one makes to the process of production as a form of social cooperation. To look at wages or interests and dividends in isolation would be to fundamentally misunderstand the nature of economic life.[49] From an ethical perspective, we look at people's *relative* rather than their *absolute* earnings to assess whether the underlying system of social cooperation is fair. As John Rawls puts it, '[c]ooperation involves the idea of fair terms of cooperation: these are terms that each participant may reasonably accept, provided that everyone else likewise accepts them. Fair terms of cooperation specify an idea of reciprocity or mutuality: all who are engaged in cooperation and who do their part as the rules and procedures require, are to benefit in some appropriate way as assessed by a suitable benchmark of comparison.'[50] As I have emphasized before, this book abstains from providing the benchmark Rawls refers to—that is, I delegate the question of deciding on a theory of justice to the democratic choice of the polity in question. But any given benchmark, in order to respect the ideal of reciprocity, needs access to information about the relative shares that individuals receive from social cooperation. For this reason, this kind of information should be considered public rather than private.

---

49. For a detailed account of the interdependencies of economic life, see Peter Dietsch, 'Distributive Lessons from the Division of Labour', *Journal of Moral Philosophy* 5, no.1 (2008): 96–117.
50. John Rawls, 'Justice as Fairness: Political not Metaphysical', in *John Rawls—Collected Papers*, ed. Samuel Freeman (Cambridge, MA: Harvard University Press, 1999), 396.

The defence of transparency on the basis of reciprocity does not stop here. The economic cooperation among the members of society has two layers. Cooperation in the productive process as outlined in the previous paragraph represents the first layer. Cooperation to finance public goods and other government activities adds a second layer. Once again, in order to evaluate whether everyone is making the contribution that the terms of cooperation assign to them, one needs information about their income.

It is worth restating the defence of transparency on the basis of reciprocity in the terminology of fiscal autonomy given in chapter 1. When exercising their autonomy prerogative, polities make democratic choices about the size of the public budget and the level of redistribution. They subsequently need to ensure that all members actually deliver the contribution that these choices assign to them. To do so, and to thereby avoid instances of free-riding by some members, access to the income information of all members is a necessary condition.

Before considering a couple of objections to the argument just presented, more needs to be said about the kind of transparency it refers to. One can distinguish strong and weak forms of transparency. The former requires that income information is publicly available to all members of the polity. The Swedish system, which allows people to access tax returns of other citizens, is a rare example of this kind of transparency. While good arguments in favour of this more radical version exist—I have argued elsewhere that it can be defended on consequentialist grounds, because it tends to promote social justice[51]—strong transparency is *not* what is required to make the membership principle work.

---

51. Strong transparency will either make it harder to walk away with an unfairly large salary or, in the more likely case of diverging opinions of what constitutes a just distribution of income to start with, transparency will at least foster a public debate on the question of what constitutes a fair income. See Peter Dietsch, 'Show Me the Money: The Case for Income Transparency', *Journal of Social Philosophy* 37, no. 2 (2006): 197–213.

For this purpose, a weaker form of transparency is sufficient, which requires that individual and corporate income information be made available to fiscal authorities, as opposed to everyone. If it turns out that the income in question actually belongs to the tax base of a different state, where the individual or corporation in question is a member, then the information has to be passed between tax authorities. There has to be transparency, in other words, between the citizen (both individual and corporate) and the state, on the one hand, and between states, on the other.[52] Transparency in the former dimension is a precondition to transparency in the latter dimension. The Swiss tax authorities can only pass on account information of U.S. citizens with Swiss banks to the IRS if they themselves have access to this kind of information. It is easy to see that bank secrecy is incompatible with transparency thus defined.

Having established the second, weak form of transparency as the corollary of the membership principle, I can now ask whether there are any serious objections to *this* kind of transparency from a normative perspective. Someone might point to the potential risks transparency implies for the individuals and corporations in question. Links between tax officials and criminals who will use kidnapping and other means to extort money from rich people are not

---

52. Rixen and Seipp distinguish four dimensions of transparency. The first concerns relations between citizens. The strong form of transparency discussed above falls into this category. The second holds between the citizen (including corporate citizens) and the state and represent one of the two dimensions invoked in the present argument about weak transparency. It requires among others things the abolition of bank secrecy and of legal trusts that obscure the ownership structures of wealth holdings. The third dimension, which is again relevant to the present argument, holds between states and calls for automatic information exchange between them. The fourth holds between state and citizen, but this time puts the onus on the state to be transparent about its finances. See Thomas Rixen and Klaus Seipp, *Mit mehr Transparenz zu einem gerechten Steuersystem*, Studie der Abteilung Wirtschafts- und Sozialpolitik der Friedrich-Ebert-Stiftung (Bonn: Friedrich-Ebert-Stiftung, 2009), 11.

unheard of. In such contexts, privacy offers a form of protection. These kinds of arguments are weak. First, even if income information were private, the indicators of wealth—mansions, yachts, expensive cars, and the like—tend to be on public display. Second, and more fundamentally, when such links between tax officials and organized crime do occur, they do not provide an argument against transparency but, rather, point to basic deficiencies with the rule of law in the country in question. The conclusion to draw is not to sacrifice transparency but to strengthen the rule of law. Incidentally, it is no coincidence that such weaknesses in the rule of law occur more frequently in countries with very high inequalities in income and wealth.

The lack of any convincing arguments *against* weak transparency is quite astonishing. As far as I can see, there is no reasonable case that can be made against transparency of income information between citizens and tax authorities, on the one hand, and between tax authorities, on the other. This strongly suggests that the resistance we observe today to increased transparency, notably through automatic information exchange between states, is entirely based on vested interests.

2.3. The second principle: A constraint on the design of fiscal policy

The membership principle prohibits poaching and, by doing so, increases the significance of luring. This section argues that some, though not all, cases of luring are problematic from an ethical perspective and that, hence, fiscal self-determination needs to be curtailed in certain ways. A limitation of sorts to fiscal self-determination should not come as a surprise. After all, it is a constitutive feature of any right that, in order to be effective across its various holders, it will have to be limited—recall the analogy with individual liberty here. Against this background, while the membership principle is designed to *protect* fiscal self-determination, the constraint on fiscal policy to be developed in the present section *circumscribes* it.

To motivate the normative relevance of instances of luring, consider the case of Ireland. For decades, Ireland had a tax rate of between 10 and 12.5 percent on corporate profits, which drew in up to 25 percent of the FDI that American corporations made in Europe.[53] This arrangement was a major factor behind the—by European standards—phenomenal growth of the Irish economy in the decades leading up to the 2008 financial crisis, and is therefore regarded by many economic commentators as a useful and effective tool of public policy. Any argument that claims luring to be problematic from a normative perspective will have to engage with this classic case for tax competition invoked by those countries that successfully employ it to promote economic growth.

So, what is wrong with luring from a normative perspective? I will discuss two potential replies to this question and argue that, while both are unsatisfactory when considered on their own, taken together they can both delineate the problematic aspects of luring and help formulate an adequate regulatory response. In a nutshell, one might object to luring either because it produces bad outcomes or because the intentions behind it are objectionable. I will start with the former.

(a) *An outcome-based constraint.* As has been demonstrated in chapter 1, tax competition undermines the fiscal prerogatives of the state. It puts pressure on the capacity of governments to realize their citizens' preferences concerning the size of the state, as well

53. See *The Economist*, 'A Survey of Ireland'.

as the level of redistribution. This would be the case even if the membership principle were fully respected, because tax competition provides economic agents with an incentive to change membership altogether.

These considerations prepare the ground for an outcome-based principle as one candidate for a constraint on fiscal policy:

A tax policy is legitimate if it does not produce a collectively suboptimal outcome. A collectively suboptimal outcome is here defined as one where the aggregate extent of fiscal self-determination of states is reduced.

Note that I use 'legitimate' here in the sense of acceptable from the perspective of the proposed normative criteria. Such a principle would not only rule out all effective tax competition—that is, tax competition that actually succeeds in luring FDI—but also would impose far more drastic limits on fiscal policy. Suppose that, in a two-country world, the English have a preference for a leaner public budget and lower level of redistribution than Swedes. Suppose also that, to realize these preferences, the English lower their corporate tax rate. This leads to an inflow of Swedish FDI to England. In that scenario, the English continue to live out their fiscal preferences to the same extent as before, whereas the Swedish face a new constraint on their fiscal sovereignty. In the aggregate, the extent of fiscal self-determination of all countries is reduced. Even though England is not purposefully luring in Swedish capital, this is the outcome of its policy, and the above principle would therefore have to consider it illegitimate. The candidate principle would place the entire burden of adjustment on England, thus undermining precisely the kind of fiscal sovereignty that the membership principle is designed to protect. In this sense, it would overshoot its target and fail to delineate mere fiscal interdependence from illegitimate tax competition.

(b) *An intention-based constraint.* Rather than trying to delineate legitimate fiscal interdependence from illegitimate tax competition by appeal to outcomes, an alternative strategy is to focus on the intention that motivates the tax policy in question. Is it not the fact that Ireland *deliberately* tries to lure foreign corporations and their capital that raises hackles and poses problems from a normative viewpoint? Could an argument be made that this is objectionable?

Such an argument can appeal to the intuition that fiscal prerogative trumps strategic intent. Consider the following two cases. First, the England-Sweden case discussed above. The tension between the fiscal prerogatives of the two countries here is constitutive of a fiscally interdependent world without tax harmonization. Privileging the fiscal prerogatives of Sweden over those of England seems unwarranted and overshoots the target. Second, think again of the Irish case. Here, the tension does not occur between two sets of fiscal prerogatives but, rather, between the strategic intent of Ireland and the fiscal prerogatives of other countries. After all, the practice of luring in more members does not form one of the fiscal prerogatives of the state. The fiscal prerogatives of other countries trump the strategic intent of the Irish in this case.

It is worth highlighting that, at least in one respect, an intention-based constraint is an improvement on the outcome-based constraint discussed above. While the latter was not able to drive a wedge between mere fiscal interdependence and tax competition, the criterion of strategic intentions does exactly that. This is a considerable advantage.

However, an appeal to intentions suffers from an important drawback of its own. If one condemns instances of strategic luring of foreign capital, does this condemnation not have to extend beyond tax competition narrowly defined? If strategic intent is the normative hitch, what should one make of investments in infrastructure or in human capital? Ruling out strategic intent across the board would not only deprive governments of substantive policy tools but might also have negative consequences in some contexts. Take the example of strategic infrastructure investments. Suppose Belgium invests in high-quality and specialized infrastructure in order to attract entrepreneurs from various countries, who benefit from the fact that many people and firms from the same sector are geographically close. Over time a highly interdependent cluster develops. These agglomeration effects will positively impact growth in the country.[54] As a reaction, other countries may follow suit in promoting infrastructure or technology clusters. The result is a race to the top. While it is true that the initial move by Belgium temporarily violates the fiscal prerogatives of other countries, the resulting economic growth and tax revenues will allow the other countries to realize their preferences in terms of fiscal prerogatives in the long run.[55] In these cases, there is no need to rule out strategic considerations.

In similar fashion to an outcome-based constraint, an intention-based constraint overshoots the target, albeit in a different way. It cannot distinguish regulatory competition with good from regulatory competition with bad collective outcomes. I submit that the difficulties of these approaches taken in isolation can be overcome by combining them into a mixed constraint.

(c) *A mixed constraint.* An adequate constraint on the design of national fiscal policies is one that weighs the necessary protection

---

54. As the literature on economic geography points out, these agglomeration economies also open up room for taxing capital without automatically leading to capital flight. See, for instance, Richard E. Baldwin and Paul Krugman, 'Agglomeration, Integration and Tax Harmonisation', *European Economic Review* 48, no. 1 (2004): 1–23.

55. That said, it remains of course an empirical question whether a race to the top actually materializes.

of fiscal sovereignty against the costs it imposes on other countries. As chapter 4 will argue, sovereignty, like any other right, comes with certain obligations and constraints attached to it. In the context of competition for FDI, these constraints should be sensitive both to the intention behind the fiscal policy in question and to the consequences on aggregate de facto fiscal sovereignty. What would such a mixed constraint look like?

Consider the intentions component first. While the basic, practical question of how to assign intentions to a state in the first place will be discussed in section 3, we are here concerned with the criterion that decides whether an intention is strategic or not. I propose the following test: *Suppose the benefits of a change in tax policy in terms of attracting tax base from abroad did not exist. Would the country still pursue the policy under this hypothetical scenario? If yes, the policy is evidently not motivated by strategic considerations and therefore is legitimate. If not, it is strategically motivated, but the verdict depends on the impact of the policy on the aggregate fiscal self-determination of all countries.*

'Strategic' here implies that a policy is justified by the prospect of luring mobile capital from abroad rather than by appeal to the autonomy prerogative. In other words, if your country experiences a capital inflow because your polity has a different ideal of how to run the country—a smaller public budget and a lower level of redistribution—then it is not considered strategic; if you experience a capital inflow because you designed your tax policy precisely with this result in mind, then it is strategic. The counterfactual nature of the criterion allows us, on a conceptual level, to elicit the motivation of a country in pursuing any given fiscal policy.[56] Note that my

---

56. The counterfactual nature of the criterion is in part inspired by Calvin Normore, 'Consent and the Principle of Fairness', in *Essays on Philosophy, Politics & Economics. Integration & Common Research Projects*, ed. Christi Favor et al. (Stanford, CA: Stanford University Press, 2010), 225–45.

criterion also captures cases of mixed motives, where a country lowers a certain tax rate *in part* because this reflects the conception of justice of its citizens, *but also* because of the strategic value of doing so for attracting foreign tax base.

One possible objection to this line of argument is to deny altogether that intentions should be relevant to our ethical assessment of a state's fiscal policy. Whether Sweden's fiscal room for manoeuvre is constrained by the diverging political preferences of the English or by the strategic intentions of the Irish, someone might say, is neither here nor there from an ethical perspective. In both cases, these actions by other states simply modify the parameters under which Swedes make their fiscal choices. Underlying this objection is a weaker conception of fiscal autonomy than the one defended in this book.[57] Whereas the present objection regards the rights to determine the size of the public budget relative to GDP and the level of redistribution as merely formal rights, I argue that they should be substantive rights in the sense that they include some notion of policy effectiveness. The discussion of fiscal sovereignty in chapter 4 will come back to this issue.

Second, the causal impact of a specific fiscal policy on the fiscal prerogatives of all affected states will have to be evaluated. The criterion for assessing this impact is the one already discussed above: *a tax policy is legitimate if it does not produce a collectively suboptimal outcome—that is, a negative impact on the aggregate extent of fiscal self-determination.* Two features of this consequentialist part of my criterion require further explanation. First, what justifies looking at the *aggregate* self-determination of other states rather than at

---

57. Laurens van Apeldoorn presents an objection along the lines sketched in this paragraph in Laurens van Apeldoorn, 'International Taxation and the Erosion of Sovereignty', in *Global Tax Governance – What is Wrong with It and How to Fix It*, ed. Peter Dietsch and Thomas Rixen (Colchester: ECPR Press, forthcoming).

the fiscal autonomy of individual states? After all, when the lowering of a tax rate by state A triggers a capital outflow from one other country, state B, is this not enough to ascertain that fiscal autonomy has been compromised?[58] This is a fair question, but note that the judgement I wish the criterion to make in this context is precisely whether this instance of undermined fiscal autonomy should be regarded as a mere instance of fiscal interdependence or as a problematic form of tax competition. In the absence of a feasible alternative that would allow us to assess fiscal autonomy trade-offs on a state-by-state basis, the aggregate self-determination provides a good proxy to make this call. In effect, it ensures that a net capital inflow to the strategic tax setter has actually occurred. This leads us to the second point. If the assessment of capital flows were based entirely on a projection into the future, it would be too speculative in nature to be reliable. Yet, as set out in detail in section 3, I propose an arbitration procedure under which countries bring forward cases that their fiscal prerogatives *have been* violated by the fiscal policy of others. The backward-looking character of this procedure renders the task of evaluating outcomes feasible. In sum, while unsatisfactory on its own, the consequentialist criterion combines with the test for strategic intention to provide a good yardstick to evaluate fiscal policies.

Even though I acknowledge that both assessing intentions and evaluating outcomes remain daunting prospects, I believe they are feasible. As section 3 will argue, there are precedents in the practice of international law that justify this optimism.

To sum up the conceptual implications of the proposed mixed constraint, as well as its advantages over the two candidate constraints discussed before, consider table 2.1. Fiscal policies that

---

58. I thank one of my anonymous referees for pushing me to develop this point further.

Table 2.1 A MIXED CONSTRAINT ON FISCAL POLICY

		Outcome	
		Good	Bad
Intent	Independent	1 ✓	2 ✓
	Strategic	3 ✓	4 ☒

are formulated independently of their impact on international capital flows *and* that have a positive outcome (quadrant 1 of the matrix) are clearly unproblematic. A domestically motivated decision to invest in infrastructure which then has positive knock-on effects on the infrastructure abroad ('race to the top') could be an example.

Fiscal policies that are formulated independently *but* that have a negative outcome (quadrant 2) are problematic, but ruling them out would impose too powerful a constraint on the design of fiscal policy (as demonstrated by the England–Sweden case).[59] Doing so is the weakness of a purely outcome-based constraint as discussed above.

Fiscal policies that are formulated strategically *but* that have a positive outcome (quadrant 3) may at first appear to violate fiscal sovereignty, but a closer look reveals they do not because they lead

59. An anonymous referee pointed out another interesting case that falls into this category. Suppose a country stratifies its tax structure in a way that frees up 'armies of lawyers and accountants' to work 'in more productive ways', thereby creating a more attractive business environment and attracting FDI. Provided this policy is formulated independently, the fiscal policy constraint deems it legitimate even if it leads to a reduction in the aggregate level of self-determination.

to a race to the top (as demonstrated by the Belgium example). A drawback of a purely intention-based constraint is that it would rule out strategically motivated policies irrespective of their effects.

Finally, policies that are formulated strategically *and* that have a negative outcome (quadrant 4) are problematic on both counts and should therefore be prohibited. This is what the mixed constraint is designed to do. The Irish case falls into this category.

Before moving on to questions of implementation, we need to discuss one potential objection to my partial appeal to intentions in evaluating fiscal policy. Suppose the citizens of a developing country are motivated by social justice reasons to build more hospitals and, in order to do so, decide to lower their country's taxes to attract the necessary capital from abroad. Is this part of their fiscal self-determination or should it count as a strategic consideration? Would we not deprive poor countries of an important source of redistribution if it turned out that such a strategic policy contributes to a race to the bottom?

I believe that the fiscal policy constraint can answer these questions. First, I submit that this policy should indeed count as motivated by strategic considerations. Capital that is attracted to the developing country to build a hospital is not available to build a hospital elsewhere. Second, this does not mean that building the hospital in the developing country is not important and does not preclude the possibility that richer countries have an obligation of assistance towards this project. But this obligation should not be discharged in the form of a bias in the way the jurisdictional structure of international taxation is set up. It should, rather, be dealt with via explicit redistribution. In sum, provided the background institutions of global governance are just, the developing country does not have the right to resort to tax competition to finance the hospital. That said, the situation is more complicated if that condition is not fulfilled. As section 2 of chapter 5 will argue, there may be circumstances in which low-income countries' using tax competition to finance development projects is justified.[60]

The last two paragraphs illustrate that a complete account of tax justice has two components: the fair rules of the game that lie at the heart of this chapter and redistributive obligations.[61] Since this book explicitly refrains from endorsing any particular theory of global justice, I bracket the latter here. Attempting to assess redistributive obligations before the fair rules of the game have been determined amounts to a Sisyphean task. Redistribution to correct for an institutional bias and injustice is analogous to swimming against the current—it takes a lot more energy while not getting you as far.

In fact, this issue is not simply hypothetical. There is a debate about the legitimacy of developing country tax havens. When OECD countries began to pressure tax havens to change their 'harmful' tax policies (see below), some of them argued that they had chosen to become tax havens because they saw no other possibility to initiate economic development.[62] As argued above, some of them can even claim to have been 'pushed' into tax competition by the low or zero taxation of developed countries on foreign-source corporate income. If institutional reform along the lines defended in this book were to take place, these countries might have a legitimate claim to compensation of some form. I will return to this issue in chapter 5.

---

60. Thank you to Christian Schemmel for pointing out the importance of this issue.
61. See also the distinction Aaron James draws between internal and external fairness issues. James, *Fairness in Practice*, 144ff.
62. See Sharman, *Havens in a Storm*.

3. IMPLEMENTATION

It is notoriously difficult to derive concrete institutions from abstract principles, because there will generally be more than one way to institutionalize a principle. In the face of this institutional indeterminacy, I limit myself here to demonstrating that there is an institutional solution that satisfies the conditions embodied in the two principles. As a further caveat, let me stress that the following sketch cannot, owing to space constraints, do full justice to the complex issues of international tax law. But it should suffice to outline some possible institutional implications of the present proposal.

Any institutional solution must: (1) provide a forum for governments to negotiate agreements on the rules of international taxation; and (2) make sure that the rules are enforced. In the following I propose the establishment of an International Tax Organisation (ITO) and discuss the basic institutional design features required to ensure it is up to the two tasks.[63] The ITO should become the forum for negotiating and defining the rules in line with the membership principle and the fiscal policy constraint. To ensure a level playing field, all states should be members and adequately represented in the ITO's decision-making procedures, which, in a world of power politics, does of course represent a challenge in its own right.[64]

---

63. Calls for an International Tax Organisation can be found in the literature; see, e.g., Vito Tanzi, 'Is There a Need for a World Tax Organization?', in *The Economics of Globalization: Policy Perspectives from Public Economics*, ed. Assaf Razin and Efraim Sadka (Cambridge: Cambridge University Press, 1999), 173–86; Frances M. Horner, 'Do We Need an International Tax Organization?', *Tax Notes International*, 8 October 2001. However, so far no attempt has been made to derive the institutional design from the functional requirements of the issue to be dealt with.

64. The decision-making procedures of the World Bank and the International Monetary Fund, which are heavily biased in favour of developed countries, provide a cautionary tale in this context. Incidentally, this is why simply extending the mandate of the WTO to include fiscal issues would likely be an unsatisfactory solution.

3.1. Institutionalizing the membership principle

On the basis of the two principles, several reforms become imperative. First, governments have to abolish all rules that make it impossible for other countries to enforce the membership principle.[65] Thus, bank-secrecy, the supply of other deliberately non-transparent legal constructs, and the refusal to exchange information with other tax administrations will be ruled out. The requirement to exchange tax-relevant information with other countries could be implemented through a system of multilateral automatic exchanges of information.

Taking these measures to promote transparency is easier said than done. Here is a list of intermediate steps that could be taken to facilitate their adoption. First, we need stronger deterrents for tax fraud. As the *Financial Times* points out in a December 2013 editorial, the fact that tax fraud 'can lead to financial penalties—even large ones—is a feeble deterrent. By contrast, people generally avoid conduct that exposes them even to the smallest risk of prosecution for a serious criminal offence.'[66] Second, this logic applies to people in their capacity not only as individuals but also as corporate executives. The person who designs or signs off on the structure of offshore vehicles that make tax fraud possible can be compared to the guy who sets up the logistics of the bank robbery—both should land behind bars. Today's penalties on white-collar crime are too lenient. Tightening them is a key step towards more transparency in the financial

---

65. At present, there is a significant discrepancy between the financial assets held in small international financial centres and the assets that are in fact reported to other countries' tax authorities. See Philip R. Lane and Gian Maria Milesi-Ferretti, 'Cross-Border Investment in Small International Financial Centres' (IMF Working Paper WP/10/38 [2010]). Increased transparency would reduce this discrepancy.

66. *Financial Times*, 'Fear of UK Taxman', 9 December 2013.

sector. Third, and relatedly, MNEs in the financial sector should be called on their alleged commitment to corporate social responsibility (CSR). Such a commitment is incompatible with making sizeable profits from the sale of tax-avoidance strategies. Paying one's taxes surely has to count among the first social responsibilities of any economic agent.[67] Fourth, regulatory responses such as the ones proposed by FATCA—loss of banking licenses, withholding payments, other forms of economic sanctions targeting both non-compliant MNEs and non-compliant states—should be considered more widely. Finally, and as a precondition to any regulatory change in these directions, steps need to be taken to eliminate conflicts of interest in politics. In recent months, several politicians in OECD countries have had to resign—across the political spectrum—because they had secret accounts in tax havens.[68] From a certain level of responsibility upwards, but certainly including all national parliamentarians, politicians should be obliged to render public their financial situation. For them more than for anyone else, tax fraud should lead to criminal prosecutions.

Moving on to the second institutional requirement that flows from the membership principle, an ITO with inclusive membership would provide an ideal forum to reconsider the membership rule in the case of MNEs. How should the rights to tax shares of the profit of an MNE be allocated among jurisdictions? This issue is a very thorny one in international tax practice that has so far been resolved through so-called separate-entity accounting and

---

67. See Dietsch, 'Asking the Fox to Guard the Henhouse'.
68. A prominent example is Jérôme Cahuzac, former economics and finance minister in the cabinet of François Hollande; see Samuel Laurent, "Si vous n'avez rien suivi de l'affaire Cahuzac", *Le Monde*, 30 August 2013, accessed 28 March 2014, <http://www.lemonde.fr/jerome-cahuzac/>.

arm's length standard (ALS) transfer pricing.[69] As set out in the description of the various forms of tax competition in chapter 1, both the indeterminacy of applying this standard and the difficulties in its enforcement can be exploited by MNEs to lower their tax bills. One possible solution would be to switch to a system of UT + FA.[70] This would require governments to agree on a common and consolidated corporate tax base. MNEs would have to determine their worldwide profit in one single report, and they would be allowed to consolidate profits and losses of entities in different countries. The worldwide profit would then be apportioned to the respective countries in which the MNE operates on the basis of a predetermined formula.

As the discussion of the UT + FA proposal by Clausing and Avi-Yonah in section 1.3 of this chapter showed, the specifics of the formula in question raise issues of distributive justice and fairness between countries. As a rule of thumb, a just formula will reflect the real economic activity in each country by referring to factors such as property, sales, and payroll—the combination of these three factors with equal weight is also known as the 'Massachusetts formula.' Such an arrangement would make it impossible for companies to engage in the shifting of paper profits—though they would still have an incentive to relocate production facilities—and would thus be a major step forward in the implementation of the membership principle in the corporate sector.

---

69. According to the ALS, foreign branches or subsidiaries of an MNE are to be taxed as if they were independent market participants, exchanging goods and services at arm's length (i.e., market) prices; see, e.g., Lorraine Eden, *Taxing Multinationals: Transfer Pricing and Corporate Income Taxation in North America* (Toronto: University of Toronto Press, 1998), 32–52.

70. There is an extensive literature in law and public finance on UT + FA and how it compares to separate entity accounting. For an overview, see, e.g., Michael J. Graetz, *Foundations of International Income Taxation* (New York: Foundation Press, 2003), 400–35.

UT + FA faces a number of technical difficulties—as, for instance, the taxation of intangibles or the attribution of sales over the Internet to a particular jurisdiction. To see what is at stake here, consider the case of Google, which uses the so-called Double Irish tax structure with subsidiaries in Ireland and in Bermuda to reduce its tax burden.[71] As the *Financial Times* reported in October 2013, 'Google funnelled 8.8bn Euros of royalty payments to Bermuda last year, a quarter more than in 2011, underlining the rapid expansion of a strategy that has saved the US internet group billions of dollars in tax. By routing payments to Bermuda, Google reduces its overseas tax rate to about 5%, less than half the rate in already low-tax Ireland, where it books most of its international sales.'[72] While tackling the difficulties of the taxation of intangibles or the attribution of Internet sales does indeed represent a challenge, it is arguably not an insurmountable one.[73] Consider the case of intellectual property. The rights to tax intellectual property of an MNE could, for instance, be allocated to states in proportion to the shares determined by the Massachusetts formula. An alternative formula might track the research and development activities of the MNE, which presumably give rise to the intellectual property in question.

As a second-best strategy or intermediate step towards UT + FA, which requires multilateral agreement, country-by-country

---

71. For a thorough analysis of this tax arrangement, see Joseph B. Darby III, 'Double Irish More than Doubles the Tax Saving: Hybrid Structures Reduces Irish, U.S. and Worldwide Taxation', *Practical US/International Tax Strategies* 11, no. 9 (2007): 2–16.

72. Vanessa Houlder, 'Google Shifts €9bn to Bermuda', *Financial Times*, 11 October 2013.

73. Going into the details of how to address these challenges lies beyond the scope of this book, but see, for instance, Arthur J. Cockfield, 'The Rise of the OECD as Informal "World Tax Organization" Through National Responses to E-commerce Tax Challenges', *Yale Journal of Law & Technology* 8 (2005–2006): 136–87.

reporting presents an alternative that can be adopted unilaterally.[74]

Chapter 5 will discuss country-by-county reporting in more detail.

3.2. Institutionalizing the fiscal policy constraint

As I have already acknowledged, defining rules that respect the fiscal policy constraint will be difficult. First, the outcome on which I focus, namely the aggregate fiscal self-determination of countries, may not be easily observed, especially across alternative regulatory regimes. However, in principle it should be possible for a government to make the case, and support it with empirical evidence, that it has lost tax base to another country that has recently changed its tax policies. Second, and more importantly, the fact that intentions are unobservable invites hypocrisy. It will be possible for governments to misrepresent their intentions—that is, to attribute any tax reforms to the preferences citizens have about the size of the public budget relative to GDP and the extent of redistribution—even if in reality they pursue the strategic aim of attracting foreign tax base. In order to avoid hypocritical political discourse and long but futile attempts to distinguish honest from dishonest representations of intentions, the institutionalization of the principle should as much as possible rely on objectively observable proxies for the defendant's intentions. To get off the hook, the defendant would need to show that the tax policy change in question has actually had beneficial effects collectively.

---

74. For a briefing paper on country-by-country reporting, see Tax Justice Network, 'Country-by-Country Reporting: How to Make Multinational Companies More Transparent' (Tax Justice Briefing, 2008), accessed 27 June 2012, <http://www.financialtaskforce.org/beta/wp-content/uploads/2009/04/why-is-country-by-country-financial-reporting-by-multinational-companies-so-important_english.pdf?9d7bd4>.

While a detailed and legally applicable definition of the objective factors that indicate a bad outcome and a strategic intention of the defendant is a task for tax lawyers, and beyond my competences, it is clear that data on capital flows, economic growth rates, or distributive results are readily available and could be used by the parties to a tax dispute. Reference to these indicators is routinely made in all kinds of debates on policy design; international fiscal policy is no exception in this respect. Nevertheless, given the many factors that affect economic outcomes and the complex relationships among them, controversies over the right interpretation of these data are likely. In case of controversy, what is needed is an accepted independent third party that can settle the dispute through an authoritative interpretation of the facts. As described in the following section, what is envisaged here is a judicial or quasi-judicial system in which disputes among governments over tax policy can be settled. Here, it is worth noting that courts assess intentions on a regular basis in the international arena. For example, the International Court of Justice (ICJ) has to assess the intentions of the alleged offender in applying the genocide convention.[75] The WTO is another case in point. Under the rules on non-tariff trade barriers, policies with protectionist effect are generally prohibited. However, in case a country pursues a policy with the intention of protecting consumers' health and safety and can prove its good intentions, an exception to the rule of non-protectionism is granted. As in the present proposal, the WTO institutionalized this rule by focusing on the observable implications of countries' intentions. A government has to

---

75. See United Nations, 'Convention on the Prevention and Punishment of the Crime of Genocide', United Nations General Assembly Resolution A/RES/260(III) (1948), Art. 2.

provide valid scientific evidence of the claimed adverse effects on consumers' health and safety.[76]

3.3. Enforcement

What would it take to effectively enforce the two principles? Monitoring compliance should be relatively straightforward because governments can be expected to launch a complaint if other governments violate either or both of the two principles. Yet, what is needed is an independent authority that will process the complaints and eventually enforce the rules. Effective enforcement is needed to ensure compliance with the two principles, because the structure of tax competition is such that every individual country has an incentive to deviate from the collectively desirable rules. The ITO should install a dispute-settlement procedure after the WTO model to satisfy this requirement.[77] In case a member state complains that the tax practices of another member violate the rules, that state can, as a first step, try to resolve the conflict in consultations. If they are unsuccessful, the case will be transferred to the dispute-settlement body (DSB), which effectively functions like an independent judiciary, because a panel report (judgment) can only be blocked if all member states unanimously agree on blocking it. Since parties know that there will be effective enforcement of decisions in the DSB, it can be expected that they will resolve many cases in consultation. This procedure has the advantage of avoiding excessive litigation and leaves room for political negotiations and decisions.

76. Bernhard Zangl, 'Judicialization Matters! A Comparison of Dispute Settlement Under GATT and the WTO', *International Studies Quarterly* 52, no. 4 (2008): 840–41.
77. For a description of the WTO dispute settlement process, see, for example, Zangl, 'Judicialization Matters!'

One potential objection to the ITO is that it is another non-majoritarian institution that is provided with substantial enforcement powers but lacks democratic accountability and legitimacy.[78] This is an important concern. Yet, the status quo, with its hollowing out of effective fiscal sovereignty through tax competition as described in chapter 1, is even more problematic in this respect. Although it *formally* guarantees democratic accountability, de facto this is not the case. Conversely, while an ITO may reduce the scope of fiscal policy issues for which there is direct democratic accountability, it would make sure that tax policy can actually work effectively in this restricted realm.

3.4. Comparison to the OECD and EU tax agendas and the question of feasibility

How does the present proposal for the future rules of international taxation compare with the institutional status quo? Is it feasible in the sense that it relies on solutions that have successfully been put to work in other contexts or policy fields?

The current situation is characterized by unjust tax competition. This fact has not gone unnoticed by governments and international organisations. Accordingly, they have launched policy initiatives to address this situation. I now very briefly summarize the results of the two most important instances— the efforts of the OECD and the EU—to see where my proposal differs.

---

78. I thank an anonymous referee for pushing me to address this issue.

For years, the OECD initiative against harmful tax competition[79] hardly brought any tangible success, partly because it lost the support of the U.S. administration shortly after it was launched in 1998. Its promotion of transparency in tax matters relied on the on-request model of information exchange, under which the requesting state has to present initial evidence of international tax evasion in order to receive the required information about foreign funds of its residents. Yet, precisely the kind of information required to mount an initial case is often secret and thus on-request information exchange is ineffective.[80] At the same time, the issue of corporate tax avoidance seemed to have vanished from the organisation's agenda.

The financial crisis has revived the OECD's initiative, no doubt in part because governments are desperate to counter the trend of spiralling public debt. In institutional terms, the OECD international tax agenda received a boost through the endorsement and promotion by the G20 since 2009. In October 2014, more than forty countries signed a new Common Reporting Standard (CRS) developed by the OECD,[81] which has widely been welcomed as a breakthrough in tax transparency and as a net improvement compared to the on-request model. While this is certainly true, the new standard is not without weaknesses.[82] For example, since

79. See, e.g., Organization for Economic Co-operation and Development (OECD), *The Global Forum on Transparency and Exchange of Information for Tax Purposes*, A Background Information Brief (Paris: OECD, 2011), accessed 6 June 2013, <www.oecd. org/tax/transparency>; OECD, *Harmful Tax Competition—An Emerging Global Issue*.

80. See, for instance, Itai Grinberg, 'The Battle Over Taxing Offshore Accounts', *UCLA Law Review* 60, no. 2 (2012): 304–83.

81. See Organization for Economic Co-operation and Development (OECD), *Standard for Automatic Exchange of Financial Account Information in Tax Matters* (Paris: OECD Publishing, 2014), <http://dx.doi.org/10.1787/9789264216525-en>.

82. The following weaknesses are discussed in a preliminary report of the Tax Justice Network on the new standard. See Andreas Knobel and Markus Meinzer, '"The End of Bank Secrecy?" Bridging the Gap to Effective Automatic Information Exchange—An Evaluation of OECD's Common Reporting Standard (CRS) and its Alternatives' (report for the Tax Justice Network, October 2014).

some of its provisions are to be implemented bilaterally rather than through the multilateral framework, tax havens will be able to cherry-pick the countries with whom signing a bilateral treaty will have minimal impact on their financial industry; accounts below a threshold of $250 000, as well as ones opened before 2016, will not be covered by the agreement, which considerably reduces its effectiveness; finally, contrary to FATCA in the United States, which retains a 30 percent withholding tax, the CRS does not have a provision of this sort. In short, while the CRS is certainly a step in the right direction, it falls short of the routine, electronic (that is, automatic), and multilateral exchange of information on the funds of nonresidents to their respective home countries required by the membership principle.[83]

As to tax competition for paper profits, the 2013 OECD report on tax-base erosion and profit shifting documents how acutely aware the organization is of the problem and of the injustice of a global fiscal infrastructure that tolerates it.[84] The ambitious action plan the OECD has subsequently put forward to combat profit shifting underlines the fact that the organisation is serious about reform.[85] However, a closer look at the OECD's strategy creates doubts whether its proposed reforms will be effective. The action plan explicitly states that a move towards UT + FA—as advocated in this book—'is not a viable way forward',[86] but that the OECD's

---

83. For more on automatic and multilateral exchange of tax information, see David Spencer, 'Tax Information Exchange and Bank Secrecy', *Journal of International Taxation* 16, no. 3 (2005): 22–30; Palan et al., *Tax Havens*, 244–45.

84. See Organization for Economic Co-operation and Development (OECD), *Addressing Base Erosion and Profit Shifting* (Paris: OECD Publishing, 2013), accessed 10 June 2013, <http://www.oecd.org/tax/beps.htm>.

85. See Organization for Economic Co-operation and Development (OECD), *Action Plan on Base Erosion and Profit Shifting* (Paris: OECD Publishing, 2013), accessed 24 February 2015, <http://dx.doi.org/10.1787/9789264202719-en>.

86. OECD, *Action Plan on Base Erosion and Profit Shifting*, 14 and 20.

preferred approach is to preserve separate-entity accounting while closing the various loopholes from which it suffers (transfer-mispricing, earnings-stripping, hybrid mismatch arrangements, and so on). This strategy is doomed to fail. Experience shows that as long as differences between national tax laws exist, the tax-avoidance industry will always be able to identify loopholes and exploit them. Separate-entity accounting is particularly vulnerable on this front, and the repeated appeal in the OECD action plan to at least partial implementation of reforms through domestic law provisions stokes the suspicion that this will not change. In other words, preserving separate-entity accounting prolongs the cat-and-mouse game between regulators and the tax-avoidance industry, a game that the latter usually wins. Perhaps the OECD is going for a system fix rather than a system change, because they believe that UT + FA would not pass in the face of indeed significant resistance by corporate lobbies. However, the latter merely confirms that the difference in effectiveness between the two strategies is indeed huge.

One more general comment on the OECD needs to be added here. While the OECD's statutes in principle allow it to issue binding recommendations, in practice the organisation usually relies on nonbinding recommendations and leaves it up to individual countries to implement them. As several commentators have pointed out, this can lead to problems of compliance. The phenomenon of 'mock compliance,' where jurisdictions adopt 'the form but not the substance of the agreement entered,' is but one of the problems encountered in this context.[87]

I like to be optimistic and believe that the OECD will overcome the challenges discussed here. In any event, it is too early

---

87. Richard Eccleston and Richard Woodward, 'Pathologies in International Policy Transfer: The Case of the OECD Tax Transparency Initiative', *Journal of Comparative Policy Analysis: Research and Practice* 16, no. 3 (2014): 216–29.

to assess its proposed reforms. Besides, the main objective of this book, recall, is not to evaluate the policy agenda of international organisations, but to formulate principles of international tax justice that such an agenda should respect.

In recent years, the EU has also taken a number of significant steps towards curtailing tax competition. In the area of portfolio tax competition, the EU has passed the Savings Tax Directive, which took effect in July 2005. This directive targets tax evasion on interest income by requiring automatic information exchange among countries on the savings of foreign residents. While the directive has significant loopholes, it is important in that it shows that automatic international information exchange can be implemented in practice.[88]

With respect to business tax competition, the Council agreed on a soft-law Code of Conduct in 1997. Member states entered into a nonbinding commitment to remove so-called preferential tax regimes. Despite being nonbinding, the code developed some bite because compliance with it was made a condition of accession for the Central and Eastern European countries. Also, the Commission applied the principles contained in the code to its state aid rules, which thus increased compliance among the EU-15 states.[89] Currently, the EU is considering adopting a system of UT + FA.[90]

---

88. Thomas Rixen and Peter Schwarz, 'How Effective Is the European Union's Savings Tax Directive? Evidence from Four EU Member States', *Journal of Common Market Studies* 50, no. 1 (2012): 151–68.

89. Philipp Genschel et al., 'Accelerating Downhill: How the EU shapes Corporate Tax Competition in the Single Market', *Journal of Common Market Studies* 49, no. 1 (2011): 12–13.

90. See European Commission, 'Proposal for a Council Directive on a Common Consolidated Corporate Tax Base (CCCTB)', European Commission COM(2011) 121/4 (2011), accessed 24 February 2015, <http://ec.europa.eu/taxation_customs/resources/documents/taxation/company_tax/common_tax_base/com_2011_121_en.pdf>. For a discussion of the European Union's plans to introduce UT + FA, see Clemens Fuest, 'The European Commission's Proposal for a Common Consolidated Corporate Tax Base', *Oxford Review of Economic Policy* 24, no. 4 (2008): 720–39.

While the above OECD and EU initiatives represent real progress, the regulatory framework defended in this book goes significantly further. In line with the normative demands of its two principles, it proposes an international framework that is much stronger than the current global tax institutions, which cannot make universally binding rules and lack international levers of enforcement. Moreover, the OECD, as today's most important international tax forum, is made up only of industrialized countries, a fact that has invited the criticism of imperialism. The proposed ITO with its encompassing membership would remedy this shortcoming.

The experience at the regional level of the EU shows that creating an institutional framework with more effective powers of enforcement is indeed feasible. The EU uses one of the specific policies recommended above, namely automatic information exchange, and is seriously debating another one, UT + FA. At the same time, note that the proposal defended here, while it does involve a redefinition of fiscal autonomy, does not require the transfer of core fiscal prerogatives to the international level. No supra-national power to tax is established. Instead, the basic idea is that the international community protects national fiscal self-determination by imposing certain limits on the fiscal choices of nation-states. The existence of the WTO is testament to the fact that creating an international organization to define and enforce these constraints is achievable.[91]

An additional argument for the feasibility of the proposal of this book is that it does not envisage harmonisation of national

---

91. As an anonymous referee rightly emphasized, the general analysis of feasibility should also be sensitive to issues of trajectory—that is, questions regarding the (dis)incentives different countries have to accept or promote a multilateral regulatory framework of international taxation. I come back to this issue in chapter 5.

tax policies. While harmonization is portrayed as the relevant alternative to tax competition in large parts of the literature,[92] it is also clear that there are strong political objections to it. The two principles put forward here can address the undesirable aspects of tax competition without implying harmonization. First, respect of the membership principle and the fiscal policy constraint does not entail harmonization. Suppose the English really do have a preference for a smaller public budget and less redistribution than the Swedish. Neither of the principles will stop them from designing a tax structure that reflects these preferences. In turn, nothing I have said will prevent the Swedes from making a democratic choice that the best way to finance a relatively generous welfare state is to shift a considerable portion of the tax burden onto labour and consumption and to tax capital lightly, as they in fact do. However, the proposed constraint on fiscal policy prohibits the very same policies if they are based on strategic considerations and have negative consequences.

Second, even in a world where different polities have divergent preferences about the size of the public budget and the extent of redistribution, the two principles will create *some* pressure towards convergence. This is so because countries with preferences for a relatively large state and/or a high level of redistribution will now have to bear the real costs of these preferences in terms of part of their tax base voting with its feet. At the other end of the spectrum, however, the danger of a race to the bottom would be eliminated by the two principles for the very same reason. Countries with smaller public budgets and a lower level of redistribution would also be forced to bear the full costs of their tax structure, rather than being able to finance part of their public services by strategically attracting foreign tax base. The fiscal externalities generated in both directions under the two principles are those minimally present under conditions of fiscal interdependence between states.[93] They ensure a maximum—though less than perfect—correspondence between the convictions of members of the respective polities and the fiscal structure of those polities. The principles have achieved my declared objective, namely to delineate unjust tax competition from fiscal interdependence that is both inevitable and benign from an ethical standpoint.

4. PRINCIPLES FOR GLOBAL BACKGROUND JUSTICE

The membership principle and fiscal policy constraint serve to protect the de facto sovereignty of states and their capacity to implement the conception of justice of their citizens domestically through their fiscal policy. And while I have explicitly abstained from endorsing any particular theory of global *distributive* justice, it is clear that these principles and the kind of global tax cooperation they call for do take a stance on global justice more broadly defined. This section shall clarify the normative status of the two principles and elaborate why they should be understood as principles of *global background justice*.

---

93. Note that these fiscal externalities suffice to impose some of the discipline in government spending that some theorists see as one of the important advantages of tax competition. See, for instance, Geoffrey Brennan and James M. Buchanan, *The Power to Tax: Analytical Foundations of a Fiscal Constitution* (Cambridge: Cambridge University Press, 1980).

The literature on global justice has been dominated by questions of distribution. The debate has been framed as one between statists and cosmopolitans or between internationalists and globalists, where, to give the briefest definition possible, the former hold that liberal-egalitarian principles of justice should be national in scope, whereas the latter maintain they should be global in scope. Put differently, while cosmopolitan theorists generally defend continuity between our principles of justice at the national and the global level, statists hold that they are distinct.[94]

Framing the global justice debate as one between cosmopolitans and statists has come under increasing fire in recent years,[95] and rightly so I believe. Here, I shall concentrate on just one dimension of this debate, namely the question of whether a global basic structure exists that gives rise to concerns of global distributive justice.[96] Several statists argue that no clear structures and rules of the required kind exist at the global level to give rise to concerns of distributive justice.[97]

---

94. See, for instance, the following two review articles: Simon Caney, 'Review Article: International Distributive Justice', *Political Studies* 49 (2001): 974–97; and Philippe Van Parijs, 'International Distributive Justice', in *A Companion to Contemporary Political Philosophy*, ed. Robert E. Goodin et al. (Oxford: Blackwell, 2007), 638–52.

95. See, for instance, Joshua Cohen and Charles Sabel, 'Extra Republicam Nulla Justicia?', *Philosophy & Public Affairs* 34, no. 2 (2006): 147–75; A. J. Julius, 'Nagel's Atlas', *Philosophy & Public Affairs* 34, no. 2 (2006): 176–92; Ronzoni, 'The Global Order'; Laura Valentini, *Justice in a Globalized World: A Normative Framework* (Oxford: Oxford University Press, 2011).

96. John Rawls defines the basic structure of society as 'the way in which the major social institutions distribute fundamental rights and duties and determine the division of advantages from social cooperation' (Rawls, *A Theory of Justice*, 6). Here, I am interested in the *global* basic structure.

97. See, for example, Andrea Sangiovanni, 'Global Justice, Reciprocity, and the State', *Philosophy & Public Affairs* 35, no. 1 (2007): 3–39; Saladin Meckled-Garcia, 'On the Very Idea of Cosmopolitan Justice: Constructivism and International Agency', *Journal of Political Philosophy* 16, no. 3 (2008): 245–71. While I distance myself from one aspect of their position here, a lot more would have to be said to do their contributions justice.

This position has recently been contested in two ways. First, some authors have argued that several of the practices of international relations are in fact *constitutive* of a global basic structure and, hence, that issues of global justice do indeed arise.[98] Second, and more importantly in our context, Miriam Ronzoni has suggested that 'the most pressing issue is not whether we *have* a global basic structure, but whether we *need* one.'[99] Ronzoni makes the case that the absence of a global basic structure in the face of inequalities should not lead us to conclude that these inequalities somehow fall outside the purview of justice, but instead calls for the *creation* of such a basic structure. Internationally as well as domestically, certain rules may be required to guarantee the fairness of interactions between individuals. Ronzoni submits that 'under circumstances of intense international interaction and interdependence the conditions of effective sovereignty, and hence of *international background justice*, may be eroded.'[100] Consequently, she advocates the creation of functionally differentiated supra-national institutions that have the (legitimate) authority to set certain rules for appropriate conduct.

Note, however, that the idea of international or global background justice does not imply a focus on *distributive* justice in the sense that it would call for direct cross-border redistribution.

---

98. Cf., for instance, Andreas Follesdal, 'The Distributive Justice of a Global Basic Structure: A Category Mistake?', *Politics, Philosophy & Economics* 10, no. 1 (2011): 46–65.

99. Ronzoni, 'The Global Order', 243.

100. Ronzoni, 'The Global Order', 248–49. A similar idea is captured by Valentini's notion of systemic coercion. 'A system of rules S is coercive if it foreseeably and avoidably places non-trivial constraints on some agents' freedom, compared to their freedom in the absence of that system' (Valentini, *Justice in a Globalized World*, 137). Fiscal interdependencies represent a form of systemic coercion at the international level. Certain rules, according to my account the regulation of tax competition, are required to justify this systemic coercion.

Instead, in line with Rawls's use of the concept of the basic structure, it focuses on an institutional framework that ensures what can be described as just rules of the game.

This is precisely the kind of argument I have made with respect to international tax competition in part I of this book. The current institutional setting undermines effective sovereignty.[101] The two principles put forward in section 1 of the present chapter are designed to restore this sovereignty and to guarantee international background justice. They do, of course, require international cooperation, but they stop short of calling for direct cross-border redistribution. In fact, Ronzoni also cites tax competition as one policy area where she considers international background justice to be violated, and she calls for more interdisciplinary research on this issue.

Now, while the account of global background justice in fiscal affairs presented here does not call for global redistribution, the institutional reforms it does recommend would clearly have significant distributive side effects. As one can easily glean from the description of the inequality-enhancing effects of tax competition laid out in chapter 1, section 2, institutional reform banning all forms of poaching and restricting luring practices would also get rid of their inegalitarian effects. The fact that the fight against these inequalities can be fought without even endorsing a theory of global *distributive* justice significantly improves the feasibility score of the necessary reforms.[102]

---

101. The case of tax competition can be viewed as one instance of what Dani Rodrik calls the political trilemma of the world economy. Rodrik claims that hyperglobalization (in this case taking the form of mobile tax bases), democratic politics, and the nation state are incompatible. See Dani Rodrik, The Globalization Paradox (New York: W.W. Norton, 2011), 372.

102. Cf. Dietsch and Rixen, 'Redistribution, Globalisation, and Multi-Level Governance'.

This short section cannot claim to present a comprehensive treatment of the rich literature on global justice. My limited objective here has been to elucidate the nature of my contribution to the literature on global justice. I have shown in what sense the membership principle and fiscal policy constraint represent principles of global background justice.

5. CONCLUSION

In order to refine our criteria of what a regulation of tax competition should look like, the chapter started out with a survey of a number of existing reform proposals and their respective weaknesses. It turned out that certain measures including a return to capital controls or imposing a floor on capital taxation on foreign-source income have to count as second-best solutions when viewed from the normative premise of fiscal self-determination at the heart of this book. However, some of these second-best solutions will become relevant again in chapter 5.

I then argued for the two core principles that should govern international tax relations and limit tax competition. The membership principle, with its corollary of transparency, calls for individuals and corporations to pay tax where they benefit from the public infrastructure. This principle prohibits any *poaching* of foreign capital—that is, the practice of attracting capital of non-members of a state. Hence, it bans two of the three forms of tax competition introduced in chapter 1. Implementing the membership principle requires getting rid of bank secrecy and other institutions that stand in the way of automatic information exchange between the fiscal authorities of different states.

The second principle, the fiscal policy constraint, prohibits certain instances of *luring*— that is, the practice of inviting foreign individuals and corporations to follow their capital and thereby change their membership affiliation. Luring is problematic if it is *both* motivated by strategic intent *and* has a negative impact on the aggregate fiscal self-determination of other states.

Moving from principles to institutions, I have called for the creation of an ITO with a mandate both to put the above principles into international law in a way that minimizes any potential loopholes and to enforce them.

The final section of the chapter introduced the notion of global background justice and explained why the principles of regulating tax competition defended in this book fall into this category.

PART II

Efficiency of what?–Assessing efficiency arguments in the context of tax competition

Thus far, this book has argued that tax competition is problematic from a normative perspective and that we should therefore regulate it. Having presented my positive argument, I will now move on to consider the principal objection advanced against it. Opponents of the kind of tax *cooperation* advocated in part I regularly defend tax competition by pointing to its efficiency. The precise formulation of these defences varies. Some argue that economic competition between jurisdictions promotes an efficient allocation of resources.[1] Others contend that tax competition helps to control government waste and can be seen as efficiency enhancing in this sense.[2] These are but the two most prominent kinds of

1. See, for instance, Wallace E. Oates and Robert M. Schwab, 'Economic Competition Among Jurisdictions: Efficiency Enhancing or Distortion Inducing?', *Journal of Public Economics* 35, no. 3 (1988): 333–54; and Dietmar Wellisch, 'Decentralized Fiscal Policy with High Mobility Reconsidered: Reasons for Inefficiency and an Optimal Intervention Scheme', *European Journal of Political Economy* 12, no. 1 (1996): 91–111. Several arguments of this type can be traced to and have been inspired by Charles M. Tiebout, 'A Pure Theory of Local Expenditures', 416–24.
2. See, for instance, Brennan and Buchanan, *The Power to Tax*; and Charles E. McLure, 'Tax Competition: Is What's Good for the Private Goose also Good for the Public Gander?', *National Tax Journal* 39, no. 3 (1986): 341–48.

appeals to efficiency that have been put forward in defence of tax competition.

Over the years, the literature has critically discussed both the modeling assumptions of contributions in favour, or sceptical of, tax competition and, closely related, the empirical adequacy of the conclusions of these models. Though I will identify the principal contributions to the literature, it is my intention neither to provide yet another model of tax competition to establish its (in-)efficiency nor to provide a comprehensive survey of the economic literature on tax competition.[3]

Instead, my goal here is of a more fundamental, methodological nature. I will argue that the concept of efficiency is used in a variety of ways in the literature on tax competition and that, despite suggestions to the contrary, the resulting arguments remain inconclusive with respect to the policy choice between tax competition and tax cooperation. In order to categorize the different notions of efficiency at play, I will build on Julian LeGrand's seminal article 'Equity Versus Efficiency: The Elusive Trade-Off.'[4] For all of the plausible uses of the concept of efficiency he identifies, it is possible to find instantiations in the literature on international taxation. While none of the conclusions I draw depends on the substance of LeGrand's own arguments, using his taxonomy of efficiency arguments allows

---

3. For such surveys, see Genschel and Schwarz, 'Tax Comptetition: A Literature Review'; Signe Krogstrup, *A Synthesis of Recent Developments in the Theory of Capital Tax Competition*, EPRU Working Paper Series 04–02 (Copenhagen: Economic Policy Research Unit, 2004), <http://www.econ.ku.dk/epru/files/wp/wp-04-02.pdf>; and John D. Wilson, 'Theories of Tax Competition', *National Tax Journal* 52, no. 2 (1999): 269. The piece by Genschel and Schwarz is particularly useful because it combines the analysis of theoretical tax competition models with an overview of empirical evidence on the predictions of these models.

4. Julian LeGrand, 'Equity versus Efficiency: The Elusive Trade-Off', *Ethics* 100, no. 3 (1990): 554–68.

us to better interpret the various appeals to efficiency under tax competition.

While the bulk of the chapter aims to rebut the objection that tax cooperation of the kind advocated in this book is inefficient, the last section goes a step further and analyzes another set of efficiency claims. Contributions to *optimal tax theory* do not take a stance on the efficiency of tax competition as such. Yet, it turns out that, under tax competition, we have to be particularly careful to interpret correctly the findings of optimal tax theory. Otherwise, so I will claim, another kind of inefficiency beckons.

1. THE DEADWEIGHT LOSS AND ITS INTERPRETATION

Before turning to the concept of efficiency, a short detour is necessary to clarify the role of taxation in economic theory. Why do economists, at least in principle, not like taxes? Cynics believe that this is due to their fundamental distrust of government. Though this may be an additional factor for some economists, it is not the fundamental reason. Economists dislike taxes (as well as other interventions in the market, as for instance tariffs or subsidies) because they lead to inefficiencies in the workings of the market mechanism.

Consider the imposition of the excise tax τ depicted in figure 3.1. The tax shifts the supply curve to the upper left to a new equilibrium at the quantity q_2 for the price p_2. However, this means that there is a quantity of goods $(q_1 - q_2)$ for which the consumer's willingness to pay is higher than the producer's marginal cost pretax, but that will not be produced due to the tax. The welfare loss that is due to this discrepancy is known as the 'deadweight loss' or

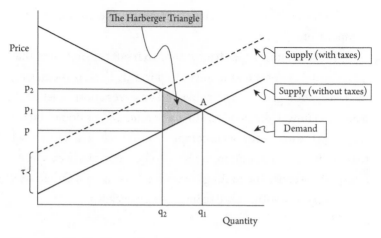

Figure 3.1. The Harberger Triangle

Credit: James R. Hines, 'Three Sides of Harberger Triangles', *Journal of Economic Perspectives* 13, no. 2 (1999): 169.

'excess burden of taxation,' and is represented by what is called the Harberger Triangle.[5] On a different, less technical description of the situation, one might say that the tax disturbs the functioning of the market mechanism as a match-maker between consumers and producers.

From the perspective of welfare economics, the virtue of a perfectly competitive market without government intervention in the form of taxes is that it is Pareto optimal—that is, it is not possible to make one person better off without making someone else worse off. The standard argument states that the situation post-tax is not Pareto optimal—without the tax, both consumers and the producer could be made better off.

5. While the notion of deadweight loss predates Harberger, it was he who not only systematized its use but also provided empirical estimates for the size of deadweight losses in various circumstances. See James R. Hines, 'Three Sides of Harberger Triangles', *Journal of Economic Perspectives* 13, no. 2 (1999): 167–88, for a discussion of the historical development of Harberger triangles, as well as the empirical literature on the concept.

I would like to make three observations. First, the standard argument implicitly assumes that the revenues raised through the tax will create an amount of welfare inferior to the deadweight loss. Two arguments highlight the implausibility of this assumption. First, as any economist will acknowledge, the market cannot function without a basic legal framework that includes contract law, certain health and safety provisions, and a number of other items. The taxation necessary to finance this *market-enabling* regulation is clearly welfare enhancing. Second, and beyond the fundamental question of giving the market a legal foundation, we know that the market fails to adequately provide certain kinds of goods, notably public goods, due to their positive externalities. Raising tax revenue to finance such *market intervention* and provision of public goods will, up to a point, again create an amount of welfare that exceeds the deadweight loss. In both of these scenarios, taxation is efficient in the sense of Pareto optimal.[6] More generally, then, in the same way as an assessment of the progressivity versus regressivity of a tax regime needs to look at the expenditure side as well as the revenue side, an assessment of the welfare implications of a tax needs to be sensitive to both, too.[7]

6. At least in his empirical work, Harberger makes an assumption that rules out such a scenario. According to Hines, he 'calculates deadweight loss triangles based on demand curves constructed by returning tax revenue to consumers in lump-sum fashion' (Hines, 'Three Sides of Harberger Triangles', 11).

7. The existence of such 'revenue offsets' to compensate for the excess burden of taxation is increasingly recognized in the literature. See, for instance, Raj Chetty, *Is the Taxable Income Elasticity Sufficient to Calculate Deadweight Loss? The Implications of Evasion and Avoidance*, NBER Working Paper No. 13844 (Cambridge: National Bureau of Economic Research, 2008), 2–3, as well as the literature cited there. At a more general level, some scholars have argued that public spending by governments, rather than acting as a break on economic growth, has in fact been a major contributor to growth as well as welfare. See Peter Lindert, *Growing Public—Social Spending and Economic Growth Since the Eighteenth Century* (Cambridge: Cambridge University Press, 2004).

Second, the standard argument is based on the assumption of a perfectly competitive market. As Lipsey and Lancaster have shown, when the assumptions of perfect competition are not met, *more* competition in the sense of less government intervention does not necessarily lead to a higher level of welfare.[8] Government intervention here includes taxation. In particular, it is possible 'that introducing distortions in one market might enhance the efficiency of the economy by mitigating the effects of distortions elsewhere.'[9] The significance of this result for the normative implications of the concept of deadweight loss can hardly be overstated.

Third, Harberger himself was well aware of the previous point, which is what motivated him to pursue empirical estimates of deadweight losses.[10] 'We do not live on the Pareto frontier [which is another way of saying we do not live in a perfectly competitive market], and we are not going to do so in the future. Yet policy decisions are constantly being made which can move us either toward or away from that frontier.'[11] Against this background, Harberger set out to measure the distortive effects of different policies on the various sectors of the economy. The point of this research programme is not to deplore government intervention per se, but to identify the least distortive policy options, which will include some government interventions that actually *promote* efficiency.

In sum, this short excursion into the history of public economics shows that the insights we gain from the concept of deadweight loss are more complex than the standard argument suggests. Whereas 'on the Pareto frontier' it is true that

8. R. G. Lipsey and Kelvin Lancaster, 'The General Theory of Second Best', *Review of Economic Studies* 24, no. 1 (1956–57): 11–32.

9. Hines, 'Three Sides of Harberger Triangles', 9.

10. Hines, 'Three Sides of Harberger Triangles', 10.

11. Arnold C. Harberger, 'The Measurement of Waste', *American Economic Review* 54, no. 3 (1964): 58–59.

government interventions including taxes dent welfare, this hypothetical conclusion does not transfer to the real world 'within' the Pareto frontier. In practice, it is an open question whether a particular government intervention is welfare enhancing or reducing. Against this background, the key question becomes an empirical one—as Harberger realized. Can we measure the various welfare effects of a policy and aggregate them to obtain an overall assessment? The research programme that builds on this question is as relevant to the evaluation of (inter)national fiscal policy and regulation as it is to any other policy sector.

Note also a conceptual implication of the above considerations for the notion of efficiency employed in calculating the deadweight loss. The shift from the Pareto frontier to the area inside the frontier mirrors a shift from questions about Pareto *optimality* to questions about Pareto *improvements*. When we realize that points on the Pareto frontier are unattainable in the real world, the contribution that efficiency in the sense of a Pareto improvement can make to policy debates is to tell us which measures can better the well-being of some without reducing that of others. While efficiency in this sense will condone Pareto superior policies and, conversely, condemn Pareto inferior policies, the concept remains silent on policies that better the situation of some while disadvantaging others. This shall become important to my argument later on.

2. TWO CONCEPTS OF EFFICIENCY

Because it probes the premises of efficiency arguments, the literature on the so-called equity–efficiency trade-off offers insights that are relevant beyond the confines of the equity–efficiency debate proper. Here, I will use one particular contribution to this debate as inspiration for my conceptual analysis of efficiency in the context of tax competition.

The discussion of the equity–efficiency trade-off has a long pedigree. For instance, it lay at the heart of the socialist calculation debate in the 1930s and 1940s.[12] Economists have attempted to narrow down the circumstances in which it is justified to speak of a trade-off between the two values in the sense that promoting one requires sacrifices in terms of the other.[13] Political philosophers have emphasized the need to render explicit the normative premises of notions of efficiency, as well as the interdependence between efficiency assessments and normative judgements.[14] All of these contributions accept the idea that there is a trade-off between equity and efficiency.

Julian LeGrand challenges this fundamental assumption.[15] The purpose of this short section consists in laying out why Le-Grand thinks it is misleading to speak of a trade-off between equity and efficiency and to distil the implications of his argument for the concept of efficiency itself. These considerations will then form the conceptual groundwork to analyse the use of efficiency in international tax theory in subsequent sections. It is important to emphasize that the lessons I propose to learn from LeGrand for the context of tax competition are limited to his analysis of efficiency. For the purposes of my argument, I do

12. See in particular Oskar Lange, 'On the Economic Theory of Socialism: Part One', *Review of Economic Studies* 4, no. 1 (1936): 53–71; and Oskar Lange, 'On the Economic Theory of Socialism: Part Two', *Review of Economic Studies* 4, no. 2 (1937): 123–42.

13. See, for instance, Arthur M. Okun, *Equality and Efficiency* (Washington, DC: Brookings Institution, 1975); and James E. Meade, *Efficiency, Equality, and the Ownership of Property* (London: G. Allen & Unwin, 1964).

14. See, for instance, Allen Buchanan, *Ethics, Efficiency, and the Market* (Totowa, NJ: Rowman and Allenhead, 1985), 2.

15. LeGrand, 'Equity Versus Efficiency'.

not need to endorse his position on the question of a trade-off between equity and efficiency.

What do people have in mind when they characterize a state of affairs as efficient? LeGrand argues that they refer to one of two things. First, efficiency can characterize the way in which two or more social objectives are being simultaneously pursued. 'An allocation of resources is efficient if it is impossible to move toward the attainment of one social objective without moving away from the attainment of another social objective.'[16] Note that this position reflects our common-sense understanding of efficiency—that is, the capacity to convert given inputs into maximal output, in this case the two social objectives—or, conversely, the capacity to reach a given output with minimal inputs. LeGrand points out that from this perspective, it is meaningless to talk of an equity–efficiency trade-off. Efficiency here 'can be defined only in relation to the ability of forms of social and economic organization to attain their primary objectives [...], [efficiency] is a secondary objective that only acquires meaning with reference to primary objectives such as equity.'[17] In other words, efficiency is not part of the trade-off between primary social objectives, but an instrumental value that characterizes our way of dealing with this trade-off.

Second, when people *do* refer to a trade-off between efficiency and, say, equity, LeGrand argues the former in fact has to be understood as a placeholder for something else. Two common underlying social objectives that efficiency frequently gets identified with are economic growth[18] or Pareto optimality.[19] However, as LeGrand demonstrates, these social objectives are far from

16. LeGrand, 'Equity Versus Efficiency', 559.
17. LeGrand, 'Equity Versus Efficiency', 560.
18. Okun, *Equality and Efficiency*, falls into this category.
19. This is standard in the welfare economics literature; see, for instance, Amartya Sen, *On Ethics and Economics* (Oxford: Blackwell, 1987), chap. 2.

uncontroversial. For example, the welfare implications of more growth may not always be positive, since increased work effort or the environmental externalities of growth can produce a disutility even as disposable income rises. The lesson to learn from this analysis is that efficiency arguments of this type not only have to render explicit the underlying social objective but, in addition, the onus is on those who defend them to justify *why* the objective in question is worth pursuing in the first place.

As we shall see in subsequent sections, the taxonomy LeGrand proposes by distinguishing between efficiency as an instrumental value and efficiency as a placeholder for a different, underlying value perfectly captures the various appeals to efficiency we find in the literature both on tax competition and on optimal taxation. In the next section, I will show that the principal economic models of tax competition all fall into the second category. When they refer to efficiency, they in fact refer to a different underlying value, albeit not always the same one. In section 4, I will argue that optimal-tax theory represents an instance of LeGrand's first category, namely efficiency understood as an instrumental value.

3. EFFICIENCY AS A PLACEHOLDER

In the economic literature on tax competition, efficiency is the undisputed criterion to assess whether the phenomenon is desirable or not. On closer inspection, however, it turns out that alleged consensus hides three different senses in which tax competition is considered either efficient or not. Put differently, when economists appeal to efficiency in the context of tax competition, efficiency plays the role of a placeholder for a different value, which ultimately serves as the criterion to evaluate tax competition. I will suggest that the three underlying values that efficiency stands in for are productive Pareto optimality, general Pareto optimality,[20] and economic growth.

3.1. Efficiency as productive Pareto optimality

The concept of Pareto optimality itself is used in a variety of ways, depending on whether it is applied to a distributive problem, a productive problem, or both of these at the same time. The last two of these possibilities should be distinguished here in order to avoid confusion.[21]

> *Productive Pareto Optimality*: 'An allocation of productive resources is Pareto Optimal if and only if there is no (technically possible) alternative allocation which would produce more of at least one good without producing less of some other good.'
>
> *(General) Pareto Optimality*: 'A state of a given system is Pareto Optimal if and only if there is no feasible alternative state of that system in which at least one person is better off and no one is worse off.'

The crucial difference between the two notions is that the latter establishes the link between production and welfare, whereas the

---

20. Some might prefer to say that efficiency just *is* Pareto optimality. While conceding this terminological point would take nothing away from my argument, note that it would then become harder to make sense of efficiency arguments that appeal either to economic growth or to productive Pareto optimality.

21. I borrow these definitions from Buchanan, *Ethics, Efficiency, and the Market*, 4. For completeness sake, I should add that, in addition to the production of goods and the well-being of individuals, the notion of Pareto optimality can apply to a set of values. The promotion of two values is Pareto optimal if the one cannot be satisfied to a higher degree without the other being satisfied to a lesser degree. I shall not be concerned with Pareto optimality in this sense here.

former does not. Only if one combines productive Pareto optimality with the assumption that welfare is a monotonic function of growth—which is a rather implausible assumption—does the difference between the two disappear.

I should note up front that most analyses of tax competition are based on general Pareto optimality (see section 3.2). However, it is worth highlighting that there are some assessments of tax competition on efficiency grounds that appeal to productive Pareto optimality.

Consider the literature on capital export neutrality (CEN) and capital import neutrality (CIN). 'CEN exists when home- and host-country investments that earn the same pre-tax return also yield the same after-tax return.'[22] Under CEN, an investor is indifferent to investing at home or investing abroad, implying a productive Pareto optimum in the above sense. On this basis, some authors have argued for residence-based taxation as a means to guarantee CEN and, in a second step, have made a case for tax competition. 'Because residence-based taxation leads to complete equalization of marginal productivities of capital across countries, it follows that tax competition generates an efficient allocation of the *world's* stock of capital.'[23] While it is confusing to claim that the latter part of the sentence 'follows,' what the authors of this quote plausibly mean is that if all countries adopt residence-based taxation, and if the pressure for convergence between their rates created by tax competition is strong enough, then it follows that

22. Avi-Yonah, 'Globalization', 1604. As Avi-Yonah points out, CEN was introduced by Peggy Musgrave, *United States Taxation of Foreign Investment Income: Issues and Arguments* (Cambridge, MA: Law School of Harvard University, 1969).
23. Jacob A. Frenkel et al., *International Taxation in an Integrated World* (Cambridge, MA: MIT Press, 1991), emphasis in original. As we shall see in section 4 of this chapter, Frenkel et al. also use efficiency in a second, different sense.

tax competition leads to a productively Pareto-efficient allocation of the world's stock of resources.

This position can be, and has been, attacked from different angles. First, by advocates of capital import neutrality. 'CIN requires that the earnings from capital in a host country be taxed at the same rate for both domestic and foreign investors.'[24] If this is not the case, if foreign investors are taxed at a preferential rate, for example, then foreign investors will save and invest more than domestic ones. This will lead to a distortion of the international allocation of savings and therefore to a productively Pareto suboptimal outcome.[25] Moreover, note that in this case, tax competition is unlikely to remedy the situation. As we have seen in chapter 1, preferential tax rates for foreigners represent a favourite weapon in the armoury of a country that wants to attract capital from abroad without sacrificing much domestic revenue.

Second, in a world characterized by differences in tax rates on capital between countries—not only as a matter of fact but also because they reflect different values and democratic choices—it is clear that we do not live on the productive Pareto frontier. Here, the measures of CEN and CIN are likely to enter into conflict. The interesting question then becomes when we should rely on which measure or mix of measures.[26] Just as Harberger emphasized in his empirical work on the measurement of deadweight losses mentioned in section 1, the question for international tax theory becomes how to develop policies whose distortive effect is

---

24. Avi-Yonah, 'Globalization', 1605. He cites Richard E. Caves, *Multinational Enterprise and Economic Analysis* (Cambridge: Cambridge University Press, 1982).
25. See Avi-Yonah, 'Globalization', 1606.
26. The article by Thomas Horst, 'A Note on the Optimal Income Taxation of International Investment Income', *Quarterly Journal of Economics* 94, no. 4 (1980): 793–98, can be interpreted as providing an answer to this question. The elasticities of the demand and supply of capital are key to his account.

minimal and hence represents a productive Pareto *improvement*.[27] The question of what role tax competition plays in this context is an empirical one.

To conclude these remarks, I shall make two observations. First, as is reflected in the diverging assessments in the literature, we cannot conclusively say whether tax competition promotes efficiency in the sense of productive Pareto optimality. Yet, as I have made clear, this is not one of the objectives of this chapter, either. Second, and more fundamentally, even if we could establish a robust link between tax competition and productive Pareto optimality, so what? As long as the latter abstains from a welfare judgement, it does not have any action-guiding import. This shortcoming of productive Pareto optimality is well known[28] and explains why most analyses of efficiency employ the more informative concept of general Pareto optimality, to which we now turn.

3.2. Efficiency as general Pareto optimality

As we shall see, most economic analyses of tax competition use general Pareto optimality as their measure of efficiency.[29] The purpose of this section is twofold. I will first document the widespread use of Pareto optimality in models of tax competition to then, in a second step, evaluate the normative import of efficiency

27. The difference between the two lies in the fact that Harberger's analysis of deadweight losses is welfare based, whereas the literature discussed here does not explicitly establish the link to welfare.

28. Buchanan formulates this point well when he says: 'By focusing only on the quantity of outputs attainable from a given set of inputs, Productive Pareto Optimality fails to engage the root idea behind the Pareto Optimality and Pareto Superiority principles: the effect of the particular form of social organization in question on the well-being of the individuals involved' (Buchanan, *Ethics, Efficiency, and the Market*, 5).

29. From now on, when I use the term 'Pareto optimality', I am referring to *general* Pareto optimality.

arguments advanced on this basis. For presentational purposes, I will divide the literature into two groups. The first contains defenders of tax competition for reasons of Pareto optimality, the second authors who condemn it on the same grounds.

(1) For a while after its publication in 1956, Tiebout's theory of local public good provision was interpreted as an argument for the efficiency of tax competition. Tiebout's basic idea is that mobile individuals self-select into jurisdictions based on the match between their preferences and the public goods these jurisdictions provide. 'There is tax competition here in the sense that a region's taxes must be kept low enough to induce individuals to reside in the region.'[30] It is clear from this characterisation that governments in an idealized, Tieboutian world employ marginal cost pricing—that is, they charge residents only for the public goods they benefit from. Under these conditions, so they claim, residents' 'voting with their feet' through migration will lead to a Pareto-optimal outcome.[31]

Today, the Tieboutian model is widely criticized as a tool to analyse tax competition, because it relies on the unrealistic assumption that there are no externalities between jurisdictions. It is one of the prominent features of tax competition that it leads to a shift in the tax base between jurisdictions, which represents such an externality. This criticism has given rise to what is today considered the 'baseline model' of tax competition, which I will discuss below. However, it is worth noting that some authors have

30. Wilson, 'Theories of Tax Competition', 272.
31. Tiebout had individuals in mind, but extensions of his models have been proposed to include firms as well. See William A. Fischel, 'Fiscal and Environmental Considerations in the Location of Firms in Suburban Communities', in *Fiscal Zoning and Land Use Controls*, ed. Edwin Mills and Wallace Oates (Lexington, MA: D.C. Heath, 1975), 119–74; and Michelle J. White, 'Firm Location in a Zoned Metropolitan Area', in *Fiscal Zoning and Land Use Controls: The Economic Issues*, ed. Edwin S. Mills and Wallace E. Oates (Lexington, MA: D.C. Heath, 1975), 31–100.

tried to rescue the claim that tax competition—under certain conditions—is Pareto optimal while remaining in the Tieboutian tradition. For example, Oates and Schwab's model contains two policy variables: a tax on capital and environmental standards.[32] They show that, provided both homogenous worker preferences with respect to the environmental standards and a zero tax on capital, a Pareto optimum will result. Wellisch offers a framework in which a number of fiscal externalities and resulting misallocations of resources can be overcome.[33] What all these models in the Tieboutian tradition have in common is their use of Pareto optimality as the criterion of a social optimum.

In addition to the Tiebout family of models, there is a second important tradition that tends to see tax competition in a favourable light. Public-choice theorists have criticized the public-finance literature for its assumption that governments act to maximize the welfare of their citizens. Instead, they should be viewed as pursuing an agenda of their own and maximizing their own utility. From this perspective, the attraction of tax competition is obvious. The 'interjurisdictional mobility of persons in pursuit of "fiscal gains" can offer partial or possibly complete substitutes for explicit constraints on the taxing power.'[34] The threat of residents voting with their feet keeps up the pressure on wasteful government spending. 'In most cases, tax competition is efficiency enhancing when the government is modeled as a Leviathan.'[35] The standard of efficiency employed in this literature once again tends to be Pareto optimality.

An interesting contribution to this debate has been made by Edwards and Keen, who analyse how the verdict on tax

32. Oates and Schwab, 'Economic Competition Among Jurisdictions'.
33. Wellisch, 'Decentralized Fiscal Policy'.
34. Brennan and Buchanan, The Power to Tax, 184.
35. Krogstrup, A Synthesis of Recent Developments, 24.

competition varies with the assumption about government behaviour.[36] When 'policy-makers are neither entirely benevolent nor wholly self-serving,' whether or not tax competition is preferable from the perspective of efficiency depends on how the higher tax revenues under tax coordination are divided between expenditures that benefit the representative citizen and measures that serve the policymakers' interests. Finally, note that, even if public-choice theorists were right about the motivations of public officials, the constraint on taxing power provided by tax competition would only apply to mobile tax bases—that is, primarily capital.

(2) One of the early sceptics of tax competition was Wallace Oates (though he subsequently adopted a more favourable position). 'In an attempt to keep taxes low to attract business investment, local officials may hold spending below those levels for which marginal benefits equal marginal costs, particularly for those programs that do not offer direct benefits to local business.'[37] As long as marginal costs remain below marginal benefits, higher spending on public goods would be a Pareto improvement.

Zodrow and Mieszkowski have formalized Oates's analysis in what is today presented as the baseline model of tax competition.[38] The central predictions of the model for a world of small identical countries are the underprovision of public goods, on the one hand, and the idea that the tax burden on capital at source falls with increasing capital mobility, on the other. Questions of income distribution are bracketed.

This baseline model has subsequently been modified in various ways. Following Genschel and Schwarz,[39] I mention two. The

36. Jeremy Edwards and Michael Keen, 'Tax Competition and Leviathan', *European Economic Review* 40, no. 1 (1996): 113–34.
37. Wallace E. Oates, *Fiscal Federalism* (New York: Harcourt Brace Jovanovich, 1972), 143.
38. Zodrow and Mieszkowski, 'Pigou, Tiebout, Property Taxation'.
39. Genschel and Schwarz, 'Tax Comptetition: A Literature Review', 341–42.

first modification concerns the size of the countries in question. Assuming a finite number of larger countries does not change the results qualitatively, but it reduces the elasticity of capital and therefore mitigates the capital outflow and the resulting government revenue loss.[40] For countries of different size[41] or different per capita endowment of capital,[42] 'the smaller country faces stronger incentives to cut tax rates than the larger country and suffers less in the competitive equilibrium.'[43] Under such asymmetric tax competition, the smaller country may in fact be better off under tax competition than otherwise. All of these models confirm the conclusion of the baseline model by Zodrow and Mieszkowski that tax competition leads to a Pareto-suboptimal allocation of resources.

In addition to the baseline model and its extensions, two further contributions to the literature should be mentioned that also come to the conclusion that tax competition is Pareto suboptimal. The first is the perspective from economic geography.[44] Taxes are but one of the many factors underlying the decisions of firms regarding where to locate; network effects due to the presence of suppliers or research firms are another. Economic geographers point out that in the presence of agglomeration rents due to such network effects, a positive tax on capital may not trigger a capital outflow.[45] This insight does not invalidate the conclusion of the baseline model but, rather, complements it. Countries that benefit

40. See also Krogstrup, *A Synthesis of Recent Developments*, 11–13.

41. Bucovetsky, 'Asymmetric Tax Competition'.

42. John D. Wilson, 'Tax Competition with Interregional Differences in Factor Endowments', *Regional Science and Urban Economics* 21, no. 3 (1991): 423–51.

43. Genschel and Schwarz, 'Tax Competition: A Literature Review', 341.

44. See Krogstrup, *A Synthesis of Recent Developments*, 30–39, whose analysis I follow here.

45. See, for instance, Rodney D. Ludeman and Ian Wooton, 'Economic Geography and the Fiscal Effects of Regional Integration', *Journal of International Economics* 52, no. 2 (2000): 331–57; Frederik Andersson and Rikard Forslid, 'Tax Competition and Economic Geography', *Journal of Public Economic Theory* 5, no. 2 (2003): 279–303; and Baldwin and Krugman, 'Agglomeration, Integration and Tax Harmonisation'.

from agglomeration rents will suffer less from tax competition, whose efficiency-reducing impact will thereby be mitigated.

The second contribution is Hans-Werner Sinn's *selection principle*:[46]

> The Selection Principle says that governments have taken over all those activities which the private market has proved to be unable to carry out. Because the state is a stopgap which fills the empty market niches and corrects the failures of existing markets, it cannot be expected that the reintroduction of the market by the back door of systems competition will lead to a reasonable allocation result.[47]

In the context of tax competition, applying the selection principle leads Sinn to two primary conclusions.

First, whether or not tax competition leads to a Pareto-optimal equilibrium depends on whether the model assumes both capital *and* labour to be mobile. Under the realistic assumption of some labour mobility, tax competition will not result in a Pareto-optimal equilibrium.[48]

Second, and more importantly in our context, Sinn stresses that 'efficiency is not equity'[49] and that 'the real problem of systems competition is not the underprovision of public goods but rather its distributional implications.'[50] Sinn highlights what many

46. Sinn, *The New Systems Competition*.
47. Sinn, *The New Systems Competition*, 6. For a legal perspective on regulatory competition, see Joel P. Trachtman, 'Regulatory Competition and Regulatory Jurisdiction', *Journal of International Economic Law* 3, no. 2 (2000): 331–48.
48. While agreeing with its conclusion, Sinn's argument differs from the one provided by the baseline model. He believes that the underprovision hypothesis put forward by Zodrow and Mieszkowski is flawed. See Sinn, *The New Systems Competition*, 51, as well as 61–63.
49. Sinn, *The New Systems Competition*, 60.
50. Sinn, *The New Systems Competition*, 56.

other models acknowledge, namely that the downward pressure on capital taxes will shift the tax burden onto immobile factors such as labour and consumption. Yet while others narrowly focus on Pareto optimality and explicitly or implicitly bracket distributional issues, Sinn points out that a situation in which labour subsidizes capital is problematic *for distributional reasons.* Sinn's analysis stands alone among the many tax-competition models in being sensitive to distributive issues.

Before moving on to the analysis of the models of tax competition just discussed, I should add a caveat to the above categorization. What the various models have in common, I have claimed, is that they all use efficiency as a placeholder for Pareto optimality. The latter is the criterion and the sense in which they judge tax competition to be either efficient or inefficient. While this assessment is justified, it suggests a level of uniformity across the various models that is misleading. Among other things, their methodology sometimes differs. For instance, whereas the Tiebout model looks at individual agents, the baseline model works with a representative agent. As a result, the way in which they formulate the Pareto-optimality condition varies, too.[51] However, I believe these differences can be put aside when establishing the general claim that all of these models use Pareto optimality as their standard of efficiency.

3.3. Making sense of the models

The fact that only one of the above models, namely Sinn's, is sensitive to distributive issues is all the more surprising in the context

---

51. I thank François Claveau for drawing my attention to this point.

of taxation, one of whose explicit functions is redistributive.[52] Two questions arise at this point. First, how can we explain that economists rely on the obviously incomplete criterion of Pareto optimality to assess tax competition and other economic phenomena? Second, and more important in our context here, what is the normative import of their analysis? In other words, what can we learn from the above models of tax competition, and what not?

The response to the first question can be found in a turn that the history of economic thought took under the influence of positivism in the 1930s. In the wake of Lionel Robbins's statement that there is no scientific basis for interpersonal comparisons of utility,[53] welfare economists had to trade their traditional utilitarian ways for assessing social arrangements for an alternative. They found it in the concept of Pareto optimality.[54] While considerably weaker than utility maximization, the criterion that we cannot make anyone better off without making someone else worse off merely requires comparing the well-being of individuals over time. However, note that just like utility maximization, this criterion does not tell us anything about the justice of a social arrangement. As Sinn acknowledges in his analysis of tax competition, this is a serious shortcoming.

Bracketing the question of distribution for a moment, let us move on to the second question. Suppose, counterfactually, there

---

52. As mentioned in the introduction, the classic functions of taxation are the raising of revenue for public goods ('the allocation function'), the redistribution of income and wealth ('the distribution function'), and the fine-tuning of the economy ('the stabilization function'). See Musgrave and Musgrave, *Public Finance in Theory and Practice*, chap. 1.

53. Lionel Robbins, *An Essay on the Nature and Significance of Economic Sciences* (London: Macmillan, 1932).

54. See Mark Blaug, *Economic Theory in Retrospect*, 5th ed. (Cambridge: Cambridge University Press, 1997), 570ff. For the reasons why economists dislike interpersonal comparisons, see Buchanan, *Ethics, Efficiency, and the Market*, 7–8.

was a consensus among economists that tax competition leads to Pareto-optimal outcomes. What would this mean? I shall argue now that it would mean preciously little. Why? Recall a central observation from section 1 of this chapter. As the theorem of second best teaches us, the conclusions we draw about the Pareto optimality of both market outcomes and economic policies under idealized conditions are not robust when we relax these conditions. In other words, conclusions established for life 'on the Pareto frontier' as it were do not travel to situations 'within' the Pareto frontier.

Now, all the economic models of tax competition discussed in the previous section are models about life *on* the Pareto frontier. They all make idealizing assumptions that imply that the economic circumstances they depict are ones unattainable for real societies. And since the conclusions we can draw on the basis of these models do not travel to the real world *within* the Pareto frontier, the only insights we can glean from them concern a hypothetical world not only far but forever removed from ours. This, I submit, is preciously little. Worse still, if we forget that the domain of application of the insights from the idealized models is limited and use them to formulate policy advice, this can be dangerously misleading.

This does not, of course, mean that efficiency assessments of tax competition in the real world cannot be provided. However, rather than asking whether tax competition leads to Pareto-optimal results under idealized conditions, such assessments should aim to establish whether tax competition will under realistic assumption produce a Pareto *improvement*, or a Pareto *deterioration*, or neither of the two.

When practised in this way, efficiency assessments of a given policy will not always yield a conclusive result. As already stated in section 1, efficiency understood in this sense will condone policies that represent Pareto *improvements* and condemn policies that represent Pareto *deteriorations*, but—crucially—will remain silent on policies that better the situation of some while disadvantaging others. To evaluate the latter, one needs to rely on precisely the kind of interpersonal comparisons that Pareto rejected. From this angle, it is plausible to understand efficiency in the sense of the Pareto condition as a *constraint* on policymaking.[55] The policies that should be ruled out on efficiency grounds are ones that lead to Pareto deteriorations—that is, policies that worsen the position of some without making anyone else better off. Figure 3.2 illustrates the idea of Pareto as a constraint on public policy.

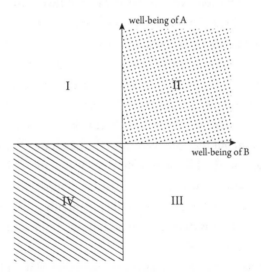

Figure 3.2. Pareto as a constraint

55. Economic theories designed to arrive at practical conclusions tend to understand the Pareto condition in this way. See, for instance, Marc Fleurbaey and François Mani-quet, *A Theory of Fairness and Social Welfare* (Cambridge: Cambridge University Press, 2011), esp. chap. 2. Put differently, looking at the Pareto criterion as a constraint makes it a necessary but not sufficient condition for social optimality. See Amartya Sen, *Inequality Reexamined* (Oxford: Clarendon Press, 1992), 136.

If a change in policy moves us from the status quo into quadrant II of figure 3.2, the policy is efficient. If it moves us into either quadrants I or III, then efficiency has nothing to say on the desirability of the policy. Only if it moves us into quadrant IV (including its boundaries)—that is, only if it reduces the well-being of one of the representative individuals without bettering that of the other—the policy will be inefficient.

Against this background, the efficiency objection against the regulation of tax competition advocated in this book has to be reformulated. To have any force, those who advance this objection would have to show that implementing the membership principle and fiscal-policy constraint defended in chapter 2 will lead to a Pareto deterioration. Now, if the analysis of this book and Sinn's assessment of tax competition are correct, we already know that the objection will *not* succeed. Why? We have seen that tax competition tends to exacerbate income inequalities, that it produces winners and losers. The same is true for tax cooperation in the form of the proposed regulation. Therefore, neither tax competition nor its regulation represents a Pareto improvement or a Pareto deterioration, but they propel us into the quadrants I or III of the above diagram. Incidentally, note that if one allowed side payments from the winners of regulating tax competition to the tax havens that lose out, regulation could potentially even be a Pareto *improvement*. In this case, efficiency considerations would *support* the project of this book.

This puts me in a position to draw two conclusions. First, from the perspective of Pareto as a constraint on public policy, the efficiency objection to regulating tax competition fails. Any attempt to classify either tax competition or its regulation as efficient in this sense is bound to be inconclusive.

Second, this means that the *autonomy prerogative* established in chapter 1, and whose contours under fiscal interdependence were sharpened in chapter 2, does not necessarily conflict with considerations of efficiency. The only scenario in which this would be the case is one where a polity sets the size of its public budget and the level of redistribution such that no one is better off and some are worse off (a Pareto deterioration). This is a rather weak constraint on the autonomy prerogative, but it nonetheless is a constraint. By contrast, for all policies that better the situation of some while worsening that of others (quadrants I and III in figure 3.2, which include tax competition and its regulation), the autonomy prerogative applies. This is as it should be. Whenever efficiency considerations alone do not yield a conclusive policy recommendation because distributive questions are involved, democratic decision making informed by arguments from theories of justice should have the final word. As we have seen throughout this book, this *desideratum* is not respected under tax competition, because the latter undermines the autonomy prerogative.

3.4. Efficiency as economic growth

There is one final potential value for which efficiency is sometimes used as a placeholder, and that is economic growth. While appeals to Pareto optimality dominate academic debates, the impact of tax competition on national competitiveness and, by extension, on economic growth is what is most frequently invoked in political discourse. Whenever low taxation on capital is defended politically today, the need to create 'favourable investment conditions' in order to promote growth and the jobs it generates are regularly invoked.

The fact that this kind of reasoning is by and large absent from academic debates has good reasons. While tax competition may indeed promote competitiveness and economic growth *locally*—that is, in the states and tax havens that manage to attract capital—it is much harder to argue that tax competition will promote economic growth *globally*. One would have to establish that economic growth is not a zero-sum game. In other words, the growth in the country that experiences the capital inflow would have to be greater than the growth forgone in the country that experiences the capital outflow. This is an open and empirical question.

However, even if the defender of tax competition on grounds of economic growth managed, unexpectedly, to clear this first hurdle, he would still have to establish the link to well-being. Does the additional growth generated by tax competition actually promote well-being? At least the standard model of tax competition would suggest that the underprovision of public goods in the country that experiences the capital outflow weighs at least as heavily as the growth in the private sector of the tax haven.

In sum, I think it is fair to say that the case for tax competition—and, conversely, the case against regulating tax competition—on grounds of economic growth is weak indeed. The only reason to include it in my discussion here is the fact, in political discourse, low taxes on capital are frequently justified by appeal to their *local* impact on economic growth.

3.5. Taking stock

Table 3.1 summarizes the analysis of the tax competition models surveyed above. Again, it has not been my objective to provide a comprehensive survey of tax-competition models; surveys of this kind exist already. My objective has been to analyse the use of the

Table 3.1 OVERVIEW OF TAX COMPETITION MODELS

Evaluation of Tax Competition / Criterion	*Tax competition is efficient*	*Tax competition is inefficient*
Productive Pareto optimality	**Capital export neutrality** Musgrave (1969)	**Capital import neutrality** Caves (1982)
Pareto optimality	**Tieboutian models** Tiebout (1956) Oates and Schwab (1988) Wellisch (1996) **Public-choice models** Brennan and Buchanan (1980)	**Baseline model and extensions** Zodrow and Mieszkowski (1986) Wilson (1991) Bucovetsky (1991) **Economic geography models** Ludema & Wooton (2000) Andersson & Forslid (2003) Baldwin & Krugman (2004)
Distributive concerns		**Selection principle** Sinn (2003)
Economic growth	**National political discourse**	**Baseline model** (see above)

concept of efficiency these models make, as well as its normative implications. Given the length of this chapter and the complexity of some of the arguments, it is worth summarizing them:

- Models based on productive Pareto optimality (line 1 of table 3.1)—that is, on a concept of efficiency that is *not* linked to well-being—do not have any normative import.
- Most models of tax competition rely on (general) Pareto optimality (line 2 of table 3.1) as their evaluation criterion. Depending on the modeling assumptions, they come to different conclusions as to whether tax competition is Pareto optimal or not.[56]
- Only one of the surveyed models of tax competition is sensitive to distributive issues (line 3 of table 3.1) and concludes—in line with chapter 1 of this book—that tax competition exacerbates income inequalities.
- The practical relevance of models that conclude, under idealized assumptions, that tax competition is either Pareto optimal or suboptimal, is limited. Since life on the Pareto frontier is unattainable, and conclusions derived for this hypothetical world are not robust when we try to transfer them to situations within the Pareto frontier, they do not have any normative import.

---

56. Sometimes, 'productive' and 'general' Pareto optimality are used simultaneously, compounding the conceptual confusion. Consider the following example: 'A fully efficient allocation cannot be achieved if tax rates differ across regions, and identical tax rates are usually not consistent with efficient differences in public goods levels across regions' (Wilson, 'Theories of Tax Competition', 276). While the first part of the sentence speaks to *productive* Pareto optimality, the latter part appeals to preferences about public goods and thereby establishes the link to well-being and *general* Pareto optimality.

- Instead of focusing on Pareto optimality, efficiency assessments of tax competition should establish whether the practice represents a Pareto improvement, or a Pareto deterioration, or neither. Conceptualized in this way, efficiency emerges as a *constraint* on public policy, sanctioning Pareto improvements, ruling out Pareto deteriorations, and remaining inconclusive on policies that fall in neither category.

- When we evaluate either tax competition or its regulation using efficiency thus understood, the result is inconclusive. Due to the redistributive impact of tax competition underscored in chapter 1 of this book, it represents neither a Pareto improvement nor a Pareto deterioration. The same is true for regulating it. Thus, on this understanding of efficiency, the efficiency objection to the project of this book fails.

- One important corollary of this conclusion is that efficiency thus understood is compatible with the autonomy prerogative in all but the most exceptional circumstances.

- When efficiency is used as a placeholder for economic growth in assessments of tax competition, the resulting argument is weak. While it is common in political discourse to promote national interests, there is no serious academic defence of the idea that tax competition could promote growth on a global scale.

Before moving on to the next section, let me for completeness' sake mention one last potential value for which efficiency could, in principle, act as a placeholder.[57] We might characterize our international fiscal system as more or less efficient depending on how well it does at promoting the value of fiscal self-determination

57. I thank Waheed Hussain for pushing me to include this point, which clarifies the relation between the efficiency objection and the normative claims made in part I.

introduced in chapter 1. If fiscal self-determination were the only value we care about, then it would follow straightforwardly from chapter 2 that the regulation of tax competition advocated in this book is efficient. If we care about several, different values, then we will also have to address questions about the hierarchy between them.

In this chapter, I have deliberately bracketed the conceptual possibility of looking at efficiency as a placeholder for fiscal self-determination because it is clearly not what economists who present efficiency arguments about tax competition versus tax cooperation have in mind. My goal here has been to show that when considering the underlying values of standard economic arguments about efficiency, namely Pareto optimality and economic growth, these standard arguments do not represent a valid objection to my regulation of tax competition.

4. EFFICIENCY AS AN OPTIMAL TRADE-OFF

While the purpose of this chapter so far has been to analyse the various conceptions of efficiency in the context of tax competition and to defuse objections to the regulation of tax competition I advocate in this book, this last section will focus on the relation between tax competition and efficiency in a different but closely related context. Ever since James Mirrlees's paper published in 1971, *optimal tax theory* has become a central tool for the design of fiscal policy.[58]

---

58. J. A. Mirrlees, 'An Exploration in the Theory of Optimum Income Taxation', *Review of Economic Studies* 38, no. 2 (1971): 175–208.

The central idea of the literature on optimal taxation that has flourished in the wake of Mirrlees's article is that the pursuit of any social welfare function comes at a cost. In particular, a more progressive income tax regime, so the argument runs, will both reduce the incentive to work and encourage those on high incomes to reduce their tax liability.[59] Against this background, the 'optimal' or efficient level of tax progressivity is that which equalizes the marginal benefit of realizing one's social welfare function and the marginal cost in terms of the above two effects. In other words, the optimal tax literature endogenizes the level of progressivity.[60]

The concept of efficiency at work here is the second in Le-Grand's taxonomy discussed above. Efficiency is understood as the optimal way to balance two primary social objectives—in this case the promotion of a social welfare function, on the one hand,[61] and a notion of equity, on the other. My goal in this section is to show that when optimal tax theory is applied under conditions of tax competition, there is a danger of misinterpreting its recommendations in a way that favours regressive fiscal policies.

While in the early days of optimal tax theory, the behavioural response to taxation was construed narrowly—focusing on labour supply—'in recent years the public finance community has recognized that *all* behavioural responses to taxation, including evasion and avoidance, are symptoms of inefficiency.'[62] The elasticity of

---

59. According to Slemrod, most economists today agree that the first of these effects, namely the effect of taxation on labour supply, is negligible. See Joel Slemrod, 'The Consequences of Taxation', *Social Philosophy and Policy* 23, no. 2 (2006): 77.

60. The use of the notion of progressivity made in this context is imprecise. Assessments of progressivity should be made of a fiscal regime as a whole—i.e., covering both revenues *and* expenditures. Progressivity as used by the optimal tax literature usually focuses exclusively on the revenue side.

61. Most contributions to the optimal tax literature work with a utilitarian social welfare function of sorts.

62. Slemrod, 'The Consequences of Taxation', 73.

taxable income has become the key parameter in determining the optimal tax structure. The higher this elasticity, the lower the optimal level of progressivity.[63] Factors that influence this elasticity include not only behavioural responses narrowly defined but also the institutional regulations that mediate them, such as loopholes in the tax code, enforcement mechanisms, and so on.

What are the implications of the optimal tax literature for international taxation? I shall emphasize two, the first of which applies both nationally and internationally. First, as Slemrod has underlined, the institutional regulations that mediate behavioural responses to taxation are themselves under government control.[64] Simply put, if a government lets citizens and companies get away with tax evasion and tax avoidance through a series of loopholes in the tax code, then it can be seen as 'choosing' a relatively high elasticity of taxable income. 'If the taxable income elasticity is not set optimally, there is no presumption that the extent of tax progressivity that is optimal, given the current value of the other instruments, is also the global optimum.'[65] As Slemrod points out, the appropriate policy response in such a situation would be to reduce the elasticity of taxable income by closing loopholes, rather than

63. Caveats have been added to this general relationship in recent years. Chetty, for instance, shows that 'one cannot conclude that the efficiency costs of taxing high income individuals is large directly from existing evidence of large taxable income elasticities' (Chetty, *Is the Taxable Income Elasticity Sufficient*, 3). Why not? Because not all of the costs of tax avoidance or tax evasion entail actual resource costs. Some of them are transfers to other agents in the economy—the government or other private agents— and therefore do not represent a deadweight loss.

64. See Slemrod, 'The Consequences of Taxation', 81.

65. Slemrod, 'The Consequences of Taxation', 82. Frenkel et al. make a similar argument when, comparing two situations in which worldwide income taxation is or is not enforceable, they come to the conclusion that tax competition in the latter case 'leads to a constrained optimum, relative to the set of tax instruments that is available' (Frenkel, *International Taxation in an Integrated World*, 206). They underline the fact that this constrained optimum is inferior to the scenario in which a broader set of tax instruments is available.

to get locked into the local optimum with its low level of progressivity.[66] That said, he cautions that determining the optimal level of resources that a society should spend on tax enforcement is not a straightforward exercise.[67]

Note that this reasoning helps to explain the flatter tax schedule of many developing countries. Since they lack the administrative resources to close loopholes and enforce their tax code, a less progressive tax structure is more efficient for them, all things considered.[68] In addition, even if they had the resources to fight tax evasion and tax avoidance, many of the policies that would lower taxable income elasticity are ones that can only be implemented in cooperation with other states. Therefore, the political choice of lowering taxable income elasticity is often not available to states unilaterally.

There are strong reasons to believe that today the taxable income elasticity is not set optimally but, rather, is too high in most countries, leading to a lower than optimal level of progressivity. The enormous size of the tax-advice industry—comprising accountants, lawyers, and banks—can be seen as an indicator of how far the local optimum (the optimal level of progressivity *given* present regulations) is from the global optimum (the optimal level of progressivity when the regulations themselves are included in the optimization).[69] It is plausible to think that the demand for tax-advice services correlates with taxable income elasticity. The more

66. Joel Slemrod, 'Fixing the Leak in Okun's Bucket—Optimal Tax Progressivity When Avoidance Can Be Controlled', *Journal of Public Economics* 55, no. 1 (1994): 41–51.

67. See Joel Slemrod, 'Cheating Ourselves: The Economics of Tax Evasion', *Journal of Economic Perspectives* 21, no. 1 (2007): 43.

68. See Joel Slemrod and Wojciech Kopczuk, 'The Optimal Elasticity of Taxable Income', *Journal of Public Economics* 84, no. 1 (2002): 91–112.

69. For some figures on the size of the tax-advice industry, see Tax Justice Network, *Tax Us if You Can*, sec. 3.

potential loopholes there are, the higher the potential payoff in hiring someone to navigate through them and, hence, the higher the demand for financial services. Conversely, a crackdown on loopholes would presumably put a significant number of tax lawyers and accountants out of work.

As to the second implication of the optimal tax literature for international taxation, it is again Slemrod who asks an intriguing question about taxing capital in an open economy:

> Consider the following experiment. Take a country and determine the optimal progressivity of its tax system. Now split the country into two, for noneconomic (say, ethnic) reasons, and allow a high degree of capital, but not labor, mobility between the two countries. Is it right that now the optimal tax system changes, and in particular lowers, the appropriate degree of progressivity and renders any attempt to tax capital a dominated strategy?[70]

Optimal tax theory has two things to say in response to Slemrod's question. First, absent tax cooperation between the now two countries that would allow them to tax capital effectively, optimal tax theory does indeed call for a low tax on capital and hence a lower level of progressivity. Second, if the two countries cooperate to minimize opportunities for tax avoidance, the global optimum of progressivity may well be close to the one prior to separation.

Slemrod's thought experiment has implications for how we should interpret the shift towards more regressive fiscal policy in

---

70. Slemrod, 'The Consequences of Taxation', 84.

many countries. While most commentators agree with the stance taken in this book—that is, they accept the idea that tax competition has caused a shift to more regressive fiscal policies—others have objected that this shift has come about independently of tax competition and for domestic reasons.[71] While Slemrod's thought experiment shows that there exists a 'rationalization' of more regressive policies on efficiency grounds, it also shows that the framework in which these efficiency considerations are formulated suffers from a bias induced by tax competition. In other words, at least some of the motivations for more regressive fiscal policy that at first sight seem exclusively domestic in nature are in fact indirectly influenced by tax competition.

Slemrod's contribution is important because it clarifies that optimal tax theory does not necessarily call for less progressivity. Indeed, such a reading of this literature is superficial and misleading. An efficient tax regime—that is, one that optimally balances equity and a minimally distortive promotion of the other aspects of the social welfare function, is not one that takes institutional parameters as given, but one that includes them in its optimization. Efforts to fight tax evasion and avoidance should themselves be optimized.

My objective in the remainder of this chapter is to argue that a world of tax and regulatory competition creates a bias against reaching the global optimum, thereby locking countries into inferior local optima with lower levels of progressivity. As a consequence, under tax and regulatory competition, the optimal tax literature sometimes sanctions low levels of progressivity as efficient in a misleading way.

---

71. See, for instance, Sven Steinmo, 'The Evolution of Policy Ideas: Tax Policy in the 20th Century', *British Journal of Politics and International Relations* 5, no. 2 (2003): 206–36.

Lower effective tax rates are only one aspect of tax competition; regulatory aspects are at least as important. In the case of poaching, they in effect allow taxpayers to sever the link between their residence (in the case of individuals) or their economic activity (in the case of corporations), on the one hand, and their taxable income, on the other.[72] Various regulatory devices could serve as illustrations of these two cases, yet I will limit my discussion here to bank secrecy and the international business corporation (IBC), respectively.

First, bank secrecy allows individuals to hide capital gains from tax authorities in their country of residence.[73] Importantly, bank secrecy is not a loophole that the residence country can fix unilaterally, but an externality created by regulations in the destination country. The result from the perspective of optimal taxation is clear: bank secrecy increases the elasticity of taxable income and will thereby lower the optimal level of capital taxation in the residence country, and with it the level of progressivity.

Second, consider IBCs. They are set up as subsidiaries or independent companies to shift profits to low-tax jurisdictions in a variety of ways.[74] IBCs in tax havens routinely benefit from laxer regulation, including secrecy of ownership, no obligation to file their accounts on public record, protection of creditors, and low incorporation costs. The British Virgin Islands alone boasted over 800,000 IBCs in 2004, though it is not clear which percentage of these is being actively used.[75] An

---

72. Recall from chapter 1 that 'poaching' includes tax competition for portfolio capital and for paper profits, but not FDI.

73. While there is increasing pressure on some of the classic bank secrecy regulations such as the Swiss one, new havens of bank secrecy such as Singapore are emerging and, in fact, are attracting private banking activity of Swiss banks. See Palan et al., *Tax Havens*, 142.

74. For an overview, see Palan et al., *Tax Havens*, 90–91.

75. Palan et al., *Tax Havens*, 57–58.

extreme form of the IBC is the exempt corporation. In response to increasing pressure from developed countries' revenue services on IBCs that are mere sham operations, exempt corporations signal a real presence of the company in question to outsiders, but are deemed to be managed and controlled 'elsewhere' by the authorities of the tax haven.[76] This means that the exempt company is not liable for tax purposes either in the tax haven or its country of operation; legally, as long as the 'elsewhere' is not specified, it operates 'nowhere', in an artificial jurisdiction that does not physically exist and is not subject to any regulation.[77] Google's Double Irish Dutch Sandwich is a prime example of how MNEs use 'stateless income' to reduce their tax bills.[78] Under such a scenario, optimal tax theory is bound to recommend tax rates on capital close to zero as efficient.

This brings us back to the thought experiment of Joel Slemrod above. What bank secrecy and IBCs have in common is that they in effect amount to a division of the country into two (or more) parts. They allow individuals and corporations to transfer their taxable income to a jurisdiction other than that of their residence or economic activity. The impact on what is regarded as the most 'efficient' taxation of capital by optimal tax theory has already been demonstrated. The exempt company pushes this logic to its extreme. Here, the destination jurisdiction into which the taxable income is transferred is a virtual entity, free of taxation or any other form of regulation.

76. Palan et al., *Tax Havens*, 87.
77. See Richard Murphy, 'Defining the Secrecy World: Rethinking the Language of "Offshore"' (2008), accessed 22 February 2015, <http://www.taxresearch.org.uk/Documents/Finding.pdf>.
78. See Edward D. Kleinbard, 'Stateless Income', *Florida Tax Review* 11, no. 9 (2011): 699–774, for an insightful discussion of the concept of stateless income. The case of Google discussed in detail by Kleinbard is but one example for a practice that is widely spread.

What should we conclude from this analysis? Three things. First, although the focus of this chapter has been on efficiency rather than on questions of justice, it has to be noted that we are faced here with a blatant form of injustice that abuses the legal system to dodge its fiscal contribution to society.

Second, when using optimal tax theory, we have to make sure to distinguish local versus global optima when interpreting its efficiency claims. Optimal tax analysis based on the premise of a regulatory framework that is too lax from the perspective of a global optimum will produce local optima whose level of 'efficient' progressivity is misleadingly low. These local optima make for bad policy advice. Optimal tax theory is a useful tool, but only when it includes the institutional parameters governing tax evasion and tax avoidance in its optimization.

Third, I have suggested that tax and regulatory competition creates a bias against reaching the global optimum and thereby locks countries into inferior local optima with lower levels of progressivity. As the phenomenon of 'pushing' described in chapter 1 shows, to some extent states have themselves to blame for letting MNEs so easily sever their tax liability from their economic activity. If they did not set the floor for the tax rate on foreign-source corporate income at zero, there would not be much point in creating IBCs and exempt companies. Given this context, however, states have an interest to keep playing the competitive game. When doing so, they will choose levels of progressivity as efficient that, from a global perspective, are too low. Note that 'too low' here does not appeal to an independent standard to assess the 'just' level of progressivity or regressivity—a judgement that this book has deliberately avoided—but, rather, refers to the political preferences expressed by citizens in exercising their autonomy prerogative.

While chapter 1 already demonstrated that tax competition exacerbates inequalities, the present argument provides, *ceteris paribus*, a 'rationalization' of the less progressive fiscal policies that contribute to these rising inequalities. For a country that cannot unilaterally influence the institutional parameters of tax evasion and tax avoidance, a more regressive fiscal policy actually turns out to be 'locally efficient.'

The deeper the world delves into the logic of offshore finance, the more 'locally efficient' regressive tax regimes become. The longer we fail to reform the rules of international finance and taxation, the more 'locally inefficient' redistributive measures will appear. In this context, the logic of deregulation comes dangerously close to being a self-fulfilling prophecy.

5. CONCLUSION

This chapter has served two different objectives. The first has been to counter the objection that regulating tax competition along the lines set out in previous chapters will be inefficient. The second has been to highlight the distorting effect that tax competition can have on the policy recommendations of optimal tax theory when the latter is applied from the perspective of a single country. I have already summarized my argument with respect to the first of these objectives at the end of section 3, which is why these concluding remarks will focus on the second objective.

When pursuing two or more policy goals that are in tension with one another, it is essential to know how they relate and, in particular, whether trade-offs exist between them. Efficiency as an instrumental value provides precisely this kind of knowledge. Against this background, the idea of optimal tax theory to endogenize progressivity, and thereby make sure that we do not unduly sacrifice other social objectives on the altar of social justice, is to be welcomed in principle. Efficiency arguments in this vein are key to the evaluation of international fiscal policy.

However, the institutional framework that determines individuals' responses to tax policy changes should itself be part of the optimization. This holds especially for opportunities to evade or avoid tax in the context of international taxation. If these are treated as parameters rather than as variables, the resulting local optima will recommend a level of progressivity as efficient that is below the level of progressivity in the global optimum where they are treated as variables.

Chapter 4

Rethinking sovereignty in international fiscal policy

In 2009, a U.S. federal court in Florida ruled that the Swiss bank UBS had to hand over client information for up to 52,000 U.S. citizens to the Internal Revenue Service. Well before the case was finally settled by an agreement between the U.S. and Swiss governments, the latter issued the following statement in anticipation of a ruling against UBS: 'The court would be substituting its own authority for that of the competent Swiss authorities, and therefore would violate Swiss sovereignty and international law.'[1] This appeal to sovereignty is only one example among many in recent years in which countries deny that outsiders have any say in their fiscal matters, even if the choices they make affect the tax base of other countries and, thereby, the well-being of their citizens. Can such appeals to sovereignty be justified and, if so, under what conditions?

What aspects of sovereignty, if any, would countries have to sacrifice under some of the proposed schemes of tax cooperation? The spectrum ranges from what has been called 'sovereignty-preserving cooperation,'[2] on the one hand, to a sort of world government with

---

1. See BBC News, 'Swiss Bank Refuses US Tax Request', accessed 13 September 2010, <http://news.bbc.co.uk/2/hi/business/8028174.stm>.
2. See Rixen, 'From Double Tax Avoidance to Tax Competition', 206. Rixen credits the term to Richard Vann, 'A Model Tax Treaty for the Asian-Pacific Region?', *Bulletin for International Fiscal Documentation* 45, no. 3 (1991): 102.

substantial powers to levy taxes, on the other. The latter amounts to shifting fiscal competences up the ladder of governance and is incompatible with the notion of state sovereignty as we understand it today. In the middle, and this is where, realistically, tax cooperation will be situated in the near future, we find what one might call 'sovereignty-compromising cooperation.' This form of cooperation, so the argument runs, requires states to give up some of their fiscal sovereignty, it potentially even involves the creation of supra-national institutions, but it stops well short of making them the centre of fiscal control. The principles defended and the ITO proposed in part I arguably fall into this category.

The first three sections of the chapter respond to the objection from sovereignty to the kind of tax cooperation defended in this book. The last two sections use insights from the analysis of sovereignty to tackle a problem that I set aside earlier. So far, I have assumed that fiscal sovereignty is underpinned by the democratic preferences of citizens. The later sections of the chapter ask what happens to the regulatory framework of tax competition of part I when this assumption is relaxed.

1. THE MANY FACETS OF SOVEREIGNTY

Sovereignty has been conceived of in multiple ways, partly because different disciplines emphasize different aspects of the concept. To avoid confusion, it is important to lay out some of the central meanings of the term. Stephen Krasner usefully distinguishes three meanings of sovereignty, namely domestic, Westphalian, and international legal sovereignty.[3] *Domestic sovereignty* is a classic

3. See Stephen D. Krasner, 'Pervasive Not Perverse: Semi-Sovereigns as the Global Norm', *Cornell International Law Journal* 30 (2007): 653–59.

concept of political theory and concerns the legitimacy and effectiveness of the authority structure within the state. Whereas the focus of domestic sovereignty is on the internal affairs of the state, *Westphalian sovereignty* is a principle meant to govern relations between states. 'The basic rule of Westphalian sovereignty is non-intervention in the internal affairs of other states,[4] guaranteeing the autonomy of the domestic political authorities over a state's territory. Westphalian sovereignty provides the foundation for the neo-realist worldview in political science, whose advocates view international relations as anarchic and assume that states are free from external constraints. As will become clear later on, non-intervention is closely linked to the idea of self-determination, which assumes a fundamental role in many of the normative foundations of sovereignty. Finally, *international legal sovereignty* defines the status of states in the international community. Whether or not a state is recognized by other states influences issues such as diplomatic immunity, membership in international organizations, and the right to sign bilateral or multilateral treaties with other states.

In the context of tax competition and tax cooperation, Westphalian sovereignty is the kind of sovereignty that will preoccupy us, though the other two facets of the concept will become relevant at several junctions of the argument. As long as economic activities and factors of production were relatively immobile, not only was the autonomy of fiscal authorities guaranteed but also fiscal policies were effective. Westphalian sovereignty in tax matters was by and large respected. However, in recent decades, the tax base—capital in particular—has become increasingly mobile. As mentioned earlier, regulatory changes such as the discontinuation

---

4. Krasner, 'Semi-Sovereigns', 656.

of capital controls by most countries in the 1960s and 1970s, as well as the abolition of withholding taxes in the 1980s, have significantly contributed to this trend. As a result, the behavioural changes of economic agents in response to taxation have become much more pronounced. They can now move their various forms of capital between countries and 'shop' for the lowest tax burden.[5] Notice that one might say Westphalian sovereignty is still respected. Countries still control their tax rates *de jure* and no other state has a say in their fiscal policy. However, due to the mobility of the tax base, de facto control over actual government revenues is weakened considerably.

While Westphalian sovereignty has been rendered meaningless under these circumstances, domestic sovereignty has been seriously undermined. In fiscal matters, domestic sovereignty manifests itself through the democratic choice of the ratio of the public budget to GDP, as well as of the level of the redistribution of income and wealth. This is simply what self-determination means in the fiscal context and what I have called the *autonomy prerogative* in chapter 1. Since tax competition puts pressure on government revenues and tends to shift the tax burden towards more regressive taxation on immobile factors such as labour and consumption, these democratic choices, and with them domestic sovereignty, are likely to be compromised by tax competition. Rixen shows that this erosion of domestic sovereignty, or autonomy as he calls it, is an unintended consequence of the international double-tax treaty regime.[6] In fact, 'profit shifting and tax arbitrage are only possible

5. See Palan et al., 'Tax Havens and the Commercialization of State Sovereignty'.
6. See Rixen, 'From Double Tax Avoidance to Tax Competition'. For the OECD tax convention that serves as foundation to this regime, see Organization for Economic Co-operation and Development (OECD), *Model Tax Convention on Income and on Capital: Condensed Version 2005* (Paris: OECD Publishing, 2005).

because countries rely on a sovereignty preserving approach to international taxation.'[7] In other words, restating the insights of chapter 1 in terms of sovereignty, it is because countries struggle to preserve their Westphalian sovereignty that arbitrage becomes possible and the erosion of domestic sovereignty results.

This tension between Westphalian and domestic sovereignty confirms the widely held belief that the different facets of the notion of 'sovereignty' do not add up to an 'integral package of mutually consistent principles and norms.'[8] Westphalian sovereignty stands in conflict with international legal sovereignty, too.[9] Consider the multiple agreements that states enter into on the basis of their legal sovereignty at the international level. Many of these will curtail Westphalian sovereignty. Most prominently in recent decades, the states of the European Union have chosen to give up substantial powers to Brussels. Human rights documents such as the European Human Rights Convention, the International

---

7. Rixen, 'From Double Tax Avoidance to Tax Competition', 13.

8. See Krasner, 'Semi-Sovereigns', 659. See also Allen Buchanan, *Justice, Legitimacy, and Self-determination: Moral Foundations for International Law* (Oxford: Oxford University Press, 2004), 56–57 and chap. 6. Authors who do not make the distinction between different aspects of sovereignty that I rely on here, such as Timothy Endicott, 'The Logic of Freedom and Power', in *The Philosophy of International Law*, ed. Samantha Besson and John Tasioulas (Oxford: Oxford University Press, 2010), 163–85; or Jan Klabbers, 'Clinching the Concept of Sovereignty: Wimbledon Redux', *Austrian Review of International and European Law* 3, no. 3 (1999): 345–67, capture these tensions as an apparent paradox of sovereignty. For international lawyers such as Klabbers, the apparent paradox of sovereignty primarily refers to the issue whether voluntarily entered to *legal* agreements can bind sovereign states at later moments in time. By contrast, this book is preoccupied with the question whether interdependent states have *moral* obligations vis-à-vis each other.

9. Recognizing this conflict undermines the position that Buchanan labels 'legal nihilism'. Paraphrasing H. L. A. Hart, Buchanan points out that 'to say that there is no international law because the sovereignty of states precludes their being bound by law is to fail to understand that the powers, rights, liberties, and immunities that constitute sovereignty are defined by international law. To be sovereign is to be a member of a system of entities defined by and subject to international law' (Buchanan, *Justice, Legitimacy, and Self-determination*, 50).

Criminal Court, or trade agreements such as those under the World Trade Organization or NAFTA that come with dispute-settlement procedures are other examples for international arrangements that compromise Westphalian sovereignty. In some cases, the recognition that comes with international legal sovereignty will even be conditional on a partial surrendering of Westphalian sovereignty, as in the case of the conditionality requirements imposed on sovereign lending by the International Monetary Fund.[10]

There is no consensus as to how these trends should be interpreted. Krasner suggests that even before these delegations of sovereignty to supra-national organizations, the idea of sovereignty based on non-intervention was a form of 'organized hypocrisy,' with states intervening in each other's affairs all the time.[11] From this realist perspective on things, the setting up of supra-national organizations is merely a different kind of intervention and one that apparently serves the national interests of the participants. Raustiala takes a different line, arguing that what looks like a loss of sovereignty to supra-national bodies is not a departure from the statist paradigm after all, because states in most cases preserve veto rights or a right to exit.[12] In this case, the above developments would not constitute cases of intervention at all. Chris Brown challenges the absoluteness of sovereignty as non-intervention in the Westphalian paradigm and shows that sovereignty has been a contested notion since the beginning of the Westphalian system.[13]

10. I take most of these examples from Krasner, 'Semi-Sovereigns', 662–64.
11. Stephen D. Krasner, *Sovereignity: Organized Hypocrisy* (Princeton, NJ: Princeton University Press, 1999).
12. Kal Raustiala, 'Rethinking the Sovereignty Debate in International Economic Law', *Journal of International Economic Law* 6, no. 4 (2003): 842–78.
13. See Chris Brown, *Sovereignty, Rights and Justice: International Political Theory Today* (Cambridge: Polity Press, 2002). He points out that 'modern thinking on actual sovereign powers stresses the extent to which they have always been limited' (pp. 5–6).

I want to make two comments on these different positions. First, it is important to distinguish between theory and practice. It is, of course, true that history since the Westphalian treaty is littered with cases of intervention and that, therefore, actual politics has not lived up to the norm of non-intervention. This is of secondary interest here. The question that preoccupies me is whether non-intervention *should* have been respected, whether political theorists can justify it as a norm fit to govern international relations. Brown rightly emphasizes that Westphalian non-intervention 'still largely dominate[s] the official self-understanding of the twenty-first century international system.'[14] Can this self-understanding be given a normative foundation?

Second, contrary to Brown, I believe that non-intervention is a constitutive feature of the Westphalian system that, if successfully challenged, will take the notion of Westphalian sovereignty down with it. You cannot have 'Westphalian sovereignty plus certain kinds of legitimate intervention' and still call the result Westphalian.[15]

The central question, then, becomes, "Why should we either stick to or abandon a notion of sovereignty that is based on non-intervention?" The basic challenge to Westphalian sovereignty is twofold. First, in an interdependent world, Westphalian sovereignty is no longer adequate, or even logically possible. If the policies of state A affect other states in ways that, although not directly exercising authority over their policies, nevertheless indirectly undermine the effectiveness of these policies, then Westphalian sovereignty is compromised. Henry Shue attributes this tension to the *form* of sovereignty as a right governing inter-state relations

14. Brown, *Sovereignty, Rights and Justice*, 35.
15. Having said that, I suspect my disagreement with Brown might be merely terminological.

itself. If sovereignty is a right, this right takes 'the form of limits on the behaviour of other agents.'[16]

The parallel with individual liberty is once again instructive here. We do not conceive of individual liberty as absolute, but my liberty is limited by guarantees of the same fundamental liberties for everyone else. Establishing these guarantees requires cooperation and the surrender of some individual liberties to the state. Calling for individual liberty to be absolute would result in a meaningless, merely formal conception of liberty, and the right to liberty would lose its effectiveness. Any substantive conception of individual liberty is one that is necessarily limited.[17]

Second, and more specific to the fiscal context, the rise in capital mobility over recent decades means that states are becoming *more* interdependent. In such a world, institutionalized cooperation and intervention will not only be inevitable but also increasingly necessary.[18] Under increasing fiscal interdependence, to put it in Shue's terms, an effective protection of the right to sovereignty will call for more substantive correlative duties on the part of other

---

16. Henry Shue, 'Limiting Sovereigny', in *Humanitarian Intervention and International Relations*, ed. Jennifer M. Welsh (Oxford: Oxford University Press, 2004), 15. Shue adds: 'Without a partially rule-governed society, there are no duties; and with no duties, there are no effective rights. This is nothing specifically to do with sovereignty but is a matter of what a right is. Thus, if sovereignty is a right, sovereignty is limited. Sovereignty is limited because the duties that are constitutive of the right, and without which there can be no right, constrain the activity of every sovereign belonging to international society' (p. 15).

17. For a more detailed development of the analogy between individual liberty and state sovereignty, see Endicott, 'The Logic of Freedom and Power'. Endicott cites Raz, who rightly emphasizes that 'autonomy is possible only within a framework of constraints' (Joseph Raz, *The Morality of Freedom* [Oxford: Oxford University Press, 1986], 155). The structure of this argument is the same as Shue's point about sovereignty.

18. See Anne-Marie Slaughter, 'Security, Solidarity, and Sovereignty: The Grand Themes of UN Reform', *American Journal of International Law* 99, no. 3 (2005): 629: 'To exercise [. . .] authority and control in a world that has become so interconnected that people, politics, and pathogens are virtually able to disregard borders requires institutionalized cooperation and intervention'.

states. This is an argument about the *content* of sovereignty rather than about its *form*. These considerations lead me to the second step of my argument. I will suggest that we drop the anachronistic idea of Westphalian sovereignty and replace it with the notion of 'sovereignty as responsibility.'

2. SOVEREIGNTY WITH STRINGS ATTACHED

In some domains of international law, the call for a redefinition of sovereignty has already been heeded. In their book *The New Sovereignty*, Chayes and Chayes set out a notion of sovereignty that is geared towards enabling states to pursue objectives through cooperation that they could once accomplish alone.[19] In the context of human rights protection in particular, the idea of a conditional sovereignty is gaining ground.[20] In the terminology introduced above, this idea calls for the recognition of international legal sovereignty to be withheld if a government violates the human rights of its citizens. Notice that theorizing about domestic sovereignty has completed the shift towards a conditional notion long ago. Whereas in the classic accounts of Hobbes and Bodin, 'order was paramount' and 'justice was secondary,' modern

19. Abraham Chayes and Antonia H. Chayes, *The New Sovereignty: Compliance with Treaties in International Regulatory Regimes* (Cambridge, MA: Harvard University Press, 1995).
20. See Buchanan, who argues 'for a kind of staged, conditional, and provisional practice of recognition, according to which in some cases an entity claiming statehood status would not be granted all the attributes of sovereignty at once, but would be accorded them in steps, contingent on satisfying certain normative standards' (Buchanan, *Justice, Legitimacy, and Self-determination*, 56). In the real world, this idea informs the 'Responsibility to Protect' (R2P) initiative of the United Nations. See United Nations, *2005 World Summit Outcome*, United Nations General Assembly Resolution A/RES/60/1 (2005), paragraphs 138–40.

conceptualizations of sovereignty ground the authority and control of the state in justice and democratic legitimacy.[21] The same is true of international legal sovereignty, where diplomatic immunity and the recognition of states are subject to a number of (fairly minimal) conditions.

The conceptual thread that runs through all these changes in our understanding of sovereignty as a norm governing relations between states is the idea that sovereignty, just as much as liberty, entails not only rights but also obligations.[22] In light of the considerable advantages that states derive from the exchange of goods and services, knowledge and ideas, values and cultural heritage, to name but a few, the suggestion that the privileges of being a member of the international community comes with certain strings attached is hardly radical. Yet, not only realists will be quick to object that 'sovereignty as responsibility,' as I will call it, is hopelessly idealistic and built on a vision of international relations that is utopian.

Granted, international politics is a long way still from internalizing the idea of sovereignty as responsibility. However, there are encouraging signs that the shift from Westphalian sovereignty to a more demanding notion is not limited to academia.[23] Starting with the report of the International Commission on Intervention and State Sovereignty (ICISS) in 2001, which establishes the

21. See Krasner, 'Semi-Sovereigns', 653–54.
22. See Shue, 'Limiting Sovereignty'. The question about the rights and obligations flowing from sovereignty targets the 'regulative' as opposed to the 'constitutive' face of the concept (see Daniel Philpott, 'Sovereignty: An Introduction and Brief History', *Journal of International Affairs* 48, no. 2 [1995]: 353–68). Whereas the latter defines the legitimate holders of sovereignty, the former asks 'what essential prerogatives in making and enforcing decisions' legitimate polities enjoy (p. 358).
23. The following information is based on Anne-Marie Slaughter's insightful comments on the UN report 'A More Secure World: Our Shared Responsibility' (Slaughter, 'Security, Solidarity, and Sovereignty').

'responsibility to protect' as an emerging principle of customary international law, the discourse of international institutions has started to match the trend observed among international legal theorists. The ICISS insists that '[t]here is no dilution of state sovereignty. But there is a necessary re-characterization involved: from sovereignty as control to sovereignty as responsibility in both internal functions and external duties.'[24] The report of the High-level Panel on Threats, Challenges and Change, instituted by the then Secretary-General of the United Nations, Kofi Annan, goes even further. 'It asserts that all signatories of the UN Charter accept a responsibility both to protect their own citizens and to meet their international obligations to their fellow nations. Failure to fulfil these responsibilities can legitimately subject them to sanctions.'[25] The panel explicitly insists that the responsibilities attached to statehood reflect the nature of contemporary international relations, '[w]hatever perceptions may have prevailed when the Westphalian system first gave rise to the notion of State sovereignty.'[26]

Of course, these lofty declarations do not mean that international relations have overnight lost their adversarial character, or that the concept of Westphalian sovereignty has lost all influence. But they show the theoretical insight that the justifications for Westphalian sovereignty no longer hold has filtered through to practice. What it takes to transform the actual legal and institutional structures at the international level to ensure

24. International Commission on Intervention and State Sovereignty, *The Responsibility to Protect. Report by the International Commission on Intervention and State Sovereignty* (Ottawa: International Research Centre, 2001), 13, accessed 13 September 2010, <http://responsibilitytoprotect.org/ICISS%20Report.pdf>.
25. Slaughter, 'Security, Solidarity, and Sovereignty', 620.
26. United Nations High-level Panel on Threats Challenges and Change, *A More Secure World: Our Shared Responsibility* (Report of the Secretary-General's High-level Panel on Threats, Challenges and Change, 2004), p. 17, accessed 23 February 2015, <http://www.un.org/en/peacebuilding/pdf/historical/hlp_more_secure_world.pdf>.

that they reflect this new understanding of sovereignty is a fascinating question, but one that I will have to set aside for present purposes. The important lesson for the context of this chapter is that sovereignty as responsibility has the potential to overcome the shortcomings and contradictions of Westphalian sovereignty.

3. BACK TO FISCAL POLICY

Under the paradigm of sovereignty as responsibility, it seems that sovereignty so understood is much less likely to conflict with tax cooperation in the first place. After all, the goal of tax cooperation is precisely to create an institutional framework under which the efforts of states to promote the fundamental interests of their citizens are not undermined by other states. As we have seen, the benefits of such a structure necessarily impose constraints on the policies of states. Yet these constraints are not to be viewed as constraints *on* sovereignty but, rather, as constraints *of* sovereignty. This is one of the central insights of this chapter. To illustrate what I mean by these constraints of sovereignty, table 4.1 summarizes the different facets of sovereignty, as well as their meaning in the context of fiscal policy.

If my conceptual analysis holds and we accept a version of sovereignty as responsibility, then the notion of sovereignty-compromising cooperation (as opposed to sovereignty-preserving cooperation as discussed in the introduction to the chapter) is misleading. Many proposals for tax cooperation, though they may compromise the anachronistic Westphalian sovereignty, actually serve to promote sovereignty as responsibility. To bring this back to the dispute between the United States and the Swiss bank UBS, handing over the names of the account holders, rather than being

Table 4.1 SOVEREIGNTY AND INTERNATIONAL TAXATION

Kinds of sovereignty	Their context of application	Definition	Relevance to international taxation
Domestic sovereignty	Internal	concerns the legitimacy and effectiveness of the authority structure within the state	entails the prerogative of the citizens of a state to choose the size of the state (public budget/GDP) and the level of redistribution
Westphalian sovereignty (obsolete)	Relation between states	is based on the principle of non-intervention and guarantees the autonomy of the domestic political authorities over a state's territory	used to protect domestic sovereignty in taxation when interdependence between states was limited
Sovereignty as responsibility (to replace Westphalian sovereignty)	Relation between states	builds on the idea that sovereignty entails obligations as well as rights and thereby shores up the effectiveness of domestic policy	serves to evaluate the legitimacy of tax competition and to spell out the obligations of states to cooperate in tax matters
International legal sovereignty	Recognition	defines the status of states in the international community	may be withheld (sanctions)[1] to enforce the obligations for tax cooperation

[1] I bracket the issue of sanctions here.

a constraint imposed on Swiss sovereignty, is a necessary condition for respecting U.S. sovereignty. The Swiss authorities' appeal to sovereignty as a defence of bank secrecy does not stand up to scrutiny.

Even if, in the abstract, the idea of sovereignty as responsibility sounds attractive, one might object that it is far from clear what follows from adopting this concept for the context of international taxation. This is a point well taken. When proposals akin to sovereignty as responsibility have challenged the mainstream view of sovereignty as non-intervention, these debates have for the most part concentrated on issues of human rights or on developing a theory of legitimate secession. The notion of sovereignty as responsibility has not yet taken hold in the fiscal context.[27] Yet, this is precisely what motivates this chapter. Fiscal policy strikes me as one of the domains of international law where Westphalian sovereignty is still dominant. One reason may be that the consequences are *prima facie* less dramatic than in the case of human rights violations. Another reason could be the fact that the power to tax has long been one of the central responsibilities, as well as the power base, of the state, explaining its reluctance to share it.

The sovereign-debt crisis plaguing many Euro-zone countries provides a powerful illustration of this last point. Ten years after its creation, the common currency has started to reveal the flaws in its design. When implementing a monetary union beyond the bounds of what reasonably can be considered an 'optimal currency area,' this monetary union needs to be complemented with substantial fiscal transfer mechanisms. In the absence of the latter, as current experience shows, the internal imbalances of the

---

27. The contrast to another economic context, namely trade, is surprising. The rules of the World Trade Organization against protectionist tariffs can be regarded as conforming to the idea of sovereignty as responsibility.

monetary union become unsustainable. However, despite these pressures to complement monetary union with fiscal integration, Euro-zone countries are reluctant to do so. It is plausible to think that this aversion to interference in their fiscal policies is informed by a Westphalian mindset.

In order to spell out what sovereignty as responsibility means for international taxation, we need to answer the following question: *What are the duties that states have towards other states in their fiscal policies?* Part I has provided one possible answer to this question. Any country's autonomy prerogative comes with the obligation of respecting the same prerogative of others. More specifically, it requires abiding by the membership principle and the fiscal policy constraint. These principles reflect the contours of a concept of fiscal sovereignty that adequately takes into account the fiscal interdependencies under mobility of capital.

4. THE TWOFOLD CONDITIONAL NATURE OF SOVEREIGNTY

I take it that the three previous sections of this chapter suffice to refute the objection from sovereignty against the kind of tax cooperation defended in part I of this book. The analysis of fiscal sovereignty presented in the process allows us a more thorough understanding of the autonomy prerogative that plays a key role in the regulation of tax competition in part I.

According to the notion of sovereignty as responsibility defended above, sovereignty is a right that comes with obligations, and a state's sovereignty will be undermined if it does not live up to its responsibilities. Its sovereignty is conditional in this sense. This conditionality manifests itself in two dimensions that mirror the two kinds of sovereignty distinguished earlier—that is, domestic sovereignty and inter-state sovereignty.

The focus of this book thus far has been on the latter. The membership principle and the fiscal policy constraint defended in chapter 2 give content to the obligations that states have towards other states in the formulation of their fiscal policies. If a state does not respect these principles, then it forfeits its own right to exercise its autonomy prerogative. Let us call this the *external* conditionality of fiscal sovereignty.

Yet what about the domestic component of fiscal sovereignty? As argued above, and as shown in table 4.1, the legitimacy of the fiscal arrangements of the state depends on whether its citizens can effectively exercise their autonomy prerogative. If citizens cannot choose—that is, adequately influence at the ballot box—the size of the public budget and the level of redistribution, then domestic fiscal sovereignty will be undermined. Let us call this the *internal* conditionality of fiscal sovereignty.

Recall that at the very beginning of my analysis, early on in chapter 1, I simply assumed that the conditions for domestic fiscal sovereignty are fulfilled by stipulating that governments track their citizens' democratic preferences. The very idea of giving any normative weight to the self-determination of states is premised on the guarantee that this self-determination is exercised in a way that reflects the preferences of citizens. Democracy, while imperfect, is the best mechanism we have to ensure that this condition is met.

5. WHAT ABOUT NON-DEMOCRATIC REGIMES?

The time has now come to relax this idealizing assumption made in chapter 1. There are many states in today's world where the internal conditions of fiscal sovereignty are clearly not met. Arguably, this poses a problem from an ethical perspective. At the same time, we do not want to have to wait until this problem is fixed before being able to implement our regulation of tax competition.[28] As things stand, this is precisely the conundrum I find myself in.

The existence of non-democratic regimes creates several difficulties for the account defended in part I of this book. Most importantly, it makes it impossible to use the fiscal policy constraint in practice. In order to identify strategic intent as one of the two components of the fiscal policy constraint, we need a benchmark fiscal policy that is not strategically motivated. The democratic preferences of citizens are what helped us to define that benchmark. Recall that if the English democratically choose a smaller public budget and less redistribution, then other countries cannot complain about the capital flows to England that result from this policy. By contrast, if they make the same choice on strategic grounds to lure foreign capital, then other countries will have a legitimate complaint if they can show that the policy has a negative impact on their aggregate fiscal self-determination.

Without democratic choices as a benchmark, it is not clear what is a strategically motivated fiscal policy and what is not. The declarations of an undemocratic regime that a certain fiscal policy is in accordance with the political preferences of its citizens may or may not be true, but there is simply no way to find out. Under such conditions, the fiscal policy constraint is not operational. But what is the point of a regulatory framework for tax competition if it only applies to democratic regimes? Clearly, to make the regulation of tax competition stick, we want countries such as China or Saudi

---

28. I thank both Daniel Weinstock and an anonymous referee for pushing me to develop this point.

Arabia to be on board. Note that non-democratic regimes do not pose a problem to the application of the membership principle. The difficulty arises 'only' with respect to the fiscal policy constraint.

Two options present themselves at this point. Either we have to drop the ideal of self-determination on the basis of democratic preferences and adjust the fiscal policy constraint accordingly, or we have to somehow extend the fiscal policy constraint in a way that covers non-democratic regimes. The first option comes at too high a price from an ethical perspective. The whole point of *self*-determination is that people have a say in decisions that affect their lives. Granting states autonomy without requiring this link to the preferences of their citizens is too weak a normative foundation for a regulatory framework as the one defended in this book. In fact, it is no normative foundation at all.

I thus turn towards the second option. The objective is to find a way to prohibit undue forms of luring of capital to non-democratic regimes. To do this, we can use one of two measures to curb tax competition discussed in chapter 2, section 1. The first possibility is to negotiate a floor for capital taxation with non-democratic states. They would have to agree to a certain definition of their tax *base* and to a minimum *rate* of capital taxation. Such a negotiation is bound to be a balancing act. It should take place under one important constraint: being a non-democratic regime should not confer fiscal advantages. At the same time, it should not unduly penalize non-democratic states, either. To achieve this, the minimum tax rate could, for instance, be set at the average tax rate among democratic member states of the ITO.

Setting a floor for capital taxation in non-democratic regimes would play the role of a proxy for the unknown fiscal preferences of their people. It takes a step further the Baucus plan discussed in chapter 2, section 1.2. The latter, recall, proposes to set a floor for the taxation of foreign-source income of domestically registered MNEs, thereby reducing the poaching of domestic tax base. To take a concrete example, General Motors would no longer have an incentive to shift its profits abroad if it knew that the reach of the IRS extended to the firm's profits declared abroad.

My proposal for a general floor on capital taxation in non-democratic regimes is more radical because it applies to *all* economic activity taking place there, not just that of MNEs registered elsewhere. Under conditions of democratic governance, this would be a violation of the autonomy prerogative of the country in question, and would run counter to the normative premises on which this book is built. However, the very foundations of the autonomy prerogative are lacking in non-democratic regimes. Under these circumstances, setting a floor for capital taxation represents a second-best solution.

Non-democratic regimes, you might rightly object, will be reluctant to agree to this kind of arrangement. If this is the case, democratic states have one more arrow in their quiver to shore up the regulation of tax competition proposed in chapter 2. If a non-democratic regime does not agree to restricting its luring by setting a floor for capital taxation, the luring can be rendered ineffective from the outside through capital controls preventing flows to the regime in question. As chapter 2, section 1.1 showed, controls on capital outflows are particularly tricky to make work, but even a partially effective regime of this kind could serve as a proxy to eliminate problematic forms of luring. The mere threat of imposing capital controls might change the payoff structure of non-democratic regimes sufficiently to make them agree to a general floor on capital taxation as proposed above.

Both of the measures I have discussed here are clearly second-best. Ideally, we turn to the democratic preferences of citizens to ascertain the legitimacy of any given change in tax policy. When we cannot do so, as in the case of non-democratic regimes, then the regulatory framework for tax competition I have defended in part I needs to be extended to guarantee a level playing field for all states. Both a general floor on capital taxation in non-democratic regimes and controls on capital flows to such countries represent possible extensions of this kind.

In closing, I should acknowledge that, in order to make the second-best solutions discussed in this section operational, we need a reasonable way of defining what counts as a democratic regime. This is a thorny issue in its own right. Coming up with a list of criteria that have to be met for the internal conditions of fiscal sovereignty to be satisfied would take us too far afield here. Suffice it to say that political scientists have devised multiple democracy indices.[29] An index of this sort that is tailored to the fiscal context could serve as a criterion to delineate democratic from non-democratic states.

6. CONCLUSION

International tax theory should follow the lead of other domains of international law in replacing the antiquated notion of Westphalian sovereignty with a concept of sovereignty that acknowledges both obligations and rights of states in their conduct towards other countries. One candidate is the notion defended above, labeled *sovereignty as responsibility.*

This conceptual shift puts into perspective the prerogatives of the state in the context of international taxation. Whereas the

---

29. See, for example, the Democracy Index published by the Economist Intelligence Unit, accessed 27 March 2014, <https://www.eiu.com/public/topical_report.aspx?campaignid=democracyindex12>.

traditional view regards tax cooperation as a constraint on sovereignty, the position laid out in this chapter holds that certain forms of tax cooperation are required by, and conducive to, the protection of sovereignty.

Of course, this argument will not suffice to eliminate political resistance to tax cooperation, because the motivations behind this resistance vary. Tax havens, for instance, understandably see it as a threat to their national interests. The argument presented here offers no magic formula to change their minds, but it shows two things. First, the appeal of tax havens to sovereignty lacks justification. Second, other countries that would, in fact, stand to gain from certain forms of tax cooperation are wrong to think it would compromise their sovereignty. This latter point might make some forms of tax cooperation seem somewhat less utopian.

Building on the analysis of the concept of sovereignty in this chapter, the last section proposed an extension of the fiscal policy constraint to a world with non-democratic regimes. Under these circumstances, either a floor on capital taxation in the non-democratic regime should be put in place to act as a proxy for the fiscal preferences of its citizens; or if no agreement on such a fiscal floor can be found, controls should be imposed on capital outflows to the country in question in order to rule out problematic instances of luring.

Chapter 5

Life with (or after) tax competition

Part I has shown both why tax competition is unjust and what reforms should be implemented to rectify this injustice. Thus, we are aware of the shortcomings of the status quo and we also know the institutional framework that we should end up with from an ethical perspective. Yet, between the starting point and the destination lies a path full of obstacles. Both prior to any serious steps towards reform and also in their aftermath, a number of ethical questions arise. One might group these under the heading of *transitional justice*.

Neglecting these kinds of questions would not only be an omission from a normative viewpoint, but it can also have a serious impact on the feasibility of the reforms themselves. To give just one general example, suppose that the proposed path towards reform does not respect basic norms of reciprocity; some states are asked to give up all poaching of foreign tax base and cut back on luring while others attempt to preserve some of their fiscal advantages. In analysing this type of question, this chapter focuses on issues of transitional justice, as well as on the impact they have on the prospects for the reform agenda presented in part I.

The chapter discusses three broad issues. First, pending reform, are there any obligations that the winners from tax competition have towards the losers under the status quo? Second, pending reform, is it ethical to deny poor countries the right to engage in tax competition in order to finance development projects? And third, after reform, are there any conditions under which former tax havens have a legitimate claim towards compensation for the loss of tax revenue, jobs, or other advantages?

1. SHOULD THE WINNERS OF TAX COMPETITION COMPENSATE THE LOSERS?

You are the beneficiary of an unjust system. It is not in your power to change the system on your own, and no wider consensus to do so is forthcoming. What ought you to do? Do you have a moral obligation to repair part of the injustice yourself? If so, which part? These kinds of questions have spawned a sizeable literature in recent years, with Peter Singer and his question of what individuals should do to fight absolute poverty when their governments fail to do so as one of the most prominent examples.[1] We can ask a parallel question in the context of tax competition: Suppose, as is still the case today, that the community of states fails to discharge its collective duty of institutional reform. What should individual states that benefit from tax competition do under these circumstances?

Someone might conclude that if certain forms of tax competition are the problem, the ethical solution from the perspective of

---

1. See Peter Singer, *Practical Ethics*, 3rd ed. (Cambridge: Cambridge University Press, 2011). For another comprehensive treatment of this question, see Garrett Cullity, *The Moral Demands of Affluence* (Oxford: Oxford University Press, 2004).

an individual state is to unilaterally change its policy and abstain from tax competition. We know already from chapter 1 that this is not the individually rational action to take, but there are two reasons to think that it is not what is ethically required, either.

The first is an argument from fairness and rests on the intuition that the state that behaves ethically should not be worse off relative to the first-best scenario of institutional reform. In other words, '[d]emands on an agent under partial compliance should not exceed what they would be under full compliance.'[2] Assuming that some other states continue to engage in tax competition, which makes for an environment of partial compliance, the state that unilaterally ceases to participate in tax competition would indeed be worse off relative to its peers, and probably even in absolute terms, compared to a situation where they all face a level playing field of just international tax rules. The unilateral abstainer would pick up the slack for the moral failure of other states to do their 'fair share.'[3] Arguably, this is too much to ask.

The second response is based on the effectiveness of a policy of unilateral abstention. While the actions of a state that unilaterally abstains from tax competition might no longer be blameworthy, they do not actually help to reduce the practice of tax competition and the resulting injustices in any way. Unilateral abstention will at most bring a marginal benefit to the losers of tax competition, while its main effect will be a capital outflow from the unilateral abstainer to those countries that continue to compete. The problem is merely displaced rather than solved.

---

2. Liam Murphy, *Moral Demands in Nonideal Theory* (Oxford: Oxford University Press, 2003), 77.
3. The terminology is Liam Murphy's, who puts forward a fair share theory to characterize the moral demands on individuals under conditions of partial compliance. See L. Murphy, *Moral Demands in Nonideal Theory*.

An alternative to unilateral abstention is compensation. As chapter 1 has shown, tax competition violates the autonomy prerogative of states. Against this background, it is plausible to think that the net winners of tax competition—that is, those states that, on balance, experience capital inflows—incur a duty to compensate the net losers. I speak of 'net' winners and losers here because states do not fall into two neat categories of havens and non-havens.[4] Instead, to varying degrees they are beneficiaries of tax competition in one domain and lose out in another. In sum, my argument here is that the net winners from tax competition incur a default obligation of compensating the net losers.[5]

1.1. What's the point of compensatory duties?

A sceptic might object that it is naïve to think that any state will ever pay compensation of this kind, and that 'arguing for these duties is a futile exercise. After all, why should compensation be any more politically feasible than institutional reform, which, by assumption, is not forthcoming?

Two kinds of responses are available to this challenge. First, one might argue that while compensatory duties are certainly subject to feasibility constraints, these are relatively weak compared to institutional reform. Why should this be so? Institutional reform, as amply documented in part I, faces a collective-action problem. This is not the case for compensatory duties, where the main obstacle to discharging them is political will. This asymmetry means that the frequently advanced claim, 'We cannot do anything by ourselves,' does not apply in the case of compensatory

4. See section 4 in chapter 1.
5. Similar compensatory duties can arise from institutional injustices in other policy areas, but these are bracketed here.

duties. Arguably, certain policies already in place today show that some countries accept they have obligations of this sort, even if they do not describe them as compensatory duties for tax competition. One example here is the Norwegian Taxation for Development Program launched in 2011, under which Norwegian tax officials train their colleagues in developing countries with the goal of making revenue collection more efficient.[6] Incidentally, this example also shows that compensatory duties could be discharged in ways other than cash transfers.

All this sounds very optimistic, the sceptic will retort, but it does not make the feasibility constraint any weaker. On closer inspection, it is precisely in those countries that will owe compensatory duties, namely tax havens of various kinds, that the necessary political will is absent. This fact, so the objection continues, makes the payment of compensatory duties just as unlikely as institutional reform.

This point is well taken. If my defence of compensatory duties depended on the hope that individual countries are more likely to listen to the moral imperative, it would indeed be pretty weak. However, there is a second, and I believe stronger case. The main reason to argue for these compensatory duties, strange as it may sound, is not actually to see them paid. Instead, they are of rhetorical value in the fight against unjust tax competition. While we already know that developing countries lose three times as much from tax competition than they receive in development aid,[7] the notion of compensatory duties allows us to point the finger and

6. See Norwegian Ministry of Foreign Affairs, 'Norway Launches Taxation for Development Program, press release 2011, accessed 10 January 2012, <http://www.regjeringen.no/en/dep/ud/press/news/2011/norway-launches-taxation-for-development.html?id=635658>.
7. See Gurria, 'The Global Dodgers'.

attribute responsibility to individual states for this embarrassing fact. While the fallout from tax competition is usually blamed on systemic features, the mere acknowledging that some states have higher stakes in this system than others can increase the pressure on these states to act. In other words, acknowledging the existence of compensatory duties and, as we shall see further along, being able to calculate them, can help improve the prospects of wider institutional reform.

The more fundamental theoretical point behind this argument is the following: As Gilabert has pointed out in his innovative work on feasibility and the notion of 'dynamic duties,' if a feasibility constraint prevents us from discharging duty X at time t_1, we may still have a duty Y to do something that will increase our likelihood of being able to discharge duty X at time t_2.[8] Applied to the present context, if the institutional reforms laid out in part I turn out to be unfeasible for political reasons today, there still are a number of things that we can and should do to make their implementation possible in the future. Making the case for compensatory duties, I argue, falls into this category. Contrary to some policies that might have a lock-in effect and make fundamental reform of the international fiscal landscape less likely—the fragmentation occurring through the signing of more and more bilateral tax treaties could be an example here—arguing for compensatory duties is likely to have a positive influence on the trajectory of events.

To give a concrete example, suppose that state X owes $200 million of compensatory duties from tax competition to state Y. During negotiations on a different policy issue, a free-trade agreement, say, state Y starts to use the compensatory duty owed as a bargaining

8. Pablo Gilabert, *From Global Poverty to Global Equality: A Philosophical Exploration* (Oxford: Oxford University Press, 2012), sec. 4.6.

chip. State X should either pay up or agree to concessions on trade. In such a situation, the effect of compensatory duties, to use the game-theoretic language of chapter 1, section 4, is to modify the payoff structure of the duty-bearing state. By modifying the payoff structure, these duties reduce the difference in the payoffs for state X between the status quo and the regulation of tax competition, thus weakening the feasibility constraint on the latter.

Note that the case for compensatory duties can be made by a number of different actors. First, states that lose out under tax competition have an incentive to do so. A few states including the United States and the UK already calculate the so-called tax gap, measuring the difference between the tax revenues they should earn given their nominal rates and their actual revenues. This kind of statistic could well be complemented by information regarding to which destinations the missing tax base actually flows out. Second, NGOs such as the Tax Justice Network could employ compensatory duties as a tool in their campaigns. Finally, taxpayer associations might find them useful for presenting fairness arguments about the distribution of the tax burden between labour and capital.

1.2. Calculating compensatory duties

In order for the idea of compensatory duties to have any bite, we need to be able to calculate them. Put differently, can we find an adequate measure to monetarize one particular state's part in the failure to implement institutional reform? This way of phrasing the question already gives an indication as to the normative benchmark that I will use to determine the level of compensatory duties. The normative benchmark will be precisely the just institutional framework whose absence the compensatory duties are designed to make up for. The magnitude of compensatory duties as a second-best solution is determined in reference to the first-best solution of institutional reform.

In the context of international taxation, the normative benchmark has been specified in chapter 2. To wit, it is an institutional structure governed by the membership principle and the fiscal policy constraint that rules out all forms of poaching of tax base, as well as some forms of luring of tax base. The challenge now consists in identifying measures to compare how individual states fare under the status quo characterized by tax competition, on the one hand, and under the hypothetical normative benchmark, on the other. In spelling out these measures, I will once again proceed by distinguishing the three kinds of tax competition described in chapter 1, targeting portfolio capital, paper profits, and foreign direct investment (FDI), respectively.

For each of these categories, the compensatory duty will track the normatively problematic shift in tax base and the resulting loss in tax revenue between the status quo and the normative benchmark. Those states whose tax base shrinks under the status quo compared to the benchmark will be called 'rights holder states' (RHS); those whose tax base expands under the status quo compared to the benchmark will be called 'duty bearer states' (DBS).

I should preface the following analysis with a caveat. Measuring shifts in tax base from one country to another is a technical exercise, in our case complicated further by the fact that the shift in question is a counterfactual one. We cannot be entirely sure what capital flows would occur under an alternative tax policy. Ultimately, this is a task for accountants and international tax lawyers who know the technical side of this work better than I do. This qualifier notwithstanding, I am confident that my normative claims are robust and that the calculations necessary to obtain the proposed measures are feasible.

Let me analyse the compensatory duties for the three kinds of tax competition in turn. It is worth noting in advance that the identity of RHS and DBS may, of course, change depending on the kind of tax competition in question. To take a hypothetical example, Switzerland may have a compensatory duty towards Ireland with respect to portfolio capital at the same time as Ireland has a compensatory duty towards Switzerland with respect to FDI.

(a) *Portfolio capital:* In theory, measuring poached portfolio capital is straightforward. Any portfolio capital of members of RHS that is held in DBS without declaring it to the tax authorities of RHS qualifies is poached.[9] The individuals and companies that are members of RHS should be paying capital gains tax there, but attempt to avoid doing so.

In practice, the illegal nature of tax evasion makes it difficult to measure poached portfolio capital. And yet, it is not impossible. Both international organizations such as the Bank of International Settlements and private companies such as consultants or banks provide estimates of wealth that is held offshore.[10] As mentioned in the introduction, one recent estimate puts the wealth held offshore at \$21–31 trillion.[11] While this is not an exact science, breaking down this data on a country-by-country basis is possible. Needless to say, greater transparency of personal and corporate financial data would also help. It might even make these calculations superfluous by handing tax authorities the means for a more effective tax collection.[12]

---

9. Recall from chapter 2 that membership is defined according to the residence principle for individuals and according to the source principle for corporations.
10. See Tax Justice Network, *Tax Us if You Can*, 12–13. My methodology to calculate the compensatory duty for portfolio capital follows this report.
11. See Henry, *The Price of Offshore Revisited*.
12. See also my discussion of transparency in section 2.2 of chapter 2.

Once we have an estimate of undeclared portfolio capital from RHS that is held in DBS, we can stipulate a reasonable rate of return on this investment—somewhere between 5 and 8 percent, say—to calculate the capital gain on which taxes *should have been* paid in RHS. Multiply the estimated capital gain with the capital gains tax rate of RHS, and you get the first component of the compensatory duty owed by DBS. To illustrate, suppose members of Germany (RHS) hold € 100 billion of undeclared portfolio capital in Luxembourg (DBS). Using a rate of return of 6 percent and assuming a capital gains tax rate of 30 percent, this gives us a capital gain of € 6 billion and lost revenues of € 1.8 billion for Germany's tax authorities. This is the compensation payment that Luxembourg owes to Germany.

(b) *Paper profits:* Using a similar method, the compensatory duty due to the poaching of paper profits can be calculated. Here, the normative benchmark I suggested in chapter 2 is a system of unitary taxation with formulary apportionment (UT + FA). Recall that under this scheme, corporate profits are assessed globally.[13] Subsequently, a consensual formula based on measures of economic activity including sales, payroll, and corporate assets is used to assign states the share of these profits they have a right to tax. Suppose the formula determined that 36 percent of Bombardier's activities took place in Canada, Canada would then have the right to tax 36 percent of Bombardier's worldwide profits at the corporate tax rate it sees fit. However, since this normative benchmark presupposes a consensus on the formula to be used to assign the right to tax, and since this consensus and the associated institutional reform are by assumption not available, it is not possible to base our calculation of the compensatory duty due to paper profits on UT + FA.

13. Or, as a second-best, regionally as for instance in the legislative proposal currently debated in the EU.

Fortunately, an alternative instrument is available in what is called country-by-country (CbC) reporting. Under this arrangement, every multinational enterprise has to declare:

> (1) [i]n which country it operates; (2) what it is called in that location; 3) what its financial performance is in every country in which it operates, identifying both third party and intra-group trade as well as labour related information; (4) how much tax (and other benefits) it pays to government locally as a consequence.[14]

The Extractive Industries Transparency Initiative is working to spread the use of CbC reporting for this sector, where profit shifting is particularly widespread.[15] Since, as mentioned in chapter 1, 60 percent of global trade today is intra-group, the impact of introducing such a measure is potentially significant—depending on the proportion of intra-group trade that is motivated by tax arbitrage. One crucial advantage of CbC reporting lies in the fact that MNEs already have the required information; they are simply not required to publish it under current accounting and corporate governance rules.

Now, with a view to calculating compensatory duties in circumstances where institutional reform is not forthcoming, asking a state to unilaterally introduce CbC reporting would be too

14. Richard Murphy, 'Why Is Country-by-Country Financial Reporting by Multinational Companies So Important?' (Report for Tax Justice Network), accessed 15 March 2012, <http://www.taxresearch.org.uk/Documents/CountrybyCountryReporting.pdf>. Other supporters of CbC reporting include Publish What You Pay (see their website, accessed 24 February 2015, http://www.publishwhatyoupay.org/).

15. For more information, see the Extractive Industries Transparency Initiative (EITI)'s website, accessed 3 June 2013, <http://eiti.org/>. For a particularly egregious instance of profit shifting in the mining sector, see Manuel Riesco et al., 'The "Pay Your Taxes" Debate: Perspectives on Corporate Taxation and Social Responsibility in the Chilean Mining Industry' (United Nations Research Institute for Social Development, Technology, Business and Society Programme Paper no. 16, 2005).

demanding.[16] However, a more moderate proposal, while sticking to standard international accounting rules[17] for tax purposes, could have individual states ask MNEs active in their territories to publish CbC reporting *in addition*. Using these two sets of information, calculating the paper profits that have been shifted from RHS to DBS would become possible. Multiplying this amount with the corporate tax rate of RHS will produce the second component of the compensatory duty owed to RHS. To illustrate, suppose that US$ 100 billion in corporate profits have been poached from Chile (RHS) by Bermuda (DBS). Using Chile's current corporate tax rate of 20 percent, Bermuda would owe Chile a compensatory duty of US$ 20 billion, a sum equivalent to the tax revenue lost to Chile's tax authorities from profit shifting.

Someone might object that the mere requirement to publish CbC accounts, even though they are not used to calculate MNEs tax bills, is too demanding towards DBSs because it would lead to just as much of a capital outflow as actually introducing CbC for tax purposes. My response to this objection comes in two parts. First, while the mere publication requirement might indeed lead to a capital outflow from DBS by eliminating some of the most blatant forms of profit shifting—notably some that are in violation of international guidelines on transfer pricing developed by the OECD[18]—it seems unlikely that MNEs would stop entirely to use

16. The reason is the same one as in my first response to the proposal to unilaterally abstain from tax competition above.

17. Unfortunately, there are two standards today, one for the United States—set by the Financial Accounting Standards Board (FASB)—and one for the rest of the world, set by the International Accounting Standards Board (IASB). Differences between these standards not only raise compliance costs but also create loopholes.

18. See Organization for Economic Co-operation and Development (OECD), *OECD Transfer Pricing Guidelines for Multinational Enterprises and Tax Administrations 2010* (Paris: OECD Publishing, 2010). See also the argument in chapter 2 that transparency can by itself have the effect of reducing tax evasion and tax arbitrage.

ways of reducing their tax burden that might be legal but nonetheless represent forms of poaching by the standards of chapter 2. That said, this is an empirical question and it would be helpful if we had a real-world experiment of a country asking MNEs to publish CbC accounts from which to learn.

The second element of my response to the demandingness objection is that any outflow of capital that results from requiring CbC accounts to be published should in principle be offset against the compensatory duty DBS has to pay to RHS. After all, calling for CbC accounts to be made publicly available can be considered a step towards institutional reform. Admittedly, any practical attempt to quantify the deduction in compensatory duty that such a step warrants will be debatable.

(c) *Foreign direct investment:* The final component of the compensatory duty that DBS owes RHS reflects the portion of FDI from RHS in DBS that falls under the fiscal policy constraint as set out in chapter 2. Recall that the fiscal policy constraint states that instances of FDI that are *both* strategically lured in *and* produce a negative outcome—that is, reduce the aggregate level of fiscal self-determination of other states—should not be tolerated under a just set of rules for international taxation. If these criteria are met, then DBS has a compensatory duty towards RHS equivalent to the corporate tax revenue forgone by the latter due to the capital outflow that can be attributed to the DBS fiscal policy in question. Note again that FDI being lured for strategic reasons from RHS to DBS is not sufficient to trigger the compensatory duty. Unless the second, consequentialist criterion is also met—that is, unless the *aggregate* level of fiscal self-determination is reduced—no compensatory duty is due.

To illustrate, suppose US$ 100 billion of FDI are lured from the United States to Ireland. Suppose also that the fiscal policy constraint is violated—that is, both conditions triggering a compensatory duty are met. To simplify, consider only the federal corporate tax rate of 35 percent. By assumption, there is no ITO where RHS could lodge a case against this instance of luring. Under this scenario, the magnitude of the compensatory duty depends on the counterfactual profits the investment would have generated had it not migrated to DBS. This figure can only be known approximately by looking at the profits the companies behind the FDI have made in DBS. Yet, as in the case of paper profits, CbC reporting would be necessary to obtain this information. Suppose the figure in question is US\$ 20 billion. Then the compensatory duty would be US\$ 7 billion.

I should add one caveat to this last component of the compensatory duty. Just as the fiscal policy constraint in chapter 2 is likely to be more controversial than the membership principle, this last component of the compensatory duty will attract more criticism than the first two. I can live with that. If the beneficiary states from tax competition paid the first two components, this would already be a big step in the right direction.

2. SHOULD LOW-INCOME COUNTRIES BE ALLOWED TO COMPETE ON TAXES?

Should *all* winners from tax competition be obliged to pay compensatory duties under the status quo? Someone might raise the following objection to this idea. Low-income countries suffer from a number of structural disadvantages in the global economy. For them, becoming a niche tax haven in some domain is arguably one of the few viable strategies for development; following this logic, for example, we see the Cayman Islands targeting the hedge fund industry, Mauritius specializing in channeling investment into India, and Panama operating as a registration centre.[19] Barring them from pursuing these strategies amounts to correcting one injustice, namely tax competition, with another, namely the creation of one more global institution that is biased in favour of the economic and fiscal interests of rich countries. Our moral stance should therefore be more permissive with respect to developing countries. Rather than demanding compensatory duties from them, we should tolerate their resorting to tax-competition practices.[20] Tax sparing arrangements—that is, high-income countries forfeiting their residual right to taxing the foreign income of MNEs when low-income countries provide low rates as incentives—represent one way to put this idea into practice.[21]

We have already encountered a version of this objection at the end of chapter 2, section 2.3. In defence of the fiscal policy constraint, I argued that *when the background institutions of global governance are just,* a developing country should not be allowed to employ tax competition to attract capital from abroad, even if it intends to spend this money on a development project or in the fight against poverty. We shall now see that when the background institutions of global justice, which I will specify further in a moment, are *unjust,* the situation is considerably more complicated.

I first have to mention two caveats, though. To begin with, as section 4 of chapter 1 has demonstrated, it takes certain characteristics

---

19. Palan et al., *Tax Havens,* 37–38.
20. I would like to thank an anonymous referee for pushing me to discuss this issue.
21. Tax sparing arrangements are controversial. For a critical discussion, see Kim Brooks, 'Tax Sparing: A Needed Incentive for Foreign Investment in Low-Income Countries or an Unnecessary Revenue Sacrifice?', *Queen's Law Journal* 34 (2009): 505–64. Note that there is a fine line between such tax sparing arrangements and situations where developed countries are pushing low-income countries into tax competition practices (see section 2 in chapter 1).

to play the tax-competition strategy successfully. Notably, large countries for which the tax rate effect outweighs the tax base effect tend to lose out under tax competition. Hence, if the present objection goes through, the only low-income countries that could potentially benefit are small states.

Second, the objection necessarily relies on a theory of justice of one sort or another. It argues that we have a reason of justice to exempt low-income countries from compensatory duties. Engaging with this discussion is not inconsistent with my general stance in part I of not endorsing any particular theory of justice to advocate the regulation of tax competition. Independently of the theories of justice I will invoke in the particular context of the objection discussed here, my overall account does not depend on them.

Different theories of justice will appeal to different reasons why low-income countries should be exempt from paying compensatory duties. An egalitarian theory broadly construed would argue that letting low-income countries compete on taxes would get us closer to equality in the relevant dimension: equality of opportunity, compensation for undeserved inequalities, or whatever the precise metric of equality of the theory may be.[22] A utilitarian theory would argue that tolerating tax competition from low-income countries will increase overall utility compared to a situation where they are obliged to pay compensatory duties.

Without entering into a discussion of the general merits of the kinds of theories just mentioned, which would take us too far afield, we can observe that neither of them emphasize the question of *why* the countries in question fall into the low-income bracket.

22. For an overview of the egalitarian literature, see Stefan Gosepath, 'Equality' (2007), in *The Stanford Encyclopedia of Philosophy*, edited by Edward N. Zalta, accessed 24 February 2015, <http://plato.stanford.edu/archives/spr2011/entries/equality/>.

Another current in the literature on global justice does precisely that and therefore turns out to be more relevant in our context. As Thomas Pogge and others have convincingly argued,[23] the developed world and the socio-economic institutions it has by and large designed bear a partial responsibility for the low level of development in many parts of the world.

One important strand of this line of argument points to colonial relations and the long-term effects they have had on the relative level of development across the world. The economic ills colonialism has caused in developing countries have not been adequately cured. Against this background, allowing low-income former colonies to compete on taxes without having to pay compensatory duties could be described as a sort of 'reverse imperialism.'[24] Conversely, not allowing them to resort to tax competition would contribute to locking them into an undeserved position of disadvantage and would hence be unjust. Incidentally, it would also dent their ability to effectively exercise their self-determination, and thus be problematic in light of the premise of autonomy on which the argument of this book is built.[25]

Parallel arguments can be put forward with respect to structural features of the global economy in the more recent past and the present. Be it trade agreements on intellectual property, the decision procedures in many international organizations, or the negative effects of volatile capital flows in response to monetary policies in the United States and Europe, the list of global economic institutions or practices that stack the deck in favour of rich

23. See Pogge, *World Poverty and Human Rights*; but also Leif Wenar, 'Property Rights and the Resource Curse', *Philosophy & Public Affairs* 36, no. 1 (2008): 2–32.
24. I owe this term to one of my anonymous referees.
25. I thank Will Roberts for drawing my attention to this point.

countries is substantial.[26] Thus, the background institutions of global justice are not limited to the fiscal realm, but include other policy areas as well.

Finally, and perhaps most significantly in the fiscal context, many low-income country tax havens have not come up with their tax policies all by themselves; they have, in fact, been explicitly or implicitly encouraged by rich countries and by international organizations such as the IMF or the World Bank to pursue them. In some cases, the reform packages accorded by the latter have even been made conditional on a number of economic policies, including low taxation of capital. Forming part of the so-called Washington consensus, this advice was premised on the idea that any significant taxation of capital would deter FDI. Incidentally, even in a context of tax competition, this turns out to be plainly bad advice when it comes to FDI in certain sectors such as mining, where the presence of the natural resource in one place rather than another offers some leeway for taxing its exploration.[27] As far as the implicit promotion of tax competition by rich countries is concerned, think back to the phenomenon of 'pushing' described in chapter 1, section 2. Deferral or exemption arrangements in rich countries for the foreign-source income of MNEs encourage low-income countries to follow suit and not exercise their right to tax the income these MNEs generate in their jurisdictions, either. In light of the facts described in this paragraph, it almost seems preposterous, let alone just, to ask low-income countries to whom these observations apply to pay compensatory duties.

26. See Michael Patrick Ryan, *Knowledge Diplomacy: Global Competition and the Politics of Intellectual Property* (Washington, DC: Brookings Institution, 1998); Ngaire Woods, 'The Challenge of Good Governance for the IMF and the World Bank Themselves', *World Development* 28, no. 5 (2000): 823–41; and Willem Buiter, 'The Fed's Bad Manners Risk Offending Foreigners', *Financial Times*, 5 February 2014, respectively, for the three examples.
27. Cf. my discussion of the economic geography literature in section 3.2 of chapter 3.

Consider the example of Panama's development as a tax haven in recent years as a testing ground for the above argument. As documented, for instance, by Palan et al., Panama has used the exempt company, bank secrecy laws, and competitive incorporation laws to position itself as a major offshore centre, in particular to attract business from North America.[28] With close to 370,000 IBCs, Panama is one of the major providers of these structures today.[29] Over the years, the economic performance of the country has improved markedly by standard measures. As shown by data of the World Bank, Panama has enjoyed GDP growth rates averaging close to 9 percent per year over the last decade, and with a gross national income (GNI) of US$15,150 per head measured at purchasing power parity in 2012, it is now classified as an upper-middle-income country by the World Bank.[30] At the same time, as reported by *The Economist*, the World Bank also observed that 'in Panama's indigenous areas, 85% live in "extreme poverty," meaning they can't afford enough calories for a normal diet.'[31]

These observations add two new dimensions to our reflection of whether, pending institutional reform, Panama should be allowed to continue competing on taxes without incurring compensatory duties. First, in the case of a past injustice, when should the books be closed? Presumably, there is a point at which the injustice of a country engaging in tax competition starts to outweigh

28. Palan et al., *Tax Havens*, in particular pp. 37 and 137. See also Alain Denault, *Paradis fiscaux: la filière canadienne* (Montréal: Les Éditions Écosociété, 2014), chap. 12; and the country briefing on Panama provided by the Tax Justice Network, 'Financial Secrecy Index'.
29. Palan et al., *Tax Havens*, 57. Cf. the discussion of the structure of the exempt company and of IBCs in section 4 of chapter 3.
30. See World Bank, data on Panama, accessed 10 March 2014, <http://data.worldbank.org/country/panama>.
31. *The Economist*, 'Inequality in Panama – A Gulf on the Isthmus', 17 June 2011.

the past injustice invoked to justify it. Identifying this threshold is bound to invite controversy. Consider just one candidate threshold. One might argue that a country should be allowed to resort to tax competition provided its GNI lies below the world average. On this criterion, Panama, whose GNI per head exceeds the world average for 2012 by almost US$3,000, would already be disqualified.[32] Yet, the verdict might well be different when appealing to alternative criteria. The question of how to correct for past injustices is notoriously difficult,[33] and it would be naïve to attempt to settle it here.

The second additional question asks whether the exemption from compensatory duties should be conditional in any way on how the country uses the fiscal advantage obtained through tax competition. What moral weight should we give to the fact that, despite being a tax haven, Panama has not managed to do better in the fight against extreme poverty? Tricky empirical and counterfactual questions arise here. Would the country have been constrained to do even less against poverty had it not been a tax haven? Could it have done more given the tax haven status? While I cannot give conclusive answers to these questions here, I believe they should play a role in our normative judgement. After all, why give a country an exemption from compensatory duties *for reasons of justice* if doing so does not end up promoting justice?

What lessons can we draw from the above discussion? In principle, it seems very plausible to think that there are situations in which low-income countries should be exempt from compensatory

32. See World Bank, *World Development Indicators website*, accessed 9 March 2014, <http://wdi.worldbank.org/table/1.1>.

33. For an insightful discussion, see Robert Nozick, *Anarchy, State, and Utopia* (New York: Basic Books, 1974), chap. 4.

duties under conditions of tax competition. In practice, however, arriving at clear-cut conclusions from an ethical perspective turns out to be much harder. For two reasons, situations in which some form of reverse imperialism is justified are likely to be rarer than one might think at first sight. First, small countries that are able to benefit from tax competition have often already done so and fall no longer in the low-income bracket according to standard economic measures—Panama, Costa Rica, and Mauritius are examples here. At some stage of development, the moral pendulum will arguably swing the other way and require these states to pay compensation for tax competition rather than being owed compensation for other reasons. Second, if states fail to use their tax haven status in ways that promote social justice, one can argue that they forfeit the moral right to be exempted from compensatory duties.

My discussion here leaves open the possibility of what might be seen as a puzzling asymmetry concerning our ethical stance vis-à-vis low-income countries. In section 2.3 of chapter 2, I argued that if the membership principle and the fiscal policy constraint were put into practice, low-income countries would *not* be allowed to keep competing on taxes. Here, I have made the case that as long as these reforms have not been adopted, there may well be cases where low-income countries *should be* allowed to engage in tax competition without incurring compensatory duties. Is this consistent? Could the same arguments I have discussed here not also be invoked in the former case?

The morally relevant feature that allows us to drive a wedge between these two cases is the fact that the regulation of tax competition advocated in part I is built on a basic premise of reciprocity. Reciprocity cuts both ways. Just as it would be unethical to ask low-income countries to pay compensatory duties while the Delawares, Luxembourgs, and Jerseys of this world are still operating, when rich states get serious about clamping down on tax competition and the reforms outlined in part I, then reciprocity will require low-income countries to play by the new rules. As I have emphasized throughout, the membership principle and the fiscal policy constraint aim at providing a level playing field for all states, including low-income countries.

Rich countries, by the way, will find it just as hard to swallow this idea of reciprocity. Despite the fact that many of them are tax havens in their own right—half of the top ten countries on the Tax Justice Network's 'Financial Secrecy Index' for 2013 are OECD member states[34]—some big players such as the United States, the UK, or Germany tend to be spared the humiliation of appearing on any of the tax haven black or grey lists produced by the OECD or by the G20. This is unsurprising given the membership of these clubs. Especially given the role some of these states have played in the past in promoting tax competition, for any real reform to take hold they have to set an example and clean up their own acts first before they can expect anyone else to join in.

A sceptic might remain unconvinced by my proposed asymmetry between the pre-reform and the post-reform world. Would the moral slate really be wiped clean once institutional reform is adopted? Even someone who agrees with me that reciprocity requires low-income countries to play by the new rules post-reform might maintain that certain claims to compensation carry over into the post-reform period. This is the issue at the heart of the last section of this chapter.

---

34. See Tax Justice Network, Financial Secrecy Index website, accessed 9 March 2014,<http://www.financialsecrecyindex.com/>.

3. UNWINDING THE SYSTEM OF TAX HAVENS

The naïve view of how to implement the reforms advocated in this book might read roughly as follows: Look, we have identified what is wrong with tax competition from an ethics perspective and we have also formulated an adequate normative and institutional response. Once this response has been translated into practice, the issue will have been settled and we can move on relying on the now level playing field.

If they could muster up the political will, the big economic players, the G7 say, would certainly have the power to pressure smaller tax havens into adopting the reforms. But would it be fair to proceed in this way? Would this be the end of the story from an ethical perspective? For someone defending the measures outlined in part I, this might seem a strange question to ask. And yet, it turns out that the implementation of the reform process itself raises several questions of moral desirability and feasibility that cannot be ignored.

The first and most significant issue arises once we relax the simplifying assumption of treating states in general, and tax havens in particular, as a single collective agent. Most tax havens are small countries—a fact that has been explained in section 4 of chapter 1 by the comparative advantage they have in an environment of tax competition. Luxembourg, Liechtenstein, the Cayman Islands, Malta, the Channel Islands of Jersey and Guernsey—none of these places has a population of even one million people. 'Shutting down' a tax haven or, to be more precise, the capital flows from which it benefits, is bound to have an enormous economic impact. What is more, and this is where the ethical challenge arises, the people who are most likely to bear the principal cost of this economic adjustment are not those who currently collect the spoils of the practices of tax competition. On the one hand, the financial sectors in small tax havens would certainly take a severe hit or even disappear, but those who have promoted and managed them are hardly in a position to complain. On the other hand, other sectors of the economy such as tourism, agriculture, or even light manufacturing, which in many cases were crowded out by the financial industry,[35] will struggle to rebuild among the ruins of a local economic meltdown. Leaving them out in the rain for a second time would be unjust.

The case of Jersey has been well documented by Hampton and Christensen,[36] and I borrow all the figures in this paragraph from them to underpin the case for assistance towards transitioning tax havens. With the expansion of the financial sector, and a 40 percent population increase between 1961 and 1991 owing to the influx of accountants and tax lawyers, Jersey over the years manoeuvred itself into a position where 90 percent of its government revenues come from the financial industry and at least 12 percent of the workforce is directly employed by it. This dependence of Jersey's economic fate on finance has a self-reinforcing effect. The booming sector drives up labour costs as well as real estate prices, thereby crowding out economic activity in other areas such as tourism or agriculture, thus further increasing reliance on finance.

The ultimate stage of economic monoculture is the capturing of local legislatures by financial interests, the writing of laws by corporations rather than by democratically elected officials.[37]

35. See Mark P. Hampton and John Christensen, 'Offshore Pariahs? Small Island Economies, Tax Havens, and the Re-configuration of Global Finance', *World Development* 30, no. 9 (2002): 1664–66.
36. See Hampton and Christensen, 'Offshore Pariahs?'; and Mark P. Hampton and John Christensen, 'Looking for Plan B: What Next for Island Hosts of Offshore Finance?', *The Round Table* 100, no. 413 (2011): 169–81.
37. See, for example, Palan, 'Tax Havens and the Commercialization of State Sovereignty'. This phenomenon is by no means limited to small island-nations—see Palan et al., *Tax Havens*, 109–11, for the instrumental role played by private law firms in the drafting of corporate legislation in the U.S. states of New Jersey and Delaware in the late 19th and early 20th century. The impact of these laws is still being felt today.

In such cases, the ability of those outside the financial sector, critical of its dominance and eager to diversify the economic landscape of their country, is severely constrained. In the terminology of chapter 4, domestic sovereignty is no longer guaranteed.

When a tax haven such as Jersey is closed, those outside its financial sector are at risk of having to pick up the social losses after not having participated in the private gains. In this sense, their position can be compared to the average taxpayer of countries hit by the financial crisis of 2008. From an ethics perspective, these individuals have a legitimate claim to compensation of some kind. In places where the governance structures themselves are in need of reform, this compensation could take the form of direct transfers from outside agencies—in the case of Jersey, direct payments to citizens or retraining programmes financed by the UK or the EU would be an option.

Fortuitously, the moral case for a targeted compensation of citizens of transitioning tax havens also weakens the feasibility constraints facing the unwinding of tax havens. Announcing compensation payments of this kind modifies the payoff structure of tax havens, and thereby increases the chances of their cooperation in the transition. This fact has already been acknowledged by a UN report in 1998.[38]

While the degree of economic dependence on the financial sector is likely to be highest in very small tax havens, the case for compensation plausibly applies to bigger ones, too. As we have already seen with the example of Panama in section 2 of this chapter, being a tax haven is not incompatible with swathes of the

---

38. See Jack A. Blum et al., 'Financial Havens, Banking Secrecy and Money Laundering' (report commissioned by the Global Programme against Money-Laundering at the Office for Drug Control and Crime Prevention of the United Nations, 1998). Accessed 24 February 2015. Available at < https://www.imolin.org/imolin/finhaeng.html>.

population living in severe poverty. In the economic downturn that putting an end to tax haven activity will necessarily trigger, the poor are bound to suffer. Once again, the international community has a moral obligation to smooth the transition for certain groups of citizens in tax havens.

This obligation will be even stronger in cases where, as I have emphasized in chapter 1, section 2, the international community or individual rich states have contributed to the economic monoculture in tax havens by 'pushing' them to play this role through their own fiscal policies.

All this being said, the richer the tax haven in question, the weaker the argument becomes for any kind of compensation. It seems hardly plausible that the argument developed in this section applies to anyone in Switzerland, Luxembourg, or Singapore.

3.1. Additional duties towards low-income countries?

The previous section asked whether there are any post-reform obligations towards certain groups of individuals in tax havens—that is, in states that are winners from tax competition today. The present section addresses the parallel question for large low-income countries as the primary losers from tax competition. As chapter 1 has shown, large low-income countries are particularly hard hit by tax competition, because both aspects of their autonomy prerogative are undermined. Under the status quo, this has a considerable impact on their potential for development.

Regulating tax competition along the lines of chapter 2 ensures that low-income countries will face a level playing field in fiscal matters in the future, but it does nothing to correct for the biases of the past. Especially given the path dependence of FDI— multinationals are more likely than not to stay where tax breaks have lured them in the past, even if these tax breaks no longer exist—the biases of the current system will throw a long shadow on a world where tax competition is regulated.

Of course, there are many good reasons for transfers from rich countries to poor ones—humanitarian concerns, reparations for harms under the colonial regime, other forms of structural injustice. But even setting these aside for a moment, there is a moral case for compensating low-income countries *for the damages they suffered specifically as a result of tax competition.*

Such obligations can be discharged in various ways, including direct transfer payments or in-kind assistance through logistical support, training programmes, and so on. One of the possibilities in this regard is of particular relevance to the regulation of tax competition advocated in this book.

Recall the idea of UT + FA defended in part I as a just way to tax MNEs. The formula that is adopted for such a unitary tax could be adjusted in ways that favour low-income countries. For example, giving less weight to the sales factor, which tends to benefit rich countries with high consumption, and more weight to the payroll factor, which usually plays into the hands of low-income countries with low labour costs, represents one way of introducing a low-income country bias.[39]

3.2. Corporate lobbies—the elephant in the room

Like any institutional change, regulating tax competition will produce winners and losers. As the earlier example of Jersey has illustrated, some groups among the losers have a legitimate claim for

---

39. For a similar proposal to 'improve the relative position of low-income countries' through a staggered rate schedule for corporate taxes in capital-exporting and capital-importing countries, respectively, see Musgrave and Musgrave, 'Inter-Nation Equity'.

compensation. One constituency that certainly does *not* have any such claim and that represents perhaps the biggest obstacle in the path to reform is the corporate sector. The stakes are highest for the facilitators of tax arbitrage, the financial services industry including banks, and accountancy and law firms that come up with ever new ways to dodge one's taxes and that are set to lose entire revenue streams under a regulation of tax competition.[40] A chapter on issues of both transitional justice and feasibility would be incomplete without addressing the question of how to counter the corporate lobby against reform.

Corporate interests, just like the various interests within a country, are not monolithic. While the financial industry, as well as the MNEs that gain from its services, benefit from the status quo, small and medium enterprises that operate without foreign subsidiaries do not. Unable to shift their profits to low-tax jurisdictions as multinational enterprises do, they pay much higher *effective* tax rates on their profits than do the latter. If *all* enterprises paid the same effective rate, this rate could be lowered without revenue loss. Given the relative importance of small and medium enterprises for job creation, their political weight is significant.

If one adds the economic interests of workers and consumers, who have had to bear the brunt of the state's efforts to maintain its revenues by shifting the tax burden onto immobile factors, a potential political coalition for regulating tax competition emerges. However, to realize this potential, their interests have to be articulated. For too long, the policies catering to the interests of mobile capital have been presented both as ultimately benefiting everyone and as an imperative that policymakers have

---

40. For an insightful overview of the role of the financial services industry, see Tax Justice Network, *Tax Us if You Can*, 28ff.

no choice but to follow. This is the so-called TINA—'There is no alternative'—policy on globalization.[41] This discourse is beginning to crumble, not least owing to the sustained efforts of a number of NGOs such as the Tax Justice Network that have contributed to firmly establish tax competition on the public agenda. Yet, a lot of work remains to be done to get the message across. Contrary to commonly advanced claims, it has to be clear that tax competition is not the friend, but the enemy, of entrepreneurship and of the small and medium firms that supply most jobs in our economies. Moreover, workers and consumers need to realize that their interests are not inseparably tied to those of capital owners.

Counting on the moral and political leadership of governments to articulate these arguments might be a long shot. However, owing to the financial crisis and the ensuing pressure on state budgets, governments currently also have an acute interest in restoring their fiscal capacity to tax capital. While many states have seemed to tolerate, for instance, the profit shifting of multinationals as the price they had to pay to keep the associated jobs, the debt crisis has stirred them to search for more innovative solutions. From this perspective, the moment for structural reform is now. Once the pressure on public budgets and debt levels eases, the motivation of governments to regulate tax competition will recede, too.

4. CONCLUSION

This chapter has shown that the ethical questions relating to tax competition are not limited to identifying the normative and

---

41. See Streeck, *Gekaufte Zeit*, 88.

institutional principles that should govern the practice. Challenging questions of transitional justice also arise both before and after institutional reform is implemented.

The first two sections looked at the moral landscape under the status quo of unbridled tax competition. I argued, first, that the winners of tax competition have a moral obligation to compensate the losers. While the prospects of such compensatory duties actually getting paid in practice might be slim, the mere fact of monetarizing the damage done to fiscal sovereignty through the poaching and luring of tax base can help to put pressure on the winners of tax competition. The principal point of compensatory duties, thus, is to modify the payoff structure of the winners from tax competition and weaken the feasibility constraint on the kind of institutional reform called for in part I. Moreover, I demonstrated how to calculate compensatory duties.

The second section acknowledged that we should be more permissive towards the use of tax competition by low-income countries under the status quo. In contrast to rich countries, it seems unethical to ask low-income countries to pay compensatory duties for their tax competition practices today. This argument is reinforced once we take into account that most of them have been actively pushed, or at the very least been encouraged by the incentive structure they face, to engage in tax competition. That said, the current standard of living and the spending patterns of the country in question may well influence our normative judgement of whether to exempt low-income countries from compensatory duties. While plausible in principle, such exemptions might be rare in practice.

Finally, I discussed a number of questions arising in a post-reform world. I made a case for structural aid towards those citizens of tax havens that do not benefit from the current boom, but who would nonetheless be hit by the inevitable economic downturn following the clampdown on fiscal arbitrage. I also suggested that residual duties of redistribution towards low-income countries exist because of the losses they incur under tax competition today. The last section of the chapter reflected on the likely resistance to reform from corporate lobbies. While MNEs can indeed be expected to fight, tooth and nail, regulation of the kind advocated in this book, a potentially very large coalition including small and medium enterprises actually stands to gain from it. Communicating that tax competition is not in the interest of *all* corporations is a necessary step in the path towards reform.

Conclusion

In its recent report on 'Base erosion and profit shifting,' the OECD acknowledges that 'the international common principles drawn from national experiences to share tax jurisdiction may not have kept pace with the changing business environment.'[1] As discussed in section 3.4 of chapter 2, both the OECD in conjunction with the G20 and the EU are currently working on important reforms of international tax governance. Numerous scientific studies on the workings and implications of tax competition have been conducted in parallel with these developments; many of them have been cited in this book. As to the interest in tax competition from national governments, it has received a further boost since the onset of the financial crisis in 2008, because finance ministers are looking for ways to raise money to restore their budgets.

While awareness of the problematic character of tax competition is clearly widespread, what has been lacking in the debate is a *comprehensive, normative* perspective on the practice. What forms of tax competition, if any, can be justified, and on what grounds? While this question has been asked, often implicitly, by contributions from within disciplines, these various strands of analysis have not been integrated. For instance, economic analyses of the

1. OECD, *Addressing Base Erosion and Profit Shifting.*

efficiency of tax competition have neither made explicit the normative foundations of their analysis nor specified how the value of efficiency relates to other normative dimensions of tax competition such as self-determination or distributive justice.

The principal objective of this book has been to fill this void and provide such a comprehensive, normative evaluation of tax competition. In short, I have argued that tax competition is problematic, principally because it undermines the value of self-determination (chapter 1). It should be regulated by prohibiting the poaching of tax bases and by restricting the luring of foreign direct investment (chapter 2). On any plausible conception of economic efficiency, existing attempts to demonstrate that the fiscal cooperation called for in this book is inefficient fail. On the contrary, it can be shown that tax competition is prone to result in inefficient fiscal arrangements (chapter 3). The normative and institutional response to the phenomenon of tax competition defended in this book is not only compatible with the sovereignty of states, but it is even required by it on a modern understanding of sovereignty (chapter 4). Finally, life under tax competition and the transition to a more just institutional framework raise ethical questions in their own right (chapter 5).

Beyond this synopsis, I do not intend to summarize the findings of the book again in detail. This has already been done at the ends of the individual chapters. Instead, I will concentrate on five central insights that emerge from the book as a whole and that deserve to be highlighted here.

First, the book advocates a transition from a regulatory context in which it is individually rational but collectively suboptimal for states to attract mobile capital through tax competition, to a regulatory framework in which fiscal cooperation allows states to regain effective fiscal control over capital. Collectively speaking, the latter is the better way to 'catch capital' in the fiscal net. As I have emphasized at several junctures, I do not defend any particular rate of capital taxation. This is a choice that should be made in the democratic decision-making process. My emphasis lies on the fact that international tax arrangements should be structured in a way that ensures an *effective right* of states to catch capital in their fiscal nets if they wish to do so.

Second, a general feature of the proposed regulation of tax competition should be underscored, namely its emphasis on institutions. Note that the 'ethics of tax competition' set out in this book has not focused on the motivations of individual persons or corporations to pay their tax bills or exploit loopholes and evade taxes. The implicit assumption here has been that the dispositions of individuals are not given but, rather, malleable; and that the key to fiscal compliance lies in designing the distribution of fiscal competences between jurisdictions in appropriate fashion. Individuals, in other words, are neither good nor bad *a priori*. Whether they pay their taxes or not depends on the incentive structure of the institutional framework they find themselves in.[2] Tax competition generates loopholes with all their temptations and, therefore, brings out the worst in individuals in terms of their fiscal behaviour. Tax cooperation of the sort advocated here tends to close loopholes and, in that sense, promotes fiscal compliance. As to the governments that underwrite the required institutions, their commitment to tax cooperation can be likened to a constitutional commitment. By ruling out the poaching of tax bases, for instance, they take certain fiscal choices off the policy menu. While these policy choices may be individually rational, ruling them out is collectively beneficial.

2. As I have argued elsewhere, pinning one's hopes on the corporate social responsibility of MNEs to pay their taxes is not a promising strategy. See Dietsch, 'Asking the Fox to Guard the Henhouse'. David Scheffer, 'The Ethical Imperative of Curbing Corporate Tax Avoidance', *Ethics & International Affairs* 24, no. 7 (2013): 361–69, is more optimistic in this regard.

Third, the structure of the normative argument defended in this book is one that potentially has relevance beyond the context of fiscal policy. Recall that my starting point has been to say that the fiscal policy of one state can generate externalities for the self-determination and distribution of income in other states. One way to formulate the central question of this book is by asking what *normative* interdependence, if any, flows from this fiscal interdependence. What are the fiscal rights but also the obligations of a state in a context of capital mobility? This question is just as relevant in other policy contexts. What are the externalities of a state's monetary or trade policy, and what should be the policy prerogatives of states in these domains against that background? While the structure of the argument would be the same, what exactly self-determination requires in these contexts depends on how monetary or trade interdependence works in our world today. I intend to look at these questions in future work.

In this context, it is worth highlighting one particular aspect of my normative response to fiscal interdependence.[3] In the face of growing capital mobility, it has become common to argue that states are losing their capacity to adequately tax capital and that, therefore, fiscal competences should be shifted upwards to a supranational level. In short, global taxes are called for to correct the dwindling fiscal capacity of the state.[4] The approach of this book is different. I contest a key empirical premise of this call for global taxation, namely the fact that capital mobility, or globalization

---

3. The argument presented in this paragraph can be found in more detail in Dietsch and Rixen, 'Redistribution, Globalisation, and Multi-Level Governance'.
4. Examples for such global taxes are the global resource dividend (see Pogge, *World Poverty and Human Rights*) or the financial transaction tax at least when defended as a means to fight poverty rather than as an instrument to stabilize financial markets (see Tobin, 'A Currency Transaction Tax, Why and How'). For discussion of a number of other global taxes, see Brock, 'Taxation and Global Justice'.

more generally, *necessarily* undermines the fiscal capacity of the state. Whether or not they do so depends on the regulatory framework. The regulation of tax competition defended in this book is precisely one aimed at restoring the effective fiscal capacity of the state. While the distributive consequences of doing so might be similar to levying global taxes, regulating tax competition is a more realistic goal than creating a global tax and transfer mechanism.

Fourth, I should add a comment on the two key regulatory principles introduced in chapter 2. As the reader will recall, the *membership principle* effectively rules out any form of poaching of tax bases, be it in the form of portfolio capital or as paper profits. The *fiscal policy constraint*, speaking to the practice of luring foreign direct investment, prohibits *some* forms of luring, namely those that are both strategically motivated and reduce the aggregate level of fiscal self-determination of other states. The fiscal policy constraint is likely to be more controversial than the membership principle. It should be emphasized that, for the purposes of reform, the two can be separated; and that enforcing the membership principle alone would already represent a significant step towards a more just system of international taxation. Tax evasion and the shifting of profits to low-tax jurisdictions represent egregious forms of free-riding on the part of capital owners and one of the most blatant injustices of modern economic society. We need to get a grip on them.

Finally, as I have argued in chapter 5, there exists a powerful potential coalition for tax cooperation. Assuming revenue-neutral reform, workers and consumers, as well as small and medium enterprises could all see their tax burden lightened if internationally mobile capital were more effectively taxed. This book hopes to contribute to the awakening of this dormant political coalition. Its strength makes tax cooperation not only a moral imperative but also a realistic political prospect. This is a rare combination in economic history. It is tempting to draw a parallel with the breaking up of monopolies in the early twentieth century. 'The advocate of the antitrust law,' John Kenneth Galbraith wrote, 'could see himself as protecting both the public interest and a substantial business interest as well.'[5] The same holds for the reforms proposed in this book. Regulating tax competition can be defended not only in the name of justice but also in the name of sound economic policy. This substantially increases the chances of seeing through the necessary reforms.

5. John Kenneth Galbraith, *A History of Economics: The Past as the Present* (London: Penguin Books, 1998), 162.

BIBLIOGRAPHY

Alesina, Alberto, et al. 'The Political Economy of Capital Controls'. NBER Working Paper 4353, 1993.

Andersson, Frederik, and Rikard Forslid. 'Tax Competition and Economic Geography'. *Journal of Public Economic Theory* 5, no. 2 (2003): 279–303.

Apeldoorn, Laurens van. 'International Taxation and the Erosion of Sovereignty'. In *Global Tax Governance – What is Wrong With It and How to Fix It*, edited by Peter Dietsch and Thomas Rixen. Colchester: ECPR Press, forthcoming.

Arnold, Brian J., and Michael J. McIntyre. *International Tax Primer*. The Hague: Kluwer Law International, 1995.

Avi-Yonah, Reuven S. 'Globalization, Tax Competition, and the Fiscal Crisis of the Welfare State'. *Harvard Law Review* 113, no. 7 (2000): 1573–676.

Avi-Yonah, Reuven S. 'Corporations, Society, and the State: A Defense of the Corporate Tax'. *Virginia Law Review* 90, no. 5 (2004): 1193–255.

Avi-Yonah, Reuven S. 'The Three Goals of Taxation'. *Tax Law Review* 60 (2006): 1–28.

Baldwin, Richard E., and Paul Krugman. 'Agglomeration, Integration and Tax Harmonisation'. *European Economic Review* 48, no. 1 (2004): 1–23.

Bamford, Douglas. 'Realising International Justice: To Constrain or to Counter-Incentivise?' *Moral Philosophy and Politics* 1, no. 1 (2014): 127–46.

Barry, Brian, and Laura Valentini. 'Egalitarian Challenges to Global Egalitarianism: A Critique'. *Review of International Studies* 35, no. 3 (2009): 485–512.

Barth, James R., et al. 'Policy Watch: The Repeal of Glass-Steagall and the Advent of Broad Banking'. *Journal of Economic Perspectives* 14, no. 2 (2000): 191–204.

Baucus, Max. 'Summary of Staff Discussion Draft: International Business Tax Reform'. U.S. Senate Committee on Finance. Accessed 25 February 2014.

<http://www.finance.senate.gov/imo/media/doc/Chairman%27s%20 Staff%20International%20Discussion%20Draft%20Summary.pdf>.

BBC News. 'Swiss Bank Refuses US Tax Request'. 1 May 2009. Accessed 13 September 2010. <http://news.bbc.co.uk/2/hi/business/8028174.stm>.

Bjorvatn, Kjetil, and Alexander W. Cappelen. 'Income Distribution and Tax Competition'. Norwegian School of Economics and Business Administration working paper 29/01 (2001). Accessed 14 May2014. <http:// www.nhh.no/Files/Filer/institutter/sam/Discussion%20papers/2001/ dp29.pdf>.

Blaug, Mark. *Economic Theory in Retrospect*. 5th ed. Cambridge: Cambridge University Press, 1997.

Bloomberg News. 'Artful Dodgers'. Accessed 6 February 2014. <http://topics. bloomberg.com/artful-dodgers/>.

Blum, Jack A., et al. 'Financial Havens, Banking Secrecy and Money Laundering'. Report commissioned by the Global Programme Against Money-Laundering at the Office for Drug Control and Crime Prevention of the United Nations, 1998. Accessed 24 February 2015. <https://www.imolin.org/imolin/finhaeng.html>.

Boston Consulting Group. *Tapping Human Assets to Sustain Growth*. Global Wealth Report. Boston, MA: Boston Consulting Group, 2007.

Brennan, Geoffrey, and James M. Buchanan. *The Power to Tax: Analytical Foundations of a Fiscal Constitution*. Cambridge: Cambridge University Press, 1980.

Brock, Gillian. 'Taxation and Global Justice: Closing the Gap between Theory and Practice'. *Journal of Social Philosophy* 39, no. 2 (2008): 161–84.

Brooks, Kim. 'Tax Sparing: A Needed Incentive for Foreign Investment in Low-Income Countries or an Unnecessary Revenue Sacrifice?' *Queen's Law Journal* 34 (2009): 505–64.

Brown, Chris. *Sovereignty, Rights and Justice: International Political Theory Today*. Cambridge: Polity Press, 2002.

Buchanan, Allen. *Ethics, Efficiency, and the Market*. Totowa, NJ: Rowman and Allenhead, 1985.

Buchanan, Allen. *Justice, Legitimacy, and Self-determination: Moral Foundations for International Law*. Oxford: Oxford University Press, 2004.

Buchanan, Allen, and Robert O. Keohane. 'The Legitimacy of Global Governance Institutions'. *Ethics & International Affairs* 20, no. 4 (2006): 405–37.

Bucovetsky, Sam. 'Asymmetric Tax Competition'. *Journal of Urban Economics* 30, no. 2 (1991): 167–81.

Buiter, Willem. 'The Fed's Bad Manners Risk Offending Foreigners'. *Financial Times*, 5 February 2014.

Caney, Simon. 'Review Article: International Distributive Justice'. *Political Studies* 49 (2001): 974–97.

Caney, Simon. 'Cosmopolitan Justice and Institutional Design: An Egalitarian Liberal Conception of Global Governance'. *Social Theory and Practice* 32, no. 4 (2006): 725–56.

Cappelen, Alexander. 'The Moral Rationale for International Fiscal Law'. *Ethics & International Affairs* 15, no. 1 (2001): 97–110.

Cappelen, Alexander. 'Responsibility and International Distributive Justice.' In *Real World Justice*, edited by Thomas Pogge and Andreas Follesdal, 215–28. Dordrecht: Springer, 2005.

Caves, Richard E. *Multinational Enterprise and Economic Analysis*. Cambridge: Cambridge University Press, 1982.

Chayes, Abraham, and Antonia H. Chayes. *The New Sovereignty: Compliance with Treaties in International Regulatory Regimes*. Cambridge, MA: Harvard University Press, 1995.

Chetty, Raj. *Is the Taxable Income Elasticity Sufficient to Calculate Deadweight Loss? The Implications of Evasion and Avoidance*. NBER Working Paper No. 13844. Cambridge: National Bureau of Economic Research, 2008.

Christensen, John, and Sony Kapoor. 'Tax Avoidance, Tax Competition and Globalization: Making Tax Justice a Focus for Global Activism'. *Accountancy Business and the Public Interest* 3, no. 2 (2004): 1–16.

Christian Aid. 'Death and Taxes: The True Toll of Tax Dodging'. Report, 2008. Accessed 9 December 2011. <http://www.christianaid.org.uk/images/deathandtaxes.pdf>.

Christians, Allison. 'Sovereignty, Taxation, and Social Contract'. *Minnesota Journal of International Law* 99 (2009): 99–153.

Christians, Allison. 'Drawing the Boundaries of Tax Justice'. In *The Quest for Tax Reform Continues: The Royal Commission on Taxation Fifty Years Later*, edited by Kim Brooks. Toronto: Carswell, 2013, 53–80.

Clausing, Kimberly A., and Reuven S. Avi-Yonah. *Reforming Corporate Taxation in a Global Economy: A Proposal to Adopt Formulary Apportionment*. Hamilton Project Discussion Paper 2007–08. Washington, DC: Hamilton Project, Brookings Institution, 2007.

Cobham, Alex. 'Tax Evasion, Tax Avoidance and Development Finance'. QEH Working Paper Series 129, 2005. Accessed 13 April 2015. <http://www3.qeh.ox.ac.uk/pdf/qehwp/qehwps129.pdf>.

Cobham, Alex. *Taxation Policy and Development*. OCCG Economy Analysis 2. Oxford: Oxford Council on Good Governance, 2005. Accessed 10 June 2013. <http://www.ocgg.org/fileadmin/Publications/EY002.pdf>.

Cockfield, Arthur J. 'The Rise of the OECD as Informal "World Tax Orgnization" Through National Responses to E-commerce Tax Challenges'. *Yale Journal of Law & Technology* 8 (2005–2006): 136–87.

Cohen, Joshua, and Charles Sabel. 'Extra Republicam Nulla Justicia?' *Philosophy & Public Affairs* 34, no. 2 (2006): 147–75.

Cullity, Garrett. *The Moral Demands of Affluence*. Oxford: Oxford University Press, 2004.

Darby III, Joseph B. 'Double Irish More than Doubles the Tax Saving: Hybrid Structures Reduces Irish, U.S. and Worldwide Taxation'. *Practical US/International Tax Strategies* 11, no. 9 (2007): 2–16.

Davis, Natalie Zemon. *Trickster Travels: A Sixteenth-century Muslim between Worlds*. New York: Hill and Wang, 2006.

de Grauwe, Paul. *The Economics of Monetary Union*. Oxford and New York: Oxford University Press, 2003.

Dehejia, Vivek H., and Philipp Genschel. 'Tax Competition in the European Union'. *Politics & Society* 27 (1999): 403–30.

de Mooij, Ruud A., and Sjef Ederveen. 'Corporate Tax Elasticities: A Reader's Guide to Empirical Findings'. *Oxford Review of Economic Policy* 24, no. 4 (2008): 680–97.

Denault, Alain. *Paradis fiscaux: la filière canadienne*. Montréal: Les Éditions Écosociété, 2014.

Devereux, Michael P. 'The Impact of Taxation on the Location of Capital, Firms and Profit: A Survey of Empirical Evidence (with Data Appendix by Giorgia Maffini)'. Oxford University Centre for Business Taxation, working paper 07/02, April 2006.

Dharmapala, Dhammika. 'What Problems and Opportunities Are Created by Tax Havens?' *Oxford Review of Economic Policy* 24, no. 4 (2008): 661–79.

Dietsch, Peter. 'Show Me the Money: The Case for Income Transparency'. *Journal of Social Philosophy* 37, no. 2 (2006): 197–213.

Dietsch, Peter. 'Distributive Lessons from the Division of Labour'. *Journal of Moral Philosophy* 5, no. 1 (2008): 96–117.

Dietsch, Peter. 'Asking the Fox to Guard the Henhouse: The Tax Planning Industry and Corporate Social Responsibility'. *Ethical Perspectives* 18, no. 3 (2011): 341–54.

Dietsch, Peter. 'Tax Competition and Its Effects on Domestic and Global Justice'. In *Social Justice, Global Dynamics: Theoretical and Empirical Perspectives*, edited by Ayelet Banai, Miriam Ronzoni, and Christian Schemmel, 95–114. London: Routledge, 2011.

Dietsch, Peter. 'The State and Tax Competition—A Normative Perspective'. In *Political Philosophy and Taxation*, edited by Martin O'Neill and Shepley Orr. Oxford: Oxford University Press, forthcoming.

Dietsch, Peter, and Thomas Rixen. 'Redistribution, Globalisation, and Multi-Level Governance'. *Moral Philosophy and Politics* 1, no. 1 (2014): 61–81.

Dietsch, Peter, and Thomas Rixen. 'Tax Competition and Global Background Justice'. *Journal of Political Philosophy* 22, no. 2 (2014): 150–57.

Dietsch, Peter, and Thomas Rixen, eds. *Global Tax Governance—What is Wrong with It and How to Fix It*. Colchester: ECPR Press, forthcoming.

Drucker, Jesse. 'Google 2.4% Rate Shows How $60 Billion Lost to Tax Loopholes'. Accessed 17 July 2012. <http://www.bloomberg.com/news/2010-10-21/google-2-4-rate-shows-how-60-billion-u-s-revenue-lost-to-tax-loopholes.html>.

Dworkin, Ronald. *Sovereign Virtue: The Theory and Practice of Equality*. 2nd ed. Cambridge, MA: Harvard University Press, 2000.

Eccleston, Richard. *The Dynamics of Global Economic Governance—The Financial Crisis, the OECD, and the Politics of International Tax Cooperation*. Cheltenham: Edward Elgar, 2013.

Eccleston, Richard, and Richard Woodward. 'Pathologies in International Policy Transfer: The Case of the OECD Tax Transparency Initiative'. *Journal of Comparative Policy Analysis: Research and Practice* 16, no. 3 (2014): 216–29.

Economist, The. 'Inequality in Panama—A Gulf on the Isthmus'. 17 June 2011.

Economist, The. 'A Survey of Ireland'. 16 October 2004.

Economist Intelligence Unit. 'Democracy Index'. Accessed 27 March 2014. <https://www.eiu.com/public/topical_report.aspx?campaignid=democracyindex12.

Eden, Lorraine. *Taxing Multinationals: Transfer Pricing and Corporate Income Taxation in North America*. Toronto: University of Toronto Press, 1998.

Edwards, Sebastian. 'How Effective Are Capital Controls?' NBER Working Paper 7413, 1999.

Edwards, Jeremy, and Michael Keen. 'Tax Competition and Leviathan'. *European Economic Review* 40, no. 1 (1996): 113–34.

Egan, Timothy. 'Under My Thumb'. *New York Times*, 14 November 2013.

Eichengreen, Barry. 'The Global Gamble on Financial Liberalization: Reflections on Capital Mobility, National Autonomy, and Social Justice'. *Ethics & International Affairs* 13, no. 1 (1999): 205–26.

Endicott, Timothy. 'The Logic of Freedom and Power'. In *The Philosophy of International Law*, edited by Samantha Besson and John Tasioulas, 163–85. Oxford: Oxford University Press, 2010.

Engel, Eduardo, et al. 'Taxes and Income Distribution in Chile: Some Unpleasant Redistributive Arithmetic'. *Journal of Development Economics* 59, no. 1 (1999): 155–92.

European Commission. 'Proposal for a Council Directive on a Common Consolidated Corporate Tax Base (CCCTB)'. European Commission COM(2011) 121/4, 2011. Accessed 24 February 2015. <http://ec.europa.eu/taxation_customs/resources/documents/taxation/company_tax/common_tax_base/com_2011_121_en.pdf>

Eurostat. Eurostat website. Accessed 19 February 2015. <http://ec.europa.eu/eurostat>.

Extractive Industries Transparency Initiative (EITI). EITI website. Accessed 3 June 2013. <http://eiti.org/>.

Financial Times. 'Fear of UK Taxman'. 9 December 2013.

Financial Times. 'Russian Money Streams Through Cyprus'. 6 February 2013.

Finke, Katharine, et al. *Impact of Tax Rate Cut Cum Base Broadening Reforms on Heterogeneous Firm's – Learning from the German Tax Reform 2008*. ZEW Discussion Paper 10–036. Mannheim: Zentrum für Europäische Wirtschaftsforschung, 2010.

Fischel, William A. 'Fiscal and Environmental Considerations in the Location of Firms in Suburban Communities'. In *Fiscal Zoning and Land Use Controls*, edited by Edwin Mills and Wallace Oates, 119–74. Lexington, MA: D.C. Heath, 1975.

Fleurbaey, Marc, and François Maniquet. *A Theory of Fairness and Social Welfare*. Cambridge: Cambridge University Press, 2011.

Follesdal, Andreas. 'The Distributive Justice of a Global Basic Structure: A Category Mistake?' *Politics, Philosophy & Economics* 10, no. 1 (2011): 46–65.

Frenkel, Jacob A., et al. *International Taxation in an Integrated World*. Cambridge, MA: MIT Press, 1991.

Frey, Bruno S., and Reiner Eichenberger. 'To Harmonize or to Compete? That's Not the Question'. *Journal of Public Economics* 60, no. 3 (1996): 335–49.

Fuest, Clemens. 'The European Commission's Proposal for a Common Consolidated Corporate Tax Base'. *Oxford Review of Economic Policy* 24, no. 4 (2008): 720–39.

Galbraith, John Kenneth. *A History of Economics: The Past as the Present*. London: Penguin Books, 1998.

Gallagher, Kevin P. 'The Myth of Financial Protectionism: The New (and Old) Economics of Capital Controls'. Political Economy Research Institute Working Paper Series 278, 2012.

Gelles, David. 'New Corporate Tax Shelter: A Merger Abroad.' *New York Times*, 8 October 2013.

Genschel, Philipp, and Peter Schwarz. 'Tax Competition: A Literature Review'. *Socio-Economic Review* 9, no. 2 (2011): 339–70.

Genschel, Philipp, et al. 'Accelerating Downhill: How the EU shapes Corporate Tax Competition in the Single Market'. *Journal of Common Market Studies* 49, no. 1 (2011): 1–22.

Gilabert, Pablo. *From Global Poverty to Global Equality: A Philosophical Exploration*. Oxford: Oxford University Press, 2012.

Glyn, Andrew. *Capitalism Unleashed: Finance, Globalization, and Welfare*. Oxford: Oxford University Press, 2007.

Gosepath, Stefan. 'Equality' (2007). *Stanford Encyclopedia of Philosophy*. Accessed 24 February 2015. <http://plato.stanford.edu/archives/spr2011/entries/equality/>.

Graetz, Michael J. *Foundations of International Income Taxation*. New York: Foundation Press, 2003.

Grinberg, Itai. 'The Battle over Taxing Offshore Accounts'. *UCLA Law Review* 60, no. 2 (2012): 304–83.

Grinberg, Itai. 'Taxing Capital Income in Emerging Countries: Will FATCA Open the Door?' *World Tax Journal* 5, no. 3 (2013): 325–67.

Gurria, Angel. 'The Global Dodgers'. *The Guardian*, 27 November 2008.

Hallerberg, Mark, and Scott Basinger. 'Internationalization and Changes in Tax Policy in OECD Countries. The Importance of Domestic Veto Players'. *Comparative Political Studies* 31, no. 3 (1998): 321–52.

Halliday, Daniel. 'Justice and Taxation'. *Philosophical Compass* 8, no. 12 (2013): 1111–22.

Hampton, Mark P., and John Christensen. 'Offshore Pariahs? Small Island Economies, Tax Havens, and the Re-configuration of Global Finance'. *World Development* 30, no. 9 (2002): 1657–73.

Hampton, Mark P., and John Christensen. 'Looking for Plan B: What Next for Island Hosts of Offshore Finance?' *The Round Table* 100, no. 413 (2011): 169–81.

Hanlon, Michelle, et al. 'Taking the Long Way Home: U.S. Tax Evasion and Offshore Investments in U.S. Equity and Debt Markets'. *Journal of Finance* 70, no. 1 (2015): 257–87.

Harberger, Arnold C. 'The Measurement of Waste'. *American Economic Review* 54, no. 3 (1964): 58–76.

Henry, James S. 'The Price of Offshore Revisited: New Estimates for "Missing" Global Private Wealth, Income, Inequality, and Lost Taxes'. Report for Tax Justice Network, 2012. Accessed 10 June 2013. <http://www.taxjustice.net/cms/upload/pdf/Price_of_Offshore_Revisited_120722.pdf>.

Hines, James R. 'Three Sides of Harberger Triangles'. *Journal of Economic Perspectives* 13, no. 2 (1999): 167–88.

HM Revenue and Customs. *Measuring Tax Gaps 2011*. London: HM Revenue and Customs, 2011. Accessed 11 December 2012. <http://www.hmrc.gov.uk/statistics/tax-gaps/mtg-2011.pdf>.

Horner, Frances M. 'Do We Need an International Tax Organization?' *Tax Notes International*, 8 October 2001.

Horst, Thomas. 'A Note on the Optimal Income Taxation of International Investment Income'. *Quarterly Journal of Economics* 94, no. 4 (1980): 793–98.

Houlder, Vanessa. 'Bound by the Call of Duty'. *Financial Times*, 27 June 2012.

Houlder, Vanessa. 'Google Shifts €9bn to Bermuda'. *Financial Times*, 11 October 2013.

International Commission on Intervention and State Sovereignty. *The Responsibility to Protect. Report by the International Commission on Intervention and State Sovereignty*. Ottawa: International Research Centre, 2001. Accessed 13 September 2010. <http://responsibilitytoprotect.org/ICISS%20Report.pdf>.

International Consortium of Investigative Journalists (ICIJ), The. "Luxembourg Leaks: Global Companies' Secrets Exposed". ICIJ website, accessed 24 February 2015, <http://www.icij.org/project/luxembourg-leaks>.

James, Aaron. *Fairness in Practice*. Oxford: Oxford University Press, 2012.

Janeba, Eckhard, and Wolfgang Peters. 'Tax Evasion, Tax Competition and Gains from Nondiscrimination: The Case of Interest Taxation in Europe'. *Economic Journal* 109, no. 452 (1999): 93–101.

Julius, A. J. 'Nagel's Atlas'. *Philosophy & Public Affairs* 34, no. 2 (2006): 176–92.

Kaufman, Nancy H. 'Fairness and the Taxation of International Income'. *Law and Policy in International Business* 29, no. 2 (1998): 145–203.

Kee, James Edwin. 'Fiscal Decentralization: Theory as Reform'. Paper presented at the VIII Congreso Internacional del CLAD sobre la Reforma del Estado y de la Administración Pública, Panamá, 28–31 October 2003.

Keen, Michael. 'Preferential Regimes Can Make Tax Competition Less Harmful'. *National Tax Journal* 54, no. 4 (2001): 757–62.

Klabbers, Jan. 'Clinching the Concept of Sovereignty: Wimbledon Redux'. *Austrian Review of International and European Law* 3, no. 3 (1999): 345–67.

Kleinbard, Edward D. 'Stateless Income'. *Florida Tax Review* 11, no. 9 (2011): 699–774.

Knobel, Andreas, and Markus Meinzer. 'The End of Bank Secrecy? Bridging the Gap to Effective Automatic Information Exchange—An Evaluation of OECD's Common Reporting Standard (CRS) and Its Alternatives'. Report for the Tax Justice Network, October 2014.

Krasner, Stephen D. *Sovereignty: Organized Hypocrisy*. Princeton, NJ: Princeton University Press, 1999.

Krasner, Stephen D. 'Pervasive Not Perverse: Semi-Sovereigns as the Global Norm'. *Cornell International Law Journal* 30 (2007): 651–80.

Krogstrup, Signe *A Synthesis of Recent Developments in the Theory of Capital Tax Competition*. EPRU Working Paper Series 04–02. Copenhagen: Economic Policy Research Unit, 2004. Accessed 13 April 2015. <http://www.econ.ku.dk/epru/files/wp/wp-04-02.pdf>.

Lane, Philip R., and Gian Maria Milesi-Ferretti. 'Cross-Border Investment in Small International Financial Centres'. IMF Working Paper WP/10/38, 2010.

Lange, Oskar. 'On the Economic Theory of Socialism: Part One'. *Review of Economic Studies* 4, no. 1 (1936): 53–71.

Lange, Oskar. 'On the Economic Theory of Socialism: Part Two'. *Review of Economic Studies* 4, no. 2 (1937): 123–42.

Laurent, Samuel, "Si vous n'avez rien suivi de l'affaire Cahuzac", *Le Monde*, 30 August 2013. Accessed 28 March 2014, <http://www.lemonde.fr/jerome-cahuzac/>.

Lyne Latulippe, 'Tax Competition: An Internalized Policy Goal'. In *Global Tax Governance – What is Wrong With It and How to Fix It*, edited by Peter Dietsch and Thomas Rixen. Colchester: ECPR Press, forthcoming.

LeGrand, Julian. 'Equity versus Efficiency: The Elusive Trade-Off'. *Ethics* 100, no. 3 (1990): 554–68.

Lindert, Peter. *Growing Public—Social Spending and Economic Growth since the Eighteenth Century*. Cambridge: Cambridge University Press, 2004.

Lipsey, R. G., and Kelvin Lancaster. 'The General Theory of Second Best'. *Review of Economic Studies* 24, no. 1 (1956–57): 11–32.

Ludema, Rodney D., and Ian Wooton. 'Economic Geography and the Fiscal Effects of Regional Integration'. *Journal of International Economics* 52, no. 2 (2000): 331–57.

Mathieson, Donald J., and Liliana Rojas-Suarez. 'Liberalization of the Capital Account: Experience and Issues'. IMF Working Paper 92/46, 1992.

McIntyre, Robert S., et al. 'The Sorry State of Corporate Taxes. What Fortune 500 Firms Pay (or Don't Pay) in the USA and What They Pay Abroad—2008 to 2012'. Report by Citizens for Tax Justice and the Institute on Taxation and Public Policy, Washington, DC, 2014. Accessed 21 March 2014. <http://www.ctj.org/corporatetaxdodgers/sorrystateofcorptaxes.pdf>.

McLure, Charles E. 'Tax Competition: Is What's Good for the Private Goose also Good for the Public Gander?' *National Tax Journal* 39, no. 3 (1986): 341–48.

Meade, James E. *Efficiency, Equality, and the Ownership of Property*. London: G. Allen & Unwin, 1964.

Meckled-Garcia, Saladin. 'On the Very Idea of Cosmopolitan Justice: Constructivism and International Agency'. *Journal of Political Philosophy* 16, no. 3 (2008): 245–71.

Mider, Zachary R. 'Moguls Rent South Dakota Addresses to Shelter Wealth Forever'. *Bloomberg News*. Accessed 6 February 2014. <http://www.bloomberg.com/news/articles/2013-12-27/moguls-rent-south-dakota-addresses-to-dodge-taxes-forever>.

Milanovic, Branko. *Worlds Apart: Measuring International and Global Inequality*. Princeton, NJ: Princeton University Press, 2005.

Mirrlees, J. A. 'An Exploration in the Theory of Optimum Income Taxation'. *Review of Economic Studies* 38, no. 2 (1971): 175–208.

Moggridge, Donald, ed. *Activities 1941–1946: Shaping the Post-war World, Bretton Woods and Reparations*. Vol. 26 of *The Collected Writings of J.M. Keynes*. Cambridge: Cambridge University Press, 1980.

Mueller, Dennis C. 'Redistribution and Allocative Efficiency in a Mobile World Economy'. *Jahrbuch für Neue Politische Ökonomie* 17 (1998): 172–90.

Murphy, Liam. *Moral Demands in Nonideal Theory*. Oxford: Oxford University Press, 2003.

Murphy, Liam, and Thomas Nagel. *The Myth of Ownership: Taxes and Justice*. Oxford: Oxford University Press, 2002.

Murphy, Richard. 'Defining the Secrecy World: Rethinking the Language of "Offshore"', 2008. Accessed 22 February 2015. <http://www.taxresearch.org.uk/Documents/Finding.pdf>.

Murphy, Richard. 'Why Is Country-by-Country Financial Reporting by Multinational Companies so Important?' Report for Tax Justice Network. Accessed 15 March 2012. <http://www.taxresearch.org.uk/Documents/CountrybyCountryReporting.pdf>.

Musgrave, Peggy. *United States Taxation of Foreign Investment Income: Issues and Arguments*. Cambridge, MA: Law School of Harvard University, 1969.

Musgrave, Peggy. 'Fiscal Coordination and Competition in an International Setting'. In *Retrospectives on Public Finance*, edited by Lorraine Eden, 276–305. Durham, NC: Duke University Press, 1991.

Musgrave, Richard A., and Peggy Musgrave. 'Inter-Nation Equity'. In *Modern Fiscal Issues: Essays in Honor of Carl S. Shoup*, edited by Richard M. Bird and John G. Head, 63–85. Toronto: University of Toronto Press, 1972.

Musgrave, Richard A., and Peggy B. Musgrave. *Public Finance in Theory and Practice*. 5th ed. New York: McGraw-Hill, 1989.

Neely, Christopher J. 'An Introduction to Capital Controls'. *Federal Reserve Bank of St. Louis Review* 81, no. 6 (1999): 13–30.

Normore, Calvin. 'Consent and the Principle of Fairness'. In *Essays on Philosophy, Politics & Economics. Integration & Common Research Projects*, edited by Christi Favor, Gerald Gaus, and Julian Lamont, 225–45. Stanford, CA: Stanford University Press, 2010.

North, Douglass C. *Structure and Change in Economic History*. New York: Norton, 1981.

Norwegian Ministry of Foreign Affairs. 'Norway Launches Taxation for Development Program'. Press release, 2011. Accessed 10 January 2012. <http://www.regjeringen.no/en/dep/ud/press/news/2011/norway-launches-taxation-for-development.html?id=635658>.

Nozick, Robert. *Anarchy, State, and Utopia*. New York: Basic Books, 1974.

Oates, Wallace E. *Fiscal Federalism*. New York: Harcourt Brace Jovanovich, 1972.

Oates, Wallace E., and Robert M. Schwab. 'Economic Competition among Jurisdictions: Efficiency Enhancing or Distortion Inducing?' *Journal of Public Economics* 35, no. 3 (1988): 333–54.

Okun, Arthur M. *Equality and Efficiency*. Washington, DC: Brookings Institution, 1975.

Olson, Mancur. 'The Principle of "Fiscal Equivalence": The Division of Responsibilities among Different Levels of Government'. *American Economic Review* 59, no. 2 (1969): 479–87.

Organization for Economic Co-operation and Development (OECD). 'Harmful Tax Competition—An Emerging Global Issue'. Paris: OECD Publications, 1998. Accessed 11 June 2013. <http://www.oecd.org/tax/transparency/44430243.pdf>.

Organization for Economic Co-operation and Development (OECD). 'Intra-industry and Intra-firm Trade and the Internationalisation of Production'. Special chapter of the OECD *Economic Outlook 71*. Paris: OECD Publishing, 2002. Accessed 9 December 2011. <http://www.oecd.org/dataoecd/6/18/2752923.pdf>.

Organization for Economic Co-operation and Development (OECD). *Model Tax Convention on Income and on Capital: Condensed Version 2005*. Paris: OECD Publishing, 2005.

Organization for Economic Co-operation and Development (OECD). *OECD Transfer Pricing Guidelines for Multinational Enterprises and Tax Administrations 2010*. Paris: OECD Publishing, 2010.

Organization for Economic Co-operation and Development (OECD). *Divided We Stand: Why Inequality Keeps Rising*. Paris: OECD Publishing, 2011. Accessed 10 June 2013. <http://www.oecd.org/els/soc/dividedwestand-whyinequalitykeepsrising.htm>.

Organization for Economic Co-operation and Development (OECD). *The Global Forum on Transparency and Exchange of Information for Tax Purposes*. A Background Information Brief. Paris: OECD Publishing, 2011. Accessed 6 June 2013.<http://www.oecd.org/tax/transparency>.

Organization for Economic Co-operation and Development (OECD). *Action Plan on Base Erosion and Profit Shifting*. Paris: OECD Publishing, 2013. Accessed 3 November 2014. <http://dx.doi.org/10.1787/9789264202719-en>.

Organization for Economic Co-operation and Development (OECD). *Addressing Base Erosion and Profit Shifting*. Paris: OECD Publishing, 2013. Accessed 10 June 2013. <http://www.oecd.org/tax/beps.htm>.

Organization for Economic Co-operation and Development (OECD). *Standard for Automatic Exchange of Financial Account Information in Tax Matters*. OECD Publishing, 2014. <http://dx.doi.org/10.1787/9789264216525-en>.

Ostry, Jonathan D., et al. 'Capital Inflows: The Role of Controls'. IMF Staff Position Note SPN/10/04, 2010.

O'Neill, Martin, and Shepley Orr, eds., *Political Philosophy and Taxation*. Oxford: Oxford University Press, forthcoming.

Owens, Jeffrey. 'Written Testimony of Jeffrey Owens, Director, OECD Center for Tax Policy and Administration before Senate Finance Committee on Offshore Tax Evasion, 3 May 2007'. Accessed 9 December 2011. <http://finance.senate.gov/imo/media/doc/050307testjo1.pdf>.

Palan, Ronen. 'Tax Havens and the Commercialization of State Sovereignty'. *International Organization* 56, no. 1 (2002): 151–76.

Palan, Ronen, Richard Murphy, and Christian Chavagneux. *Tax Havens: How Globalization Really Works*. Ithaca, NY: Cornell University Press, 2010.

Philpott, Daniel. 'Sovereignty: An Introduction and Brief History'. *Journal of International Affairs* 48, no. 2 (1995): 353–68.

Piketty, Thomas. *Capital in the Twenty-First Century*. Cambridge, MA: Belknap Press, 2014.

Pogge, Thomas. 'Cosmopolitanism and Sovereignty'. *Ethics* 103, no. 1 (1992): 48–75.

Pogge, Thomas. *World Poverty and Human Rights: Cosmopolitan Responsibilities and Reforms*. 2nd ed. Cambridge: Polity Press, 2008.

Publish What You Pay. Publish What You Pay website. Accessed 24 February 2015. <http://www.publishwhatyoupay.org/>.

Raustiala, Kal. 'Rethinking the Sovereignty Debate in International Economic Law'. *Journal of International Economic Law* 6, no. 4 (2003): 842–78.

Rawls, John. 'Justice as Fairness: Political not Metaphysical.' In *John Rawls—Collected Papers*, edited by Samuel Freeman, 388–414. Cambridge, MA: Harvard University Press, 1999.

Rawls, John. *A Theory of Justice*. 2nd ed. Cambridge, MA: Belknap Press, 1999.

Raz, Joseph. *The Morality of Freedom*. Oxford: Oxford University Press, 1986.

Razin, Assaf, and Efraim Sadka. 'Efficient Investment Incentives in the Presence of Capital Flight'. *Journal of International Economics* 31 (1991): 171–81.

Riesco, Manuel, et al. 'The "Pay Your Taxes" Debate: Perspectives on Corporate Taxation and Social Responsibility in the Chilean Mining Industry'. UN Research Institute for Social Development, Technology, Business and Society Programme Paper no. 16, 2005.

Rixen, Thomas. *The Political Economy of International Tax Governance*. Basingstoke: Palgrave Macmillan, 2008.

Rixen, Thomas. 'From Double Tax Avoidance to Tax Competition: Explaining the Institutional Trajectory of International Tax Governance'. *Review of International Political Economy* 18, no. 2 (2010): 197–227.

Rixen, Thomas. 'Tax Competition and Inequality: The Case for Global Tax Governance'. *Global Governance: A Review of Multilateralism and International Organizations* 17, no. 4 (2011): 447–67.

Rixen, Thomas, and Peter Schwarz. 'How Effective Is the European Union's Savings Tax Directive? Evidence from Four EU Member States'. *Journal of Common Market Studies* 50, no. 1 (2012): 151–68.

Rixen, Thomas, and Klaus Seipp. *Mit mehr Transparenz zu einem gerechten Steuersystem*. Studie der Abteilung Wirtschafts- und Sozialpolitik der Friedrich-Ebert-Stiftung. Bonn: Friedrich-Ebert-Stiftung, 2009.

Robbins, Lionel. *An Essay on the Nature and Significance of Economic Sciences*. London: Macmillan, 1932.

Rodrik, Dani. *The Globalization Paradox*. New York: W.W. Norton, 2011.

Ronzoni, Miriam. 'The Global Order: A Case of Background Injustice? A Practice-Dependent Account'. *Philosophy & Public Affairs* 37, no. 3 (2009): 229–56.

Rubin, Richard. 'Wealthy N.Y. Residents Escape Tax with Trusts in Nevada'. *Bloomberg News*. Accessed 6 February 2014. <http://www.bloomberg.com/news/articles/2013-12-18/wealthy-n-y-residents-escape-tax-with-trusts-in-nevada>.

Ryan, Michael Patrick. *Knowledge Diplomacy: Global Competition and the Politics of Intellectual Property*. Washington, DC: Brookings Institution, 1998.

Sabaini, Gómez, et al. *La equidad distributiva y el sistema tributario: un análisis para el caso argentino*. Serie Gestión Pública. Santiago de Chile: Comisión Económica para América Latina, 2002.

Saez, Emmanuel. 'Striking it Richer: The Evolution of Top Incomes in the United States'. Accessed 21 March 2014. <http://elsa.berkeley.edu/users/saez/saez-UStopincomes-2012.pdf>.

Sangiovanni, Andrea. 'Global Justice, Reciprocity, and the State'. *Philosophy & Public Affairs* 35, no. 1 (2007): 3–39.

Scheffer, David. 'The Ethical Imperative of Curbing Corporate Tax Avoidance'. *Ethics & International Affairs* 24, no. 7 (2013): 361–69.

Schwarz, Peter. 'Does Capital Mobility Reduce the Corporate-Labor Tax Ratio?' *Public Choice* 130, no. 3 (2007): 363–80.

Sen, Amartya. *On Ethics and Economics*. Oxford: Blackwell, 1987.

Sen, Amartya. *Inequality Reexamined*. Oxford: Clarendon Press, 1992.

Sharman, Jason C. *Havens in a Storm: The Struggle for Global Tax Regulation*. Ithaca, NY: Cornell University Press, 2006.

Sharman, Jason C. 'Shopping for Anonymous Shell Companies: An Audit Study of Anonymity and Crime in the International Financial System'. *Journal of Economic Perspectives* 24, no. 4 (2010): 127–40.

Sharman, Jason C. 'Testing the Global Financial Transparency Regime'. *International Studies Quarterly* 55 (2011): 981–1001.

Shaxson, Nicholas. *Treasure Islands—Uncovering the Damage of Offshore Banking and Tax Havens*. Basingstoke: Palgrave Macmillan, 2011.

Shome, Parthasarathi. 'Taxation in Latin America: Structural Trends and Impact of Administration'. IMF Working Paper 99/19, 1999.

Shue, Henry. 'Limiting Sovereigny'. In *Humanitarian Intervention and International Relations*, edited by Jennifer M. Welsh, 11–28. Oxford: Oxford University Press, 2004.

Singer, Peter. *Practical Ethics*. 3rd ed. Cambridge: Cambridge University Press, 2011.

Sinn, Hans-Werner. 'The Selection Principle and Market Failure in Systems Competition'. *Journal of Public Economics* 66, no. 2 (1997): 247–74.

Sinn, Hans-Werner. *The New Systems Competition*. Yrjö Jahnsson Lectures. Oxford: Blackwell, 2003.

Slaughter, Anne-Marie. 'Security, Solidarity, and Sovereignty: The Grand Themes of UN Reform'. *American Journal of International Law* 99, no. 3 (2005): 619–31.

Slemrod, Joel. 'Fixing the Leak in Okun's Bucket—Optimal Tax Progressivity when Avoidance Can Be Controlled'. *Journal of Public Economics* 55, no. 1 (1994): 41–51.

Slemrod, Joel. 'The Consequences of Taxation'. *Social Philosophy and Policy* 23, no. 2 (2006): 73–87.

Slemrod, Joel. 'Cheating Ourselves: The Economics of Tax Evasion'. *Journal of Economic Perspectives* 21, no. 1 (2007): 25–43.

Slemrod, Joel, and Jon Bakija. *Taxing Ourselves. A Citizen's Guide to the Great Debate over Tax Reform*. 3rd. ed. Cambridge, MA: MIT Press, 2004.

Slemrod, Joel, and Wojciech Kopczuk. 'The Optimal Elasticity of Taxable Income'. *Journal of Public Economics* 84, no. 1 (2002): 91–112.

Spencer, David. 'Tax Information Exchange and Bank Secrecy'. *Journal of International Taxation* 16, no. 3 (2005): 22–30.

Steinmo, Sven. 'The Evolution of Policy Ideas: Tax Policy in the 20th Century'. *British Journal of Politics and International Relations* 5, no. 2 (2003): 206–36.

Story, Louise. 'As Companies Seek Tax Deals, Governments Pay High Price'. *New York Times*, 1 December 2012.

Streeck, Wolfgang. *Gekaufte Zeit—Die vertagte Krise des demokratischen Kapitalismus*. Berlin: Suhrkamp, 2013.

Tanzi, Vito. 'Is There a Need for a World Tax Organization?' In *The Economics of Globalization: Policy Perspectives from Public Economics*, edited by Assaf Razin and Efraim Sadka, 173–86. Cambridge: Cambridge University Press, 1999.

Tax Justice Network. 'Tax Us if You Can. *The True Story of a Global Failure*. London: Tax Justice Network, 2005. Accessed 9 December 2011. <http://www.taxjustice.net/cms/upload/pdf/tuiyc_-_eng_-_web_file.pdf>.

Tax Justice Network. 'Country-by-Country Reporting: How to Make Multinational Companies More Transparent'. Tax Justice Briefing, 2008. Accessed 27 June 2012. <http://www.financialtaskforce.org/beta/wp-content/uploads/2009/04/why-is-country-by-country-financial-reporting-by-multinational-companies-so-important_english.pdf?9d7bd4>.

Tax Justice Network. 'Financial Secrecy Index' website. Accessed 17 February 2014. <http://www.financialsecrecyindex.com/>.

Thielemann, Ulrich. 'Grundsätze fairen Steuerwettbewerbs—Ein wirtschaftsethisches Plädoyer für einen Steuerleistungswettbewerb'. In *Regulierung oder Deregulierung der Finanzmärkte*, edited by Bernd Britzelmaier, Stephan Geberl, Hans-Rüdiger Kaufmann, and Marco Menichetti, 113–32. Heidelberg: Physica, 2002.

Thorpe, Nick. 'Romania's "Nokia City" Hopes Dashed'. *BBC News*. Accessed 6 February 2014. <http://www.bbc.co.uk/news/world-europe-16290078>.

Tiebout, Charles M. 'A Pure Theory of Local Expenditures'. *Journal of Political Economy* 64, no. 5 (1956): 416–24.

Tobin, James. 'A Proposal for International Monetary Reform'. *Eastern Economic Journal* 4, nos. 3–4 (1978): 153–59.

Tobin, James. 'A Currency Transaction Tax, Why and How'. *Open Economies Review* 7, no. 1 (1996): 493–99.

Trachtman, Joel P. 'Regulatory Competition and Regulatory Jurisdiction'. *Journal of International Economic Law* 3, no. 2 (2000): 331–48.

United Nations. 'Convention on the Prevention and Punishment of the Crime of Genocide'. United Nations General Assembly Resolution A/RES/260(III), 1948.

United Nations. '2005 World Summit Outcome'. United Nations General Assembly Resolution A/RES/60/1, 2005.

United Nations Development Programme. *Human Development Report 2006: Beyond Scarcity–Power, Poverty and the Global Water Crisis*. Basingstoke: Palgrave Macmillan, 2006.

United Nations High-level Panel on Threats Challenges and Change. 'A More Secure World: Our Shared Responsibility'. Report of the Secretary-General's High-level Panel on Threats, Challenges and Change, 2004. Accessed 23 February 2015. <http://www.un.org/en/peacebuilding/pdf/historical/hlp_ more_secure_world.pdf>.

U.S. Department of Treasury. Department website. Accessed 25 February 2014. <http://www.treasury.gov/resource-center/tax-policy/treaties/Pages/ FATCA.aspx>.

U.S. Internal Revenue Service (IRS). IRS website. Accessed 25 February 2014. <http://www.irs.gov/Businesses/Corporations/Foreign-Account-Tax-Compliance-Act-(FATCA)>.

U.S. Office of Tax Policy at the Department of the Treasury. 'The Deferral of Income Earned Through U.S. Controlled Foreign Corporations'. Report, 2000. Accessed 6 February 2014. <http://www.treasury.gov/resource-center/ tax-policy/Documents/subpartf.pdf>.

U.S. Senate Committee on Finance. 'Baucus Unveils Proposals for International Tax Reform'. Press release. Accessed 25 February 2014. <http:// www.finance.senate.gov/newsroom/chairman/release/?id=f946a9f3-d296-42ad-bae4-bcf451b34b14>.

Valentini, Laura. *Justice in a Globalized World: A Normative Framework*. Oxford: Oxford University Press, 2011.

Valentini, Laura. 'Ideal vs. Non-ideal Theory: A Conceptual Map'. *Philosophical Compass* 7, no. 9 (2012): 654–64.

Vann, Richard. 'A Model Tax Treaty for the Asian-Pacific Region?' *Bulletin for International Fiscal Documentation* 45, no. 3 (1991): 99–111.

Van Parijs, Philippe. 'International Distributive Justice'. In *A Companion to Contemporary Political Philosophy*, edited by Robert E. Goodin, Philip Pettit, and Thomas Pogge, 638–52. Oxford: Blackwell, 2007.

Weintraub, Jeff, and Krishan Kumar. *Public and Private in Thought and Practice: Perspectives on a Grand Dichotomy*. Chicago: Chicago University Press, 1997.

Wellisch, Dietmar. 'Decentralized Fiscal Policy with High Mobility Reconsidered: Reasons for Inefficiency and an Optimal Intervention Scheme'. *European Journal of Political Economy* 12, no. 1 (1996): 91–111.

Wenar, Leif. 'Property Rights and the Resource Curse'. *Philosophy & Public Affairs* 36, no. 1 (2008): 2–32.

White, Michelle J. 'Firm Location in a Zoned Metropolitan Area'. In *Fiscal Zoning and Land Use Controls: The Economic Issues*, edited by Edwin S. Mills and Wallace E. Oates, 31–100. Lexington, MA: D.C. Heath, 1975.

Williamson, Hugh. 'German Protests Grow over Nokia Relocation'. *Financial Times*, 19 January 2008.

Wilson, John D. 'Tax Competition with Interregional Differences in Factor Endowments'. *Regional Science and Urban Economics* 21, no. 3 (1991): 423–51.

Wilson, John D. 'Theories of Tax Competition'. *National Tax Journal* 52, no. 2 (1999): 269.

Wilson, John D., and David E. Wildasin. 'Capital Tax Competition: Bane or Boon'. *Journal of Public Economics* 88, no. 6 (2004): 1065–91.

Woods, Ngaire. 'The Challenge of Good Governance for the IMF and the World Bank Themselves'. *World Development* 28, no. 5 (2000): 823–41.

World Bank. *World Development Indicators 2007*. Washington, DC: World Bank, 2007.

World Bank. *World Development Indicators website*. Accessed 9 March 2014. <http://wdi.worldbank.org/table/1.1>.

World Bank. Data on Panama. Accessed 10 March 2014. <http://data.worldbank.org/country/panama>.

World Trade Organization (WTO). 'Agreement on Implementation of Article VII of GATT 1994 ("The Customs Valuation Agreement")', 1994. Accessed 4 June 2013. <http://www.wto.org/english/docs_e/legal_e/20-val.pdf>.

Zangl, Bernhard. 'Judicialization Matters! A Comparison of Dispute Settlement under GATT and the WTO'. *International Studies Quarterly* 52, no. 4 (2008): 825–54.

Zodrow, George R. 'Capital Mobility and Source-based Taxation of Capital Income in Small Open Economies'. *International Tax and Public Finance* 13 (2006): 269–94.

Zodrow, George R., and Peter Mieszkowski. 'Pigou, Tiebout, Property Taxation, and the Underprovision of Local Public Goods'. *Journal of Urban Economics* 19, no. 3 (1986): 356–70.

INDEX

"f" indicates material in figures. "n" indicates material in footnotes. "t" indicates material in tables.